Vacant
Spaces
NY

Vacant Spaces NY

Introduction

This project began by walking around our neighborhood noticing empty storefronts. Once we saw them, they were everywhere. They followed us, appearing quietly throughout New York City. Many with no signage, no "for rent," no "coming soon." Usually empty, sometimes dusty, sometimes with brown paper covering the glass. Now, vacancy has only increased. In the densest city in the United States. During a housing crisis. Throughout a pandemic. The quantity of vacant spaces is anyone's best guess. It's only partially documented. They hide in plain sight.

Within the city, there are multiple vacancies – retail, commercial, office – but storefronts and street-level spaces are the most noticeable. A majority are claimed as losses for tax write-offs. As we have found, some large vacancies persist for years. An insistence on higher rents inflates profits and value, maintaining inflated property values throughout the city. Meanwhile, an immense housing shortage grows worse.

The basic provocation of this study is that we do not need to solve large-scale problems with large-scale solutions, with more building, with additional infrastructure, with huge investments. Solutions exist that avoid developers and those who have continuously profiteered off of what should be considered a fundamental right. Possibilities exist that don't take 5–8 years to develop, that reinvigorate street life, that don't require massive investment with disproportionate returns, that are incremental and equitably distributed throughout the city. Housing and other social services should infiltrate our city through vacant space!

We look at these immense retail vacancies as akin to the loft spaces left as Lower Manhattan deindustrialized in the late 1950s and early '60s. During this time, light manufacturing such as plastic warehouses, paper recycling facilities, and garment factories, moved from SoHo out of the city or went out of business entirely.[1] Manufacturing changed. Vacant lofts transformed into inexpensive live-work spaces. Still zoned for industrial use, these loft apartments were illegal at first. But community groups formed quickly and fought successfully for policy changes. Sometimes solutions to problems are already here, around us, if we rethink our assumptions, if we imagine other possibilities, and if we organize.

This research documents a small portion of the vacant spaces in Manhattan: those that have been reported. We worked with students from Princeton University's School of Architecture along with our architecture office, MOS, to document and draw the available data. New York City does not keep track of business or residential vacancies, instead relying on private

Introduction

companies to document and provide information. In their 2019 report on retail vacancy between 2007–2017, the City Comptroller contracted a private company, LiveXYZ, to document vacancies in the city. The information is opaque; their sources and methodologies aren't clear. Larger, corporate real estate holders often report their vacancies as losses, but many others do not. Because of this, it is nearly impossible to understand the extent of vacant spaces in New York. Most data is under reported. Harlem, where we live, is one neighborhood that is under-reported. Our observations do not align with the reported data; we live our daily lives alongside entire blocks of vacant storefronts that are missing from data.

The following document is organized from large to small, general to specific. It begins by looking at vacancy within the United States and continues down to each Manhattan neighborhood, where we zoom into specific vacant spaces, where we have provided case studies that imagine some possibilities for transforming current vacant spaces into housing or social services. There is also a section on Covid 19, which pervaded New York during our research.

As a whole, this document is not meant to provide specific solutions. The data is incomplete. Case studies are limited. We are not policy experts or data analysts or urban planners. Instead, it is simply meant to show something we have taken for granted, vacant spaces, taking part in a collective process of imagining a better city.

1. See Aaron Shkuda, *The Lofts of SoHo: Gentrification, Art, and Industry in New York, 1950–1980* (Chicago: University of Chicago Press, 2016).

Introduction

Vacancy in the US

Vacant spaces are everywhere. In cities, towns, and communities across the US. And also across the world. The effects of vacancies on their neighborhoods are generally not positive. They lower neighboring property values, increase fire risk, and are associated with higher crime rates. And they often form a cycle. Vacancies compound into more vacancies. Following the 2008 housing crisis, there have been various attempts to lower retail vacancy rates through policy – everything from tax increases on vacant storefronts and the local governments possessing vacant apartments, leasing them for a period of time as affordable units.[1]

Vacancies are typically connoted by words like *dilapidated*, *blighted*, *run-down*, *foreclosed*, and *abandoned*. Spaces that are no longer useful or that no one wants. Spaces that are forgotten and should be demolished to make way for brand new ones. Our research suggests vacancy is much more complicated. We define vacancy not in terms of these, which carry negative aesthetic associations, but as empty. Rich with details, histories, and contexts. As improvisational and flexible.

Buildings do not become vacant on their own. So we begin by looking at larger, general economic trends of real estate and commerce that drive vacancy. Retail monopolies forcing small businesses to close in rural US towns. Online distribution platforms and big-box stores offering low prices due to production scale. Unchecked market speculation from global real estate investments causing rising property values. Corporate landlords using loopholes to receive tax breaks while keeping properties vacant, waiting for the highest paying tenants. Banks denying potential owners loans, a discriminatory calculation of credit and debt.

In this context, we understand vacancy not as the consequence of a lack of demand and surplus of space, but the result of neoliberalization. Redistributing property from something accessible to a majority of individuals to just a wealthy minority, investors, and financial institutions. Properties are transformed into liquid portfolio assets. Capital that would normally be redistributed within the community and local economy is abstracted and globalized.

1. In May 2020, San Francisco voted to approve new legislation taxing, per street-front foot, properties that remained vacant for longer than 6 months. This tax increases incrementally based on elapsed time. Similarly, Barcelona's housing department is able to possess apartments that are vacant for more than 2 years and rent them as affordable housing for 4 to 10 years before returning to the owners.

US Vacancy

Housing Vacancy

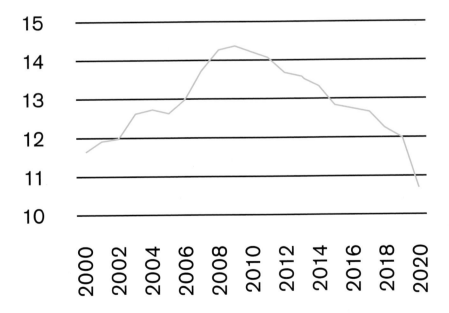

Yearly Average Percent Vacant of Total US Housing Inventory
(US Census Bureau, Current Population Survey/Housing Vacancy Survey,
July 28, 2020)

US Vacancy

The US Neighborhood and Community Shopping Center vacancy rate is 10.2 for Quarter 2 2020

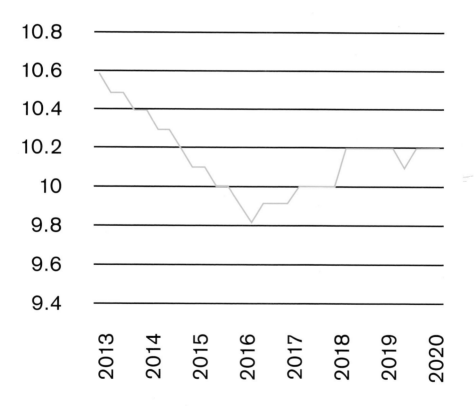

US Neighborhood and Community Shopping Center Vacancy Rate
(Reis, Moody's Analytics)

US Vacancy

Ratio of top 1 percent income to bottom 99 percent income

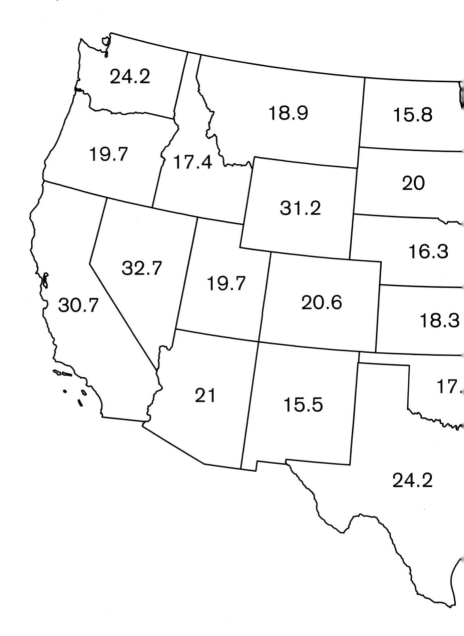

US Vacancy

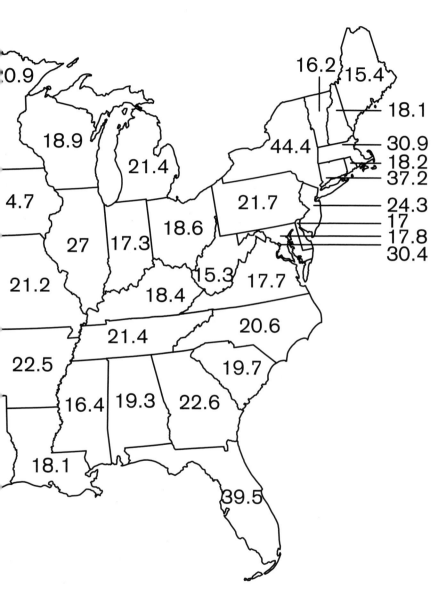

Percentage, (Estelle Sommeiller and Mark Price, *The New Gilded Age*
(Washington, DC: Economic Policy Institute, 2018)

US Vacancy

Owner-Occupied Homeownership

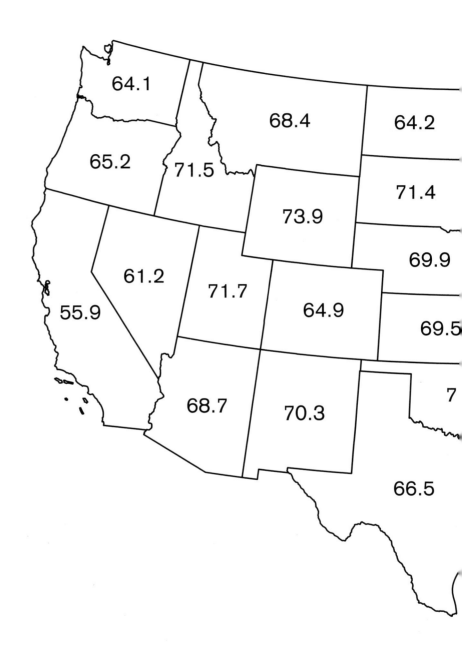

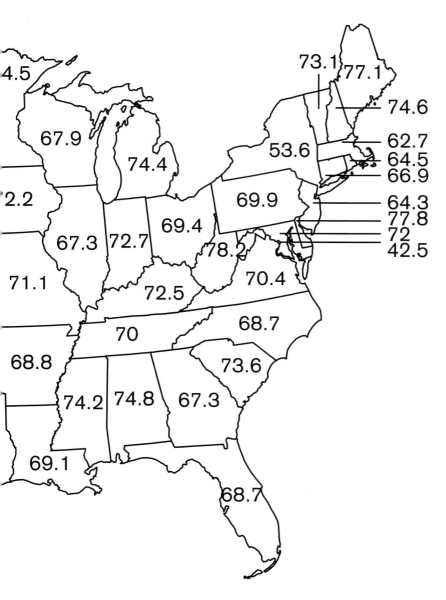

Percentage, (Estelle Sommeiller and Mark Price, *The New Gilded Age* (Washington, DC: Economic Policy Institute, 2018)

US Vacancy

Total Vacant Office SF

New York City	55,331,137
Chicago	49,384,003
Dallas	44,890,061
Houston	44,203,164
New Jersey	40,403,387
Los Angeles	30,835,121
Northern Virginia	29,758,373
Atlanta	29,288,342
Boston	25,283,383
Philadelphia	21,465,691
Denver	19,893,395
Washington, DC	19,837,626
Phoenix	17,217,559
Seattle/Puget Sound	14,664,272
Orange County	14,477,894
Minneapolis	14,302,073
Detroit	13,842,358
Suburban Maryland	12,933,590
St. Louis	12,837,403
Baltimore	10,974,645
San Diego	10,784,797
San Francisco	10,718,951
Pittsburgh	10,481,139
Fairfield County	9,423,162
Portland	9,093,399
East Bay 680 Corridor	8,847,013
Cleveland	8,331,562
Salt Lake City	8,141,566
Kansas City	7,798,165

US Vacancy

Austin	7,574,359
Fort Worth	7,478,054
Raleigh-Durham	7,400,947
Indianapolis	7,095,908
Miami	6,996,969
Westchester County	6,943,213
Cincinnati	6,872,088
Charlotte	6,384,506
Silicon Valley	6,301,549
Nashville	6,247,333
Sacramento	6,196,155
Milwaukee	6,056,004
Tampa Bay	6,041,552
San Antonio	5,088,784
Jacksonville	3,677,147
Fort Lauderdale	3,644,654
Orlando	3,629,175
North Bay	3,307,907
Richmond	2,866,913
Louisville	2,526,499
Des Moines	2,396,028
Grand Rapids	1,093,242
Total	721,262,217

SF calculated using Total SF and Total Vacancy Rate, (JLL Office Insights, Quarter 4 2020)

US Vacancy

Total Office Vacancy Rate

Cleveland	29.3
New Jersey	25.6
Houston	25.5
Westchester County	24.6
Fairfield County	24.0
Dallas	23.2
Suburban Maryland	21.5
Fort Worth	20.8
Indianapolis	20.4
Detroit	20.3
Milwaukee	20.3
Northern Virginia	20.0
Chicago	19.4
Cincinnati	19.4
Atlanta	19.4
Pittsburgh	19.2
Phoenix	18.2
Miami	18.1
Jacksonville	17.4
Denver	17.2
Minneapolis	16.6
East Bay 680 Corridor	16.3
Los Angeles	16.3
Fort Lauderdale	16.2
San Antonio	16.0
Des Moines	15.9
Tampa Bay	15.9
Baltimore	15.8
Washington, DC	15.8

Philadelphia	15.4
Portland	15.3
North Bay	15.1
Orange County	15.1
Boston	14.9
St. Louis	14.9
Nashville	14.9
Seattle/Puget Sound	14.7
Raleigh-Durham	14.3
Kansas City	14.0
Sacramento	13.9
San Francisco	13.6
San Diego	13.3
Austin	13.0
Louisville	12.4
New York City	12.1
Salt Lake City	12.1
Charlotte	11.8
Orlando	11.6
Richmond	11.6
Grand Rapids	10.1
Silicon Valley	9.9

Percentage, (JLL Office Insights, Quarter 4 2020)

US Vacancy

North American Amazon sales increased 44% between Quarter 2 2020 and Quarter 2 2019

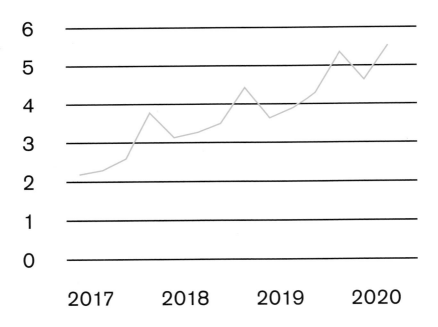

Amazon's Sales in North America in Ten Billions, (Amazon Earnings Release)

US Vacancy

E-commerce accounted for 16.1% of total US retail sales in Quarter 2 2020

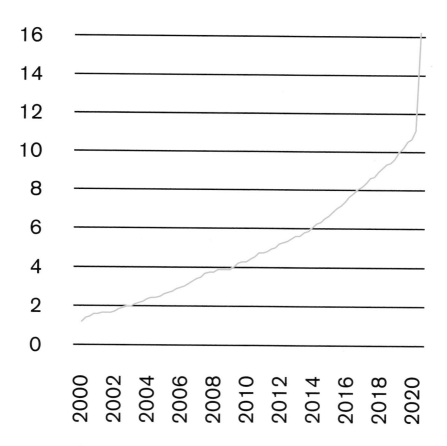

Estimated Quarterly US Retail Sales: E-commerce, (Retail Indicators Branch, US Census Bureau)

US Vacancy

Vacancy in New York City

New York City is made of 5 boroughs:
Manhattan, Brooklyn, Staten Island, Queens, and
the Bronx. 1.6 million people live in Manhattan.
67 thousand people per square mile, although
the population grows by another 2.4 million
during the weekdays with the influx of visitors
and commuters from out of the city.[1] Yet, despite
having one of the densest populations in the
United States, New York also has a growing
vacancy rate.

Vacancy exists in the city in commercial, office,
and retail spaces, as well as housing. At an
estimated 55.3 million, New York City has the
most square feet of vacant office space in the
country. Between 2017 and 2020, the New
York housing vacancy rate for rental units nearly
doubled and correlated with their price – the
more expensive the rental bracket, the higher
the vacancy rate. In order to afford a rental unit
without being rent burdened, the median renter
would need to make 106,000 dollars, 107
percent more than the median renter income.

Vacancies have been historically omitted in city
policy and real estate development decisions
that directly and indirectly cause them. While
landlords who own just one or two buildings
likely experience a financial burden keeping their
property vacant in the hopes of a high-paying
tenant, many buildings in Manhattan are owned

by large companies or diversified landlords who are less impacted by a single vacant space. The extent of these corporations is hard to identify. Of just the vacant Vornado Realty Trust properties we documented – 666 5th Avenue, 11 Penn Plaza, 715 Lexington Avenue, 334 Canal Street, and 304 Canal Street – we found 17 subsidiaries.[2] Most do not include its name:

> 666 Fifth Cleaning LLC, 666 Fifth Management LLC, WOC 666 Fifth Retail TIC Owner LLC, WDC 666 Fifth Retail TIC Owner LLC, Green Acres 666 Fifth Retail EAT TIC Owner LLC, Green Acres 666 Fifth Retail TIC Owner LLC, VNO 666 Fifth Holding LLC, VNO 666 Fifth Lender LLC, VNO 666 Fifth Member LLC, VNO 666 Fifth Retail TIC Lessee LLC, Vornado Eleven Penn Plaza LLC, Vornado Eleven Penn Plaza Owner LLC, 715 Lexington Avenue LLC, 715 Lexington Avenue TIC II LLC, 715 Lexington Avenue TIC LLC, 304-306 Canal Street LLC, 334 Canal Street LLC

The highest number of reported ground-floor vacancies are not in lower economic areas, but luxury retail ones, places where the building values and rents are highest. The top 5 Neighborhood Tabulation Areas include: Midtown, Midtown South; SoHo, TriBeCa, Civic Center, Little Italy; Hudson Yards, Chelsea,

Flatiron, Union Square; and the West Village.
In these popular retail areas, vacancies are
caused by maintaining artificially high property
values; however, in lower income areas, vacancies suppress surrounding property values.
According to a 2019 City Comptroller report on
retail vacancy, the empty space in Manhattan
grew from 2.1 million square feet in 2007 to
4.3 million square feet in 2017, mostly due to a
higher penalty for not submitting Real Property
Income and Expense (RPIE) statements.[3]
We find that this is only a small percentage,
estimating the collected area of reported vacancies in Manhattan could be as much as 31.2
million square feet.[4] Nearly a third of all available
retail space in Manhattan.

1. Mitchell L. Moss and Carson Qing, *The Dynamic Population of Manhattan* (New York: New York University, 2012).
2. Securities and Exchange Commission, *Vornado Realty Trust Form 10-K: Subsidiaries of the Registrant as of December 31, 2017, Exhibit 21, 2017,* https://www.sec.gov/Archives/edgar/data/899689/000089968918000009/ ex21.htm.
3. The City Comptroller published a report on vacancies in 2019 that found storefront vacancy rates as high as 20 percent in some retail sections of Manhattan and Brooklyn. The New York City Council passed Local Law 2019/157 in December 2019, requiring landlords to register the status of their retail space in their Real Property Income and Expense (RPIE) report. Only storefronts that were sold or became vacant between January 1, 2020 and June 30, 2020 had to be recorded initially. The information has not been made public.
4. According to our research using LiveXYZ, there were 5,313 reported vacant spaces viewable from the street in Manhattan prior to Covid 19. The company's data is formatted as latitude and longitude coordinates. We extrapolated this point data by identifying the building parcel in the Primary Land Use Tax Lot Output (PLUTO) they fell within. PLUTO contains extensive land use data by tax lot. Our estimation of the total square footage of vacant space in Manhattan is subject to inconsistencies where tax lots are further subdivided into multiple stores.

New York City Vacancy

15.3% of Manhattan retail units were reported vacant prior to Covid 19

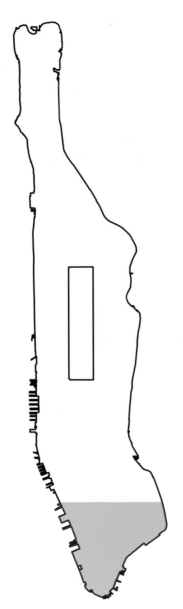

Manhattan retail vacancy determined by overlaying LiveXYZ and Primary Land Use Tax Lot Output (PLUTO) data.

Neighborhood Tabulation Areas

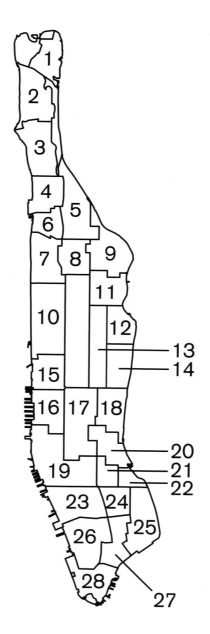

Neighborhood Tabulation Areas (NTAs), (NYC Department of City Planning)

New York City Vacancy

Inwood, Marble Hill	1
Washington Heights North	2
Washington Heights South	3
Hamilton Heights	4
Central Harlem North	5
Manhattanville	6
Morningside Heights	7
Central Harlem South	8
East Harlem North	9
Upper West Side	10
East Harlem South	11
Yorkville	12
Upper East Side, Carnegie Hill	13
Lenox Hill	14
Lincoln Square	15
Clinton	16
Midtown, Midtown South	17
Turtle Bay, East Midtown	18
Hudson Yards, Chelsea, Flatiron, Union Square	19
Murray Hill, Kips Bay	20
Gramercy	21
Stuyvesant Town, Cooper Village	22
West Village	23
East Village	24
Lower East Side	25
SoHo, TriBeCa, Civic Center, Little Italy	26
Chinatown	27
Battery Park City, Lower Manhattan	28

Manhattan contains over 50 loosely defined neighborhoods. It is broken down into different statistical regions: Community Districts, Census Tracts, and Neighborhood Tabulation Areas.

Census Tracts are used by the US Census Bureau. There are 288 in Manhattan, typically made of a population of 3,000–4,000.

Community Boards of the New York City government are appointed advisory groups of the community districts, advising on land use and zoning, participating in the city budget process, and addressing service delivery in their district. There are 12 in Manhattan.

Neighborhood Tabulation Areas (NTAs) were originally created for PlaNYC, the City's 2000–2030 sustainability plan. There are 28 NTAs in Manhattan. To avoid sampling error, NTAs combine traditionally recognized neighborhoods, such as "SoHo, TriBeCa, Civic Center, Little Italy."

We use NTAs because they offer a good compromise between census tracts and community districts in scale, and are compatible with many datasets.

Vacant Retail Spaces

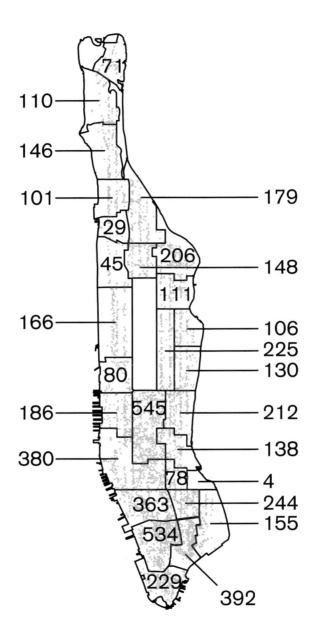

(LiveXYZ, 2020)

New York City Vacancy

Midtown, Midtown South	545
SoHo, TriBeCa, Civic Center, Little Italy	534
Chinatown	392
Hudson Yards, Chelsea, Flatiron, Union Square	380
West Village	363
East Village	244
Battery Park City, Lower Manhattan	229
Upper East Side, Carnegie Hill	225
Turtle Bay, East Midtown	212
East Harlem North	206
Clinton	186
Central Harlem North	179
Upper West Side	166
Lower East Side	155
Central Harlem South	148
Washington Heights South	146
Murray Hill, Kips Bay	138
Lenox Hill, Roosevelt Island	130
East Harlem South	111
Washington Heights North	110
Yorkville	106
Hamilton Heights	101
Lincoln Square	80
Gramercy	78
Marble Hill, Inwood	71
Morningside Heights	45
Manhattanville	29
Stuyvesant Town, Cooper Village	4

New York City Vacancy

Vacant Retail Spaces Square Footage

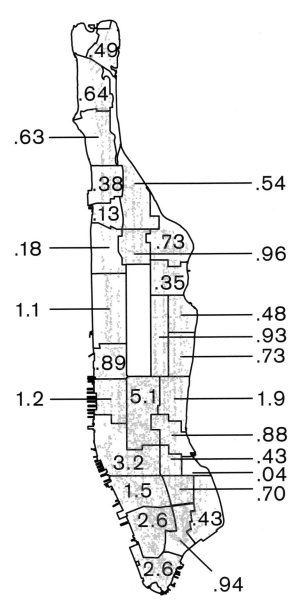

Manhattan retail vacancy SF determined by overlaying LiveXYZ latitude and longitude points and Primary Land Use Tax Lot Output (PLUTO) data.

New York City Vacancy

Midtown, Midtown South	5,134,750
Hudson Yards, Chelsea, Flatiron, Union Square	3,162,716
SoHo, TriBeCa, Civic Center, Little Italy	2,627,210
Battery Park City, Lower Manhattan	2,566,957
Turtle Bay, East Midtown	1,858,881
West Village	1,504,792
Clinton	1,236,991
Upper West Side	1,160,604
Central Harlem South	955,943
Chinatown	939,754
Upper East Side, Carnegie Hill	925,222
Lincoln Square	892,138
Murray Hill, Kips Bay	884,993
Lenox Hill, Roosevelt Island	732,084
East Harlem North	726,053
East Village	697,349
Washington Heights North	644,692
Washington Heights South	628,107
Central Harlem North	543,963
Marble Hill, Inwood	486,366
Yorkville	484,630
Lower East Side	433,800
Gramercy	430,190
Hamilton Heights	376,453
East Harlem South	348,868
Morningside Heights	176,749
Manhattanville	129,602
Stuyvesant Town, Cooper Village	42,041

New York City Vacancy

Inventory of Manhattan Office Space

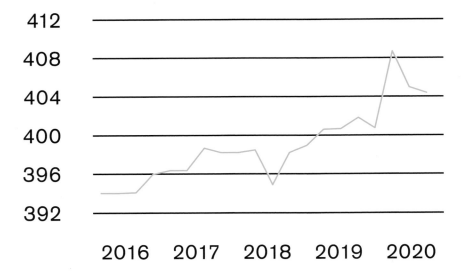

In millions, Manhattan Office MarketBeat (Cushman & Wakefield). Manhattan office space is reported quarterly by real estate firm Cushman & Wakefield. These summaries only include office spaces below 65th Street, split into 3 submarkets: Midtown, Midtown South, and Downtown (despite sharing similar names, these do not correspond to NTAs). The amount of vacant office space for all of Manhattan is almost certainly higher.

45.1 million SF of Manhattan office space was vacant in Quarter 2 of 2020

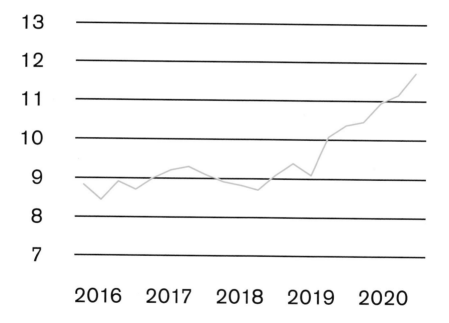

Manhattan Office MarketBeat, (Cushman & Wakefield)

New York City Vacancy

New York City Population

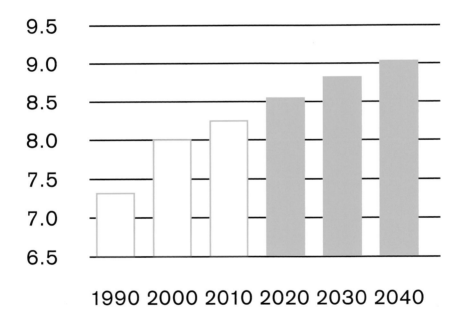

Population   Projected

New York City Population Projections by Age/Sex and Borough in millions,
(The City of New York and the Department of City Planning, 2013)

Manhattan Population

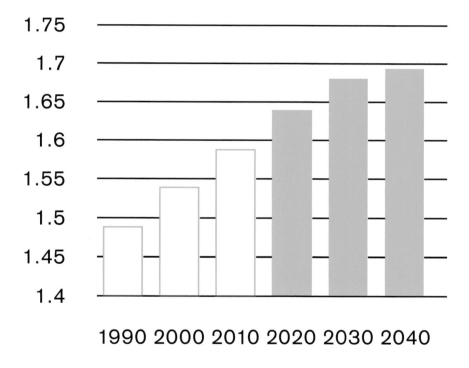

Population   Projected

New York City Population Projections by Age/Sex and Borough in millions,
(The City of New York and the Department of City Planning, 2013)

         New York City Vacancy

Ethnicity, Hispanic or Latinx Households

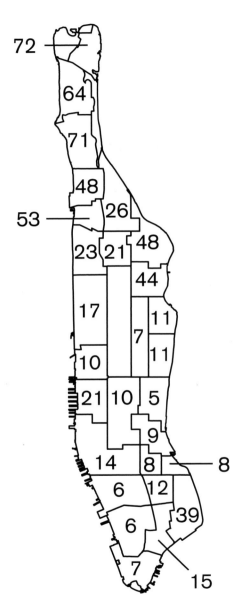

Percentage, (2014–2018 American Community Survey Database, Census Bureau ACS Demographic Profile)

Ethnicity, White Households

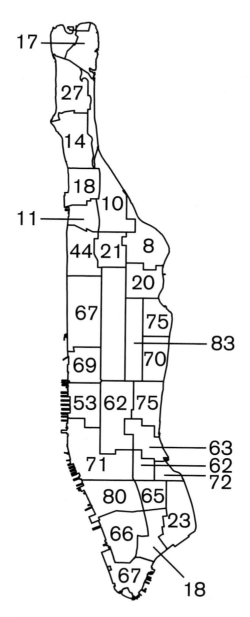

Percentage, (2014–2018 American Community Survey Database, Census Bureau ACS Demographic Profile)

New York City Vacancy

Ethnicity, Black Households

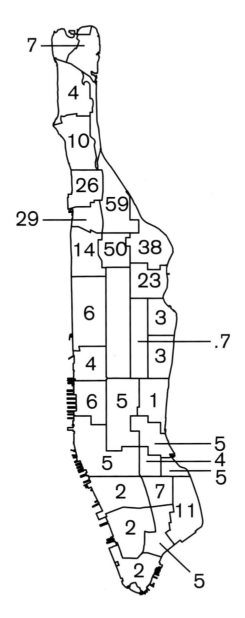

Percentage, (2014–2018 American Community Survey Database, Census Bureau ACS Demographic Profile)

Ethnicity, Asian Households

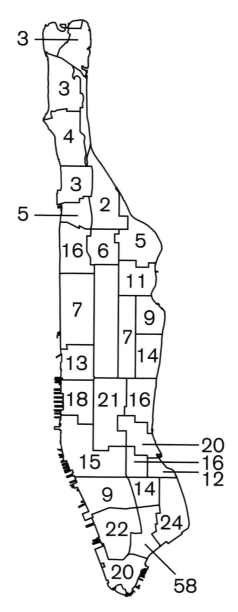

Percentage, (2014–2018 American Community Survey Database, Census Bureau ACS Demographic Profile)

Households making less than 35k

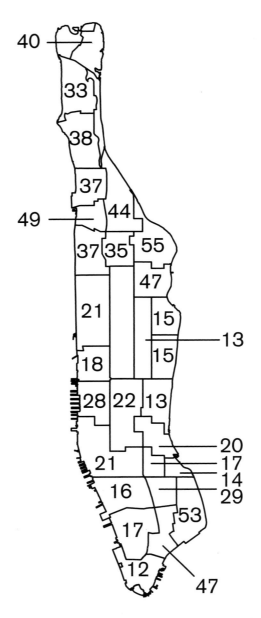

Percentage, (2014–2018 American Community Survey Database, Census Bureau ACS Demographic Profile)

Households making more than 150k

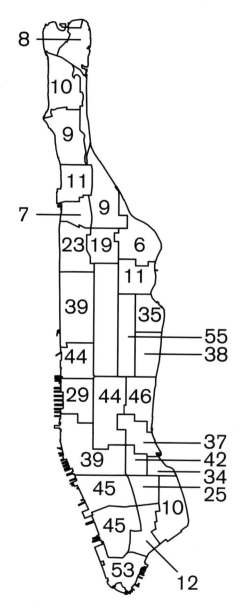

Percentage, (2014–2018 American Community Survey Database, Census Bureau ACS Demographic Profile)

Household Median Income

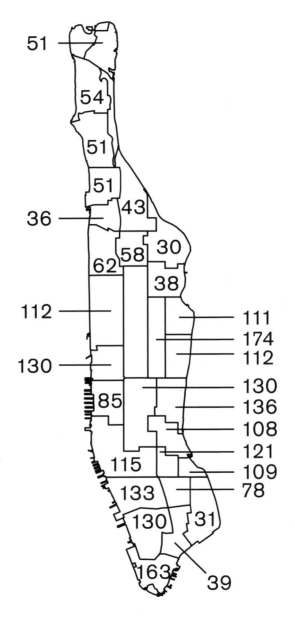

51

54

51

51

43

36

58 30

62

38

112 ——————— 111

174

130 ——————— 112

130

85 136

108

121

115 109

133 78

130 31

163 39

In thousand dollars, (2014–2018 ACS Database, Census Bureau ACS Demographic Profile)

Median Gross Rent

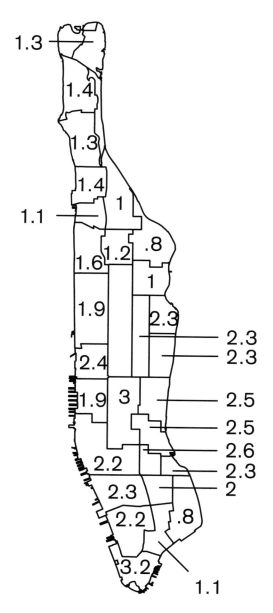

In thousand dollars, (2014–2018 ACS Database, Census Bureau ACS Demographic Profile)

New York City Vacancy

New York City Housing Units

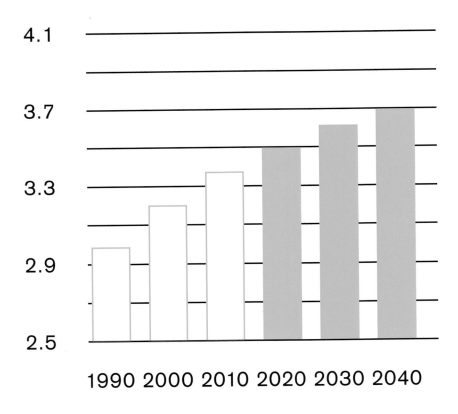

In millions, New York City Population Projections by Age/Sex and Borough, (The City of New York and the Department of City Planning, 2013)

New York City Vacancy

Manhattan Housing Units

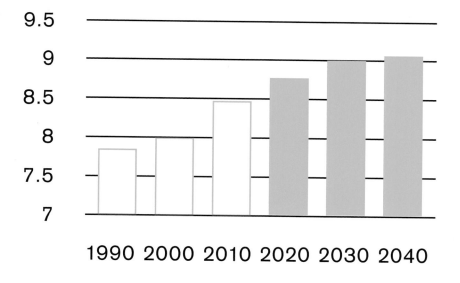

In hundred thousands, New York City Population Projections by Age/Sex and Borough, (The City of New York and the Department of City Planning, 2013)

New York City Vacancy

63% of New York City housing units are rentals

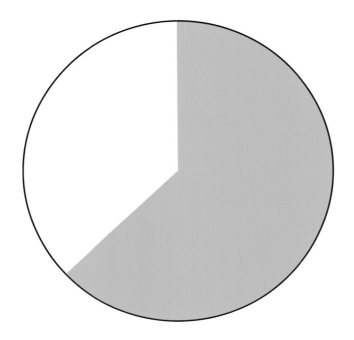

Of the city's total housing stock in 2017, 2,183,064 were rentals and
1,038,200 were owned, (US Census Bureau, New York City Housing and
Vacancy Survey, 2017)

New York City Vacancy

Vacant Housing Availability

Vacant housing units available for rent have increased since 2005. Unavailable vacant housing has increased even more dramatically.

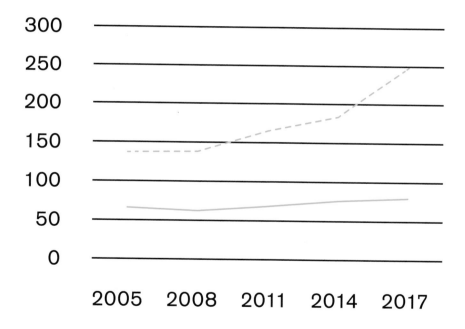

Available for Rent   --- Not Available

In thousands, (US Census Bureau, New York City Housing and Vacancy Surveys 2005–2017)

Vacant rental units unavailable because held for occasional, seasonal, or recreational use

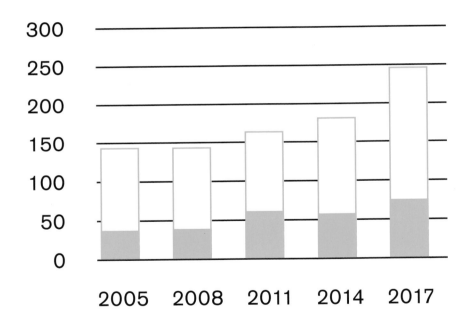

Total Unavailable   Occasional Use

In thousands, (US Census Bureau, New York City Housing and Vacancy Surveys 2005–2017)

Vacant rental units unavailable because awaiting or undergoing renovation

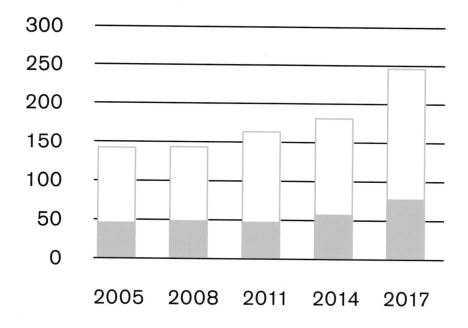

Total Unavailable   Renovation

In thousands, (US Census Bureau, New York City Housing and Vacancy Surveys 2005–2017)

The median household spends 31.3% of income on rent

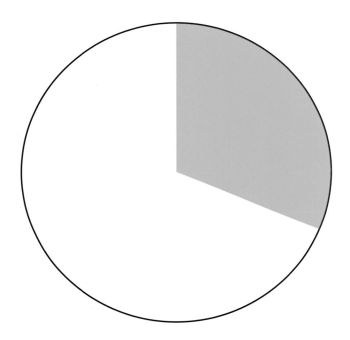

Median Contract Rent as a Percentage of Household Income in 2017, (Selected Initial Findings of the 2017 New York City Housing and Vacancy Survey, US Census Bureau, February 2018)

29.6% of households spend 50% or more of income on rent

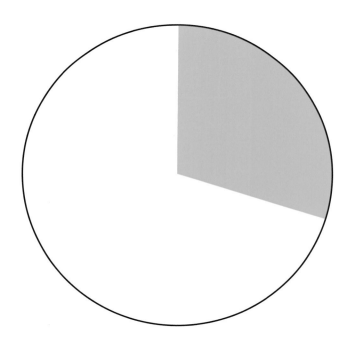

(Selected Initial Findings of the 2017 New York City Housing and Vacancy Survey, US Census Bureau, February 2018)

New York City Vacancy

Median Gross Rent as a Percentage of Household Income

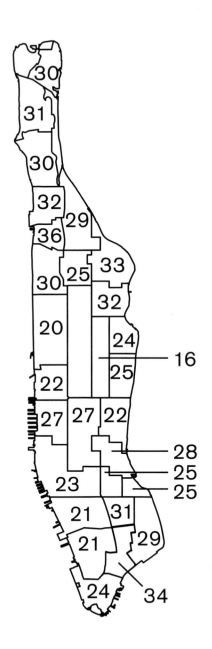

(US Census Bureau)

New York City Vacancy

Monthly Housing Costs as a Percentage of Household Income

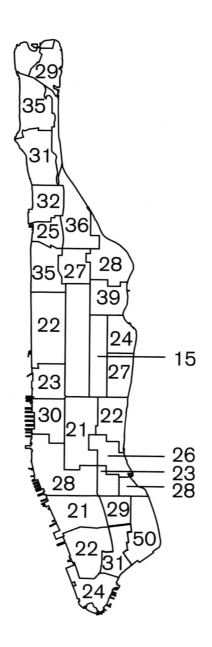

(US Census Bureau)

New York City Vacancy

Rental units unaffordable when earning median income

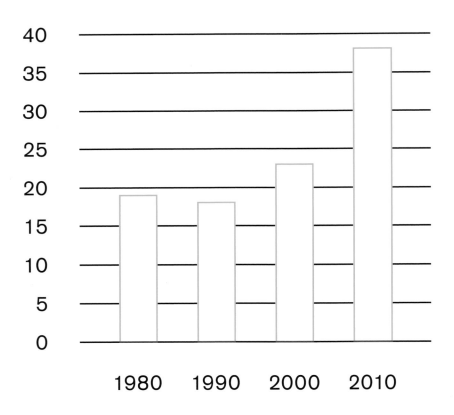

Percentage, (US Census Bureau, 1980–2010)

The median income of renters in New York City was 49,150 dollars in 2017. The median asking price of rental units was 1,875 dollars. In order to afford a rental unit without being rent burdened, the median renter would need to make 75,000 dollars, 52.6 percent more than the median income of a renter.

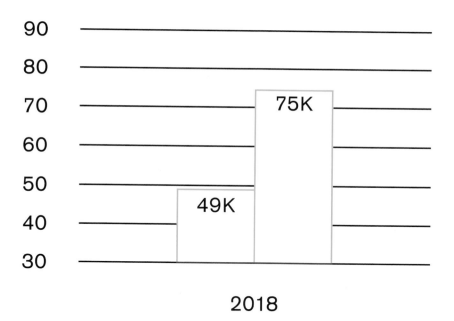

2018

(New York University Furman Center, Core Data)

New York City Vacancy

Vacant rental units costing less than $1,000 decreased by 36% between 2011 and 2017

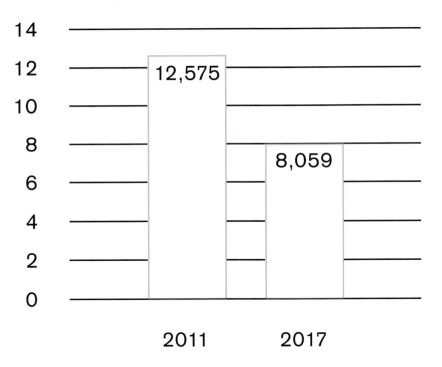

	2011	2017
	12,575	8,059

Rentable vacant units less than $1,000, (New York City Housing and Vacancy Survey 2011 and 2017, US Census Bureau)

Vacant rental units costing more than $2,000 increased by 181% between 2011 and 2017

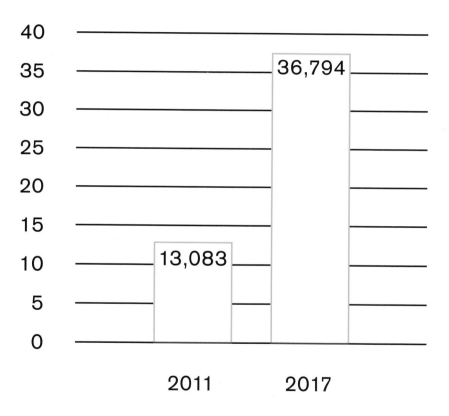

Rentable vacant units more than $2,000, (New York City Housing and Vacancy Survey 2011 and 2017, US Census Bureau)

New York City Vacancy

Renters paying 30% or more of income on rent

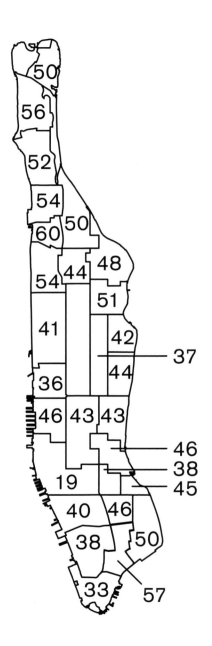

Percent, (US Census Bureau)

New York City Vacancy

Renters paying 50% or more of income on rent

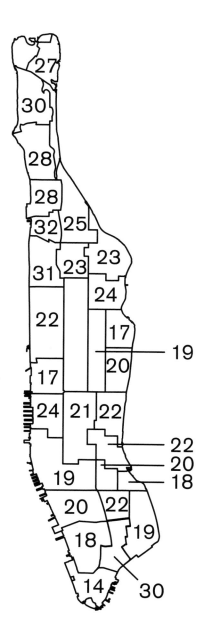

Percent, (US Census Bureau)

New York City Vacancy

Vacancy in Manhattan

Because the data on vacant spaces in New York City is opaque, we made our own observations. Photographing vacancies in each neighborhood, recording their property owner, time since the last documented occupancy, and rentable square footage. These represent only a small percentage of our findings, and are proportional to the number of reported vacancies in each neighborhood.

Of the 550 vacancies we documented, the average time left vacant was 1,316 days, or 3.6 years.[1] Vacancies in areas with high real estate value were more likely to have listings posted by real estate brokers. Although vacancies are located geographically in each of these neighborhoods, the tax relief associated with them often benefit financial institutions or individuals outside of the community; most people in the neighborhood only feel their negative impacts.

Unlisted vacant storefronts (82 of the documented vacancies) were primarily found in Central Harlem North (16); Chinatown (9); SoHo, TriBeCa, Civic Center, Little Italy (9); and East Harlem South (6). Vacancies for rent by their owner (34) were mainly found in Chinatown (8). Similarly, we found that vacancies in areas with lower real estate value were typically underreported. In Harlem, we have observed

Manhattan Vacancy

many vacancies that were unrecorded in the LiveXYZ data.

1. Time vacant was calculated using the Google Maps Timeline. The month and year were recorded for the most recent image of the vacancy and the most recent photo of it occupied.

Manhattan Vacancy

27% of ground-level units, 22% of retail space was reported vacant in Midtown, Midtown South

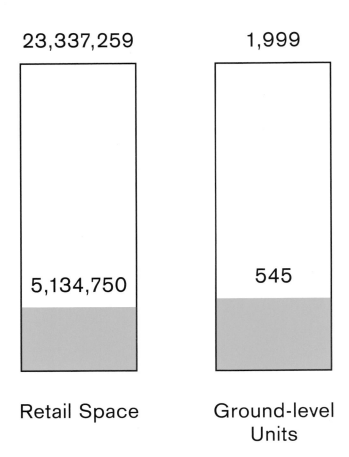

23,337,259

1,999

5,134,750

545

Retail Space

Ground-level
Units

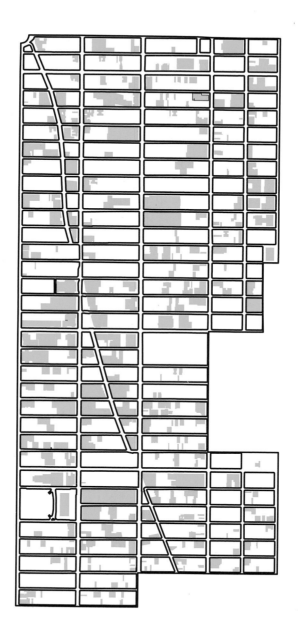

Manhattan Vacancy

Median Gross Rent as Percentage of Household Income

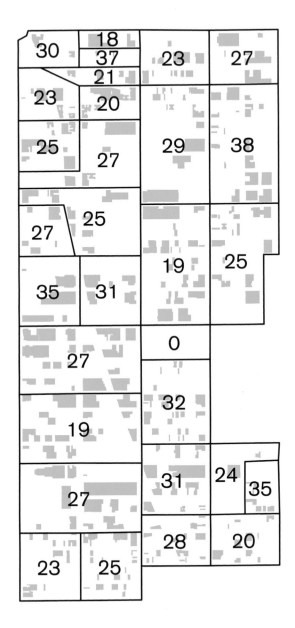

Reported Retail Vacancy SF

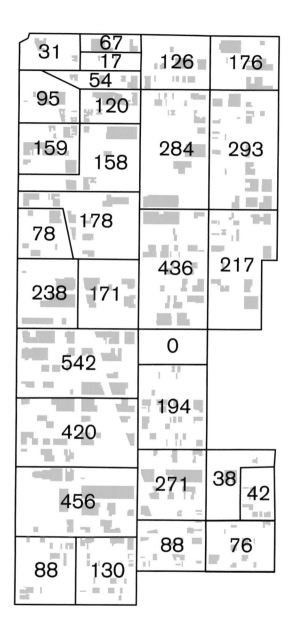

(In thousands)

Manhattan Vacancy

1700 Broadway, Jun 2019, Broadway 52nd Lp, $31M Land Val, $15.4M Tot Val, 3609 SF, 1400 days since logged occupancy.

167 West 48 Street, Jun 2019, 167 Borrower Llc, $237K Land Val, $915K Tot Val, Unlisted SF, 1339 days since logged occupancy.

601 8 Avenue, Nov 2019, 601 8th Ave Mue Llc, $3.38M Land Val, $8.8M Tot Val, Unlisted SF, 1095 days since logged occupancy.

102 Madison Avenue, Jun 2019, The Ruth Assoc I Llc, $4.5M Land Val, $15.3M Tot Val, 8240 SF, 638 days since logged occupancy.

48 West 56 Street, Jun 2019, Estate Of Irving Goldman, $989K Land Val, $3.17M Tot Val, 1700 SF, 426 days since logged occupancy.

488 7 Avenue, Jun 2019, 488 Seventh Llc, $1.54M Land Val, $14.4M Tot Val, Unlisted SF, 577 days since logged occupancy.

Manhattan Vacancy

1675 Broadway, Jun 2019, Broadway 52nd Lp, $31M Land Val, $154M Tot Val, 4402 SF, 1126 days since logged occupancy.

1693 Broadway, Jun 2019, Broadway Sky Llc, $630K Land Val, $2.60M Tot Val, 1500 SF, 1643 days since logged occupancy.

28 East 57 Street, Aug 2019, Norsel Realties Llc, $21.3M Land Val, $102M Tot Val, 4500 SF, 1765 days since logged occupancy.

134 West 42 Street, Nov 2019, Unavailable Owner, $4.84M Land Val, $37.8M Tot Val, 17000 SF, 457 days since logged occupancy.

601 Madison Avenue, May 2019, J-2, $2.93M Land Val, $13.1M Tot Val, 4226 SF, 1338 days since logged occupancy.

711 5 Avenue, Jun 2019, 711 Fifth Ave Prin Owner Llc, $24.4M Land Val, $178M Tot Val, 6859 SF, 608 days since logged occupancy.

Manhattan Vacancy

1710 Broadway, Jun 2019, 1710 Bway Llc, $1.55M Land Val, $10.5M Tot Val, 2773 SF, 1704 days since logged occupancy.

14 East 58 Street, Jun 2019, 14 East 58th Llc, $450K Land Val, $2.98M Tot Val, 5456 SF, 1765 days since logged occupancy.

1530 Broadway, Dec 2019, Bertelsmann Property, $31.2M Land Val, $317M Tot Val, 8641 SF, 1186 days since logged occupancy.

1440 Broadway, Nov 2019, 1440 Broadway NY Owner Llc, $32.4M Land Val, $107M Tot Val, 5130 SF, 2648 days since logged occupancy.

1335 6 Avenue, Jun 2019, Unavailable Owner, $90.1M Land Val, $247M Tot Val, 2515 SF, 1003 days since logged occupancy.

680 5 Avenue, Jun 2019, 680 Fifth Avenue Assoc Lp, $19.5M Land Val, $56.9M Tot Val, Unlisted SF, 426 days since logged occupancy.

Manhattan Vacancy

675 5 Avenue, Jun 2019, Yeung Chi Shing Inc, $1.28M Land Val, $4.49M Tot Val, 3700 SF, 942 days since logged occupancy.

142 West 57 Street, Aug 2019, Metropolitan Tower Condo, $27.1M Land Val, $98.1M Tot Val, Unlisted SF, 304 days since logged occupancy.

550 Madison Avenue, May 2019, OAC 550 Owner Llc, $28.5M Land Val, $184M Tot Val, 2800 SF, 1369 days since logged occupancy.

621 Madison Avenue, Jun 2019, 625 Mad Realty Llc, $32.2M Land Val, $176M Tot Val, Unlisted SF, 304 days since logged occupancy.

212 West 42 Street, Jun 2019, NYCEDC, $5.76M Land Val, $250M Tot Val, Unlisted SF, 669 days since logged occupancy.

597 5 Avenue, Jun 2019, 597 Scribner Llc, $3.59M Land Val, $25.5M Tot Val, Unlisted SF, 1795 days since logged occupancy.

Manhattan Vacancy

509 Madison Avenue, May 2019, 509 Madison Ave Assoc, $6.93M Land Val, $34.7M Tot Val, 1674 SF, 607 days since logged occupancy.

463 Fashion Avenue, Jun 2019, Arsenal Company, $12.9M Land Val, $45.6M Tot Val, 1515 SF, 1003 days since logged occupancy.

3 Times Square, Jun 2019, NYCEDC, $19.2M Land Val, $232M Tot Val, 36000 SF, 1065 days since logged occupancy.

5 Times Square, Jun 2019, NYCEDC, $19.2M Land Val, $232M Tot Val, Unlisted SF, 577 days since logged occupancy.

215 West 42 Street, Jun 2019, NYCEDC, $2.11M Land Val, $7.99M Tot Val, 8648 SF, 1857 days since logged occupancy.

209 West 37 Street, Jun 2019, 500 Seventh Avenue, $7.07M Land Val, $70.5M Tot Val, 4475 SF, 3000+ days since logged occupancy.

Manhattan Vacancy

512 7 Avenue, Jun 2019, 500 Seventh Avenue, $3.29M Land Val, $66M Tot Val, 3871 SF, 2861 days since logged occupancy.

990 Avenue Of The Amer, Oct 2019, VBG 990 AOA Llc, $9M Land Val, $52M Tot Val, 4500 SF, 2252 days since logged occupancy.

404 5 Avenue, Oct 2019, 404 Fifth Owner Llc, $7.38M Land Val, $16.2M Tot Val, 8552 SF, 1918 days since logged occupancy.

666 5 Avenue, Jun 2019, Unavailable Owner, $86M Land Val, $395M Tot Val, 2030 SF, 1400 days since logged occupancy.

1701 Broadway, Jun 2019, Bryant Associates, $1.71M Land Val, $14.4M Tot Val, 5175 SF, 3956 days since logged occupancy.

200 West 58 Street, Jun 2019, 200 West 58th Street Llc, $2.36M Land Val, $10.2M Tot Val, 2400 SF, 608 days since logged occupancy.

Manhattan Vacancy

1392 6 Avenue, Jun 2019, 60 West 57 Realty Inc, $6.75M Land Val, $36.9M Tot Val, 1238 SF, 1369 days since logged occupancy.

535 5 Avenue, Jun 2019, 535–545 Fee Llc, $9.32M Land Val, $52.5M Tot Val, 12843 SF, 638 days since logged occupancy.

578 9 Avenue, Jun 2019, 578 Ninth Avenue Associates Llc, $495K Land Val, $2.75M Tot Val, 380 SF, 1643 days since logged occupancy.

11 Penn Plaza, Oct 2019, Vornado 11 Penn Plz Own Llc, $30.8M Land Val, $163M Tot Val, Unlisted SF, 457 days since logged occupancy.

7 Penn Plaza, Jun 2019, 370 Seventh Ave Fee Own Llc, $6.17M Land Val, $53.2M Tot Val, 3110 SF, 638 days since logged occupancy.

605 Madison Avenue, May 2019, Stove Properties USA Inc, $851K Land Val, $7.61M Tot Val, 2200 SF, 1673 days since logged occupancy.

Manhattan Vacancy

120 West 49 Street, Jun 2019,
1221 Avenue Holdings Llc, $197M
Land Val, $502M Tot Val, 15000
SF, 1126 days since logged
occupancy.

Manhattan Vacancy

21% of ground-level units, 35% of retail space was reported vacant in SoHo, TriBeCa, Civic Center, Little Italy

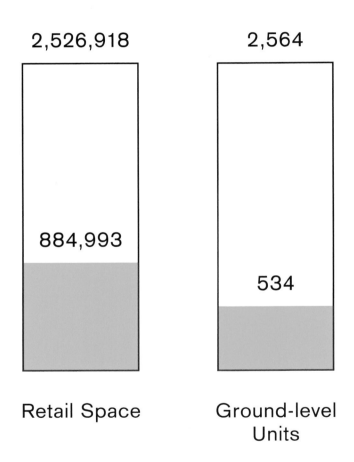

2,526,918

2,564

884,993

534

Retail Space

Ground-level Units

Manhattan Vacancy

534 Vacancies in SoHo, TriBeCa, Civic Center, Little Italy

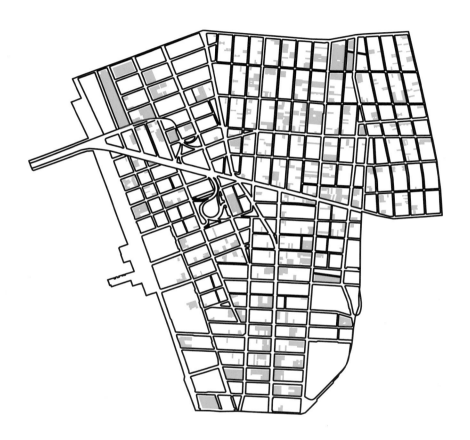

Manhattan Vacancy

Median Gross Rent as Percentage of Household Income

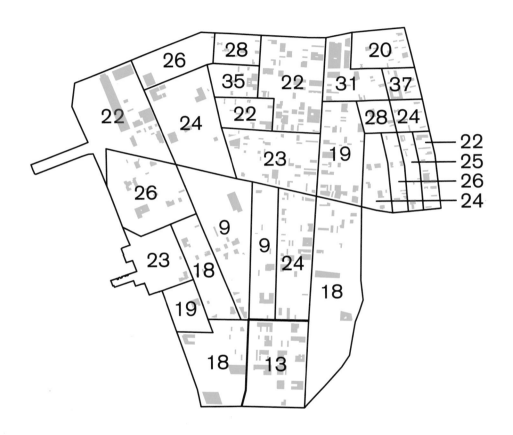

Reported Retail Vacancy SF

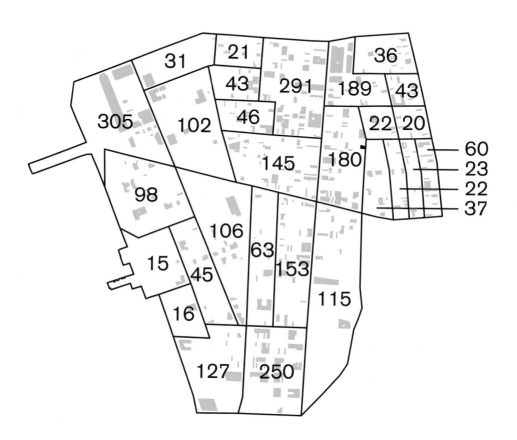

(In thousands)

Manhattan Vacancy

321 Greenwich Street, Oct 2019, Unavailable Owner, $198K Land Val, $2.89M Tot Val, Unlisted SF, 3805 days since logged occupancy.

140 West Broadway, Oct 2019, 82 Thomas St Realty, $270K Land Val, $5.22M Tot Val, 4000 SF, 1187 days since logged occupancy.

35 Walker Street, Oct 2019, Cornice Llc, $125K Land Val, $539K Tot Val, 1700 SF, 3835 days since logged occupancy.

88 Franklin Street, Oct 2019, 2374 Concourse Assoc Llc, $251K Land Val, $788K Tot Val, Unlisted SF, 760 days since logged occupancy.

209 Mulberry Street, Oct 2019, Wah Kok Realty Corp, $356K Land Val, $3.74M Tot Val, Unlisted SF, 699 days since logged occupancy.

15 Mercer Street, Jun 2019, 15 Mercer Condominium, $286K Land Val, $8.97M Tot Val, 6798 SF, 638 days since logged occupancy.

Manhattan Vacancy

490 Broadway, Jun 2019, Stable 49 LTD, $1.09M Land Val, $4.35M Tot Val, 7974 SF, 1765 days since logged occupancy.

355 Greenwich Street, Oct 2019, Unavailable Owner, $387K Land Val, $3.72M Tot Val, 4140 SF, 92 days since logged occupancy.

60 Lispenard Street, Jun 2019, 60–62 Lispenard Llc, $1.50M Land Val, $9.93M Tot Val, 3800 SF, 3713 days since logged occupancy.

277 Canal Street, Jun 2019, AJJ Canal, $743K Land Val, $4.81M Tot Val, Unlisted SF, 577 days since logged occupancy.

304 Canal Street, Oct 2019, 304–306 Canal St Llc, $416K Land Val, $3.06M Tot Val, 3741 SF, 1948 days since logged occupancy.

334 Canal Street, Oct 2019, 334 Canal Street Llc, $367K Land Val, $4.95M Tot Val, 4410 SF, 3044 days since logged occupancy.

Manhattan Vacancy

169 Hester Street, Oct 2019, 169 Hester Street Corp, $113K Land Val, $778K Tot Val, 1200 SF, 457 days since logged occupancy.

330 West Broadway, Jul 2019, West Broadway 330 Llc, $154K Land Val, $3.64M Tot Val, 2940 SF, 1856 days since logged occupancy.

37 Crosby Street, Jun 2019, Flagstaff1 Llc, $170K Land Val, $2.45M Tot Val, 2250 SF, 577 days since logged occupancy.

481 Broadway, Oct 2019, 418 Realty Corp, $1.17M Land Val, $6.56M Tot Val, 3600 SF, 699 days since logged occupancy.

449 Broadway, Aug 2020, 449 Broadway Llc, $310K Land Val, $6.04M Tot Val, 4974 SF, 168 days since logged occupancy.

391 Broadway, Oct 2019, D & Y Negrin Realty, $188K Land Val, $1.38M Tot Val, 5600 SF, 3014 days since logged occupancy.

Manhattan Vacancy

102 Greene Street, Jun 2019, 102 Greene Fee Owner Llc, $150K Land Val, $817K Tot Val, 5124 SF, 1034 days since logged occupancy.

54 Mercer Street, Aug 2020, 418 Realty Corp, $1.17M Land Val, $6.56M Tot Val, 3600 SF, 153 days since logged occupancy.

113 Wooster Street, Jun 2019, 108–114 Wooster St Corp, $2.25M Land Val, $9.74M Tot Val, 9400 SF, 638 days since logged occupancy.

74 Wooster Street, Jun 2019, 74 Wooster Holding Llc, $55K Land Val, $1.68M Tot Val, 1700 SF, 2526 days since logged occupancy.

120 Wooster Street, Jun 2019, 120 Wooster, $2.27M Land Val, $15.9M Tot Val, 4500 SF, 638 days since logged occupancy.

186 Franklin Street, Jun 2019, Franklin Street Lofts Llc, $1.40M Land Val, $7.54M Tot Val, 3705 SF, 2130 days since logged occupancy.

Manhattan Vacancy

356 Broome Street, Oct 2019, 356 Broome Llc, $205K Land Val, $441K Tot Val, 4400 SF, 122 days since logged occupancy.

371 Broadway, Jun 2011, Unavailable Owner, $628K Land Val, $17.1M Tot Val, 3000 SF, Last logged in Jun 2011.

423 Broadway, Jun 2019, 419 MM Llc, $1.41M Land Val, $2.01M Tot Val, 2500 SF, 1734 days since logged occupancy.

70 Prince Street, Jul 2020, Hoffman Peter, $126K Land Val, $1.35M Tot Val, Unlisted SF, Closed due to Covid 19.

106 Spring Street, Jul 2020, Workspace Inc, $291K Land Val, $3.68M Tot Val, 12000 SF, 2191 days since logged occupancy.

132 Wooster Street, Jul 2020, Harold Milgrom TR, 1.1M Land Val, 4.43M Tot Val, Unlisted SF, 426 days since logged occupancy.

Manhattan Vacancy

115 Mercer Street, Jun 2019, Unavailable Owner, $1.13M Land Val, $10.1M Tot Val, 4000 SF, 1064 days since logged occupancy.

118 Prince Street, Jul 2020, Tanner Prince Realty, $447K Land Val, $3.49M Tot Val, Unlisted SF, Temporarily closed due to Covid 19.

122 Spring Street, Jul 2020, 122 Spring Green Inc, $221K Land Val, $2.71M Tot Val, Unlisted SF, Temporarily closed due to Covid 19.

123 Lafayette Street, Jul 2020, 123 Lafayette Llc, $275K Land Val, $3.74M Tot Val, Unlisted SF, Temporarily closed due to Covid 19.

129 Lafayette Street, Jul 2020, Unavailable Owner, $720K Land Val, $10.7M Tot Val, Unlisted SF, 426 days since logged occupancy.

112 Mercer Street, Jul 2020, Castiron Court Corp, $1.22M Land Val, $11.8M Tot Val, 1107 SF, 426 days since logged occupancy.

Manhattan Vacancy

139 Wooster Street, Jul 2020, Unavailable Owner, $789K Land Val, $10.3M Tot Val, 4057 SF, 426 days since logged occupancy.

150 Wooster Street, Jul 2020, Unavailable Owner, $756K Land Val, $7.01M Tot Val, 6196 SF, 1064 days since logged occupancy.

155 Wooster Street, Jul 2020, 155 Wooster Street Inc, $900K Land Val, $9.13M Tot Val, Unlisted SF, Temporarily closed due to Covid 19.

156 Wooster Street, Jul 2020, 152 Wooster St Corp, $348K Land Val, $4.32M Tot Val, 4400 SF, 1642 days since logged occupancy.

166 Mott Street, Jul 2020, Hunan Llc, $64K Land Val, $818K Tot Val, Unlisted SF, 426 days since logged occupancy.

191 Centre Street, Jul 2020, Centre Plaza Llc, $473K Land Val, $7.21M Tot Val, Unlisted SF, 1003 days since logged occupancy.

Manhattan Vacancy

226 Elizabeth Street, Jul 2020, 13 Prince Owner NY Llc, $130K Land Val, $1.77M Tot Val, Unlisted SF, Permanently closed due to Covid 19.

243 Canal Street, Jul 2020, City Urban Member Llc, $395K Land Val, $1.75M Tot Val, Unlisted SF, 2160 days since logged occupancy.

240 Canal Street, Jul 2020, Eglesau Estates Ltd, $324K Land Val, $2.98M Tot Val, Unlisted SF, Temporarily closed due to Covid 19.

248 Mott Street, Jul 2020, M&E Mott Llc, $268K Land Val, $8.84M Tot Val, 450 SF, 426 days since logged occupancy.

259 Canal Street, Jul 2020, K/K Associates, $545K Land Val, $2.11M Tot Val, Unlisted SF, 669 days since logged occupancy.

433 Broadway, Jul 2020, 433 Broadway Co Llc, $2.49M Land Val, $8.69M Tot Val, Unlisted SF, 426 days since logged occupancy.

Manhattan Vacancy

490 Broadway, Jul 2020, Ponte Gadea New York Llc, $1.32M Land Val, $13.0M Tot Val, 7974 SF, 2191 days since logged occupancy.

444 Broadway, Jul 2020, Anisal Realty Corp, $900K Land Val, $3.84M Tot Val, 3073 SF, 2191 days since logged occupancy.

449 Broadway, Jul 2020, 449 Broadway Llc, $310K Land Val, $6.04M Tot Val, Unlisted SF, 426 days since logged occupancy.

465 Broadway, Jul 2020, 462 Bdwy Land Lp, $4.50M Land Val, $17.9M Tot Val, Unlisted SF, Temporarily closed due to Covid 19.

600 Broadway, Jul 2020, 600 Broadway Partners Llc, $11.3M Land Val, $42.3M Tot Val, 2300 SF, 426 days since logged occupancy.

547 Broadway, Jul 2020, 547 Bdwy Realty Inc, $257K Land Val, $3.83M Tot Val, Unlisted SF, 304 days since logged occupancy.

Manhattan Vacancy

542 Broadway, Jul 2020, Unavailable Owner, $194K Land Val, $5.41M Tot Val, Unlisted SF, Temporarily closed due to Covid 19.

550 Broadway, Jul 2020, Royal Crospin Corp, $788K Land Val, $5.93M Tot Val, 1500 SF, 304 days since logged occupancy.

555 Broadway, Jul 2020, Scholastic 557 Broadway Llc, $4.50M Land Val, $45.8M Tot Val, 16052 SF, 304 days since logged occupancy.

560 Broadway, Jul 2020, 560 Associates Llc, $4.77M Land Val, $46.0M Tot Val, 30509 SF, 426 days since logged occupancy.

580 Broadway, Jul 2020, Broad Prince Realty Corp, $2.25M Land Val, $19.6M Tot Val, 7516 SF, 304 days since logged occupancy.

579 Broadway, Jul 2020, Lord Shivas Properties Llc, $1.92M Land Val, $9.35M Tot Val, 4750 SF, 1429 days since logged occupancy.

Manhattan Vacancy

583 Broadway, Jul 2020, 583–587 Broadway Condo Assoc, $1.47M Land Val, $28.7M Tot Val, 12810 SF, 1003 days since logged occupancy.

595 Broadway, Jul 2020, 168 Mercer Street Llc, $1.13M Land Val, $6.04M Tot Val, 2300 SF, 426 days since logged occupancy.

Manhattan Vacancy

Chinatown

Manhattan Vacancy

24% of ground-level units, 28% of retail space was reported vacant in Chinatown

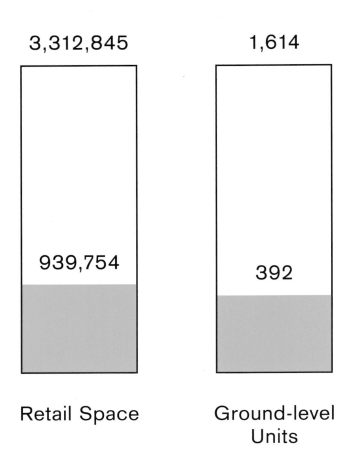

3,312,845

1,614

939,754

392

Retail Space

Ground-level
Units

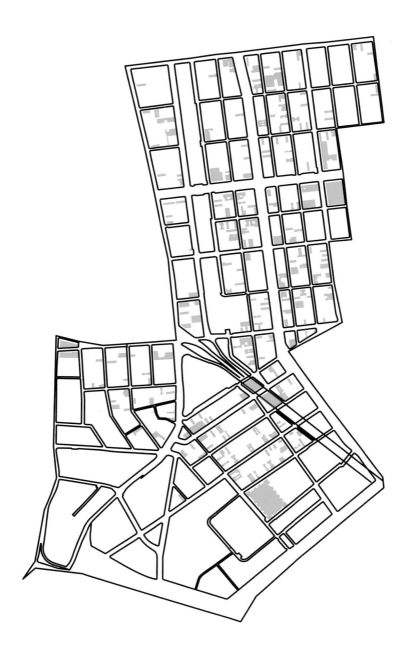

Manhattan Vacancy

Median Gross Rent as Percentage of Household Income

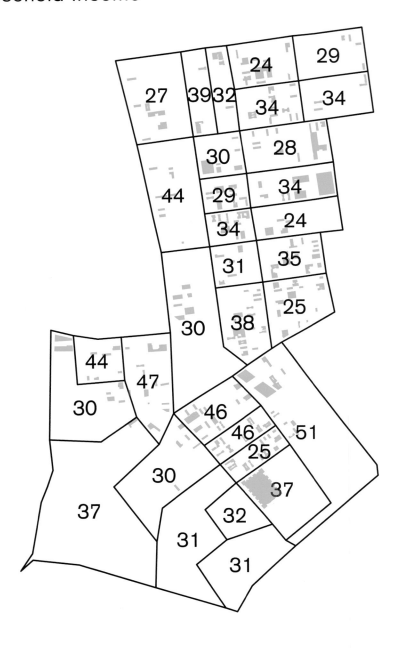

Manhattan Vacancy

Reported Retail Vacancy SF

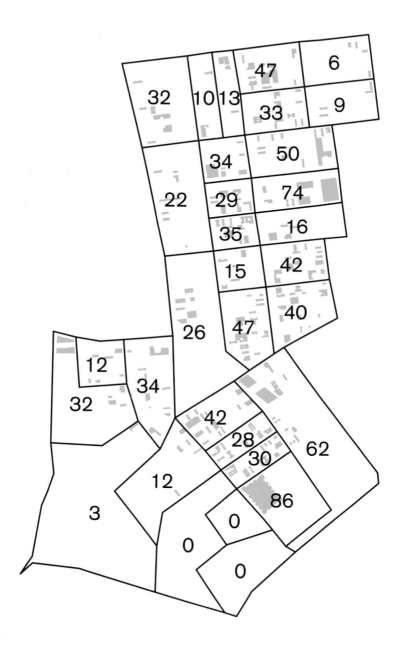

(In thousands)

Manhattan Vacancy

141 Allen Street, Oct 2019, MA88 Llc, $527K Land Val, $1.21M Tot Val, 1400 SF, 487 days since logged occupancy.

130 Division Street, Jun 2019, Sun Woohing Inc, $151K Land Val, $914K Tot Val, 1550 SF, 4383+ days since logged occupancy.

34 Allen Street, Oct 2019, Happy Spring Rlty Inc, $182K Land Val, $698K Tot Val, Unlisted SF, 122 days since logged occupancy.

88 East Broadway, Jun 2019, NYS DOT, $2.19M Land Val, $9.51M Tot Val, Unlisted SF, 2495+ days since logged occupancy.

63 Canal Street, Oct 2019, Yuan Tong Buddhist Tmpl, $294K Land Val, $895K Tot Val, Unlisted SF, 3075 days since logged occupancy.

39 East Broadway, Jun 2019, Wing Hing E Broadway Llc, $464K Land Val, $3.85M Tot Val, Unlisted SF, 2648 days since logged occupancy.

Manhattan Vacancy

136 Eldridge Street, Oct 2019, Edmund Rlty Corp, $158K Land Val, $699K Tot Val, 500 SF, 1125 days since logged occupancy.

32 Orchard Street, Jun 2019, Globalserv Prop One Llc, $139K Land Val, $767K Tot Val, 1300 SF, 638 days since logged occupancy.

237 Eldridge Street, Oct 2019, AILHDFC, $405K Land Val, $2.24M Tot Val, Unlisted SF, 122 days since logged occupancy.

234 Canal Street, Jul 2020, 224 Canal Street Llc, $918K Land Val, $7.90M Tot Val, Unlisted SF, 396 days since logged occupancy.

86 Canal Street, Jun 2019, Unavailable Owner, $2.05M Land Val, $9.22M Tot Val, Unlisted SF, 1767 days since logged occupancy.

198 Allen Street, Oct 2019, Allen Orchard Llc, $188K Land Val, $643K Tot Val, 1000 SF, 2252 days since logged occupancy.

Manhattan Vacancy

182 Allen Street, Oct 2019, Allenorchard Llc, $111K Land Val, $320K Tot Val, 1000 SF, 760 days since logged occupancy.

180 Allen Street, Oct 2019, DC Realty Corp, $315K Land Val, $1.72M Tot Val, 300 SF, 122 days since logged occupancy.

30 East Broadway, Jun 2019, Yen Kee Corp, $169K Land Val, $1.95M Tot Val, Unlisted SF, 1034 days since logged occupancy.

80–82 Canal Street, Oct 2019, HCKD Canal Realty Corp, $122K Land Val, $957K Tot Val, Unlisted SF, 1826 days since logged occupancy.

19 Eldridge Street, Jun 2019, TBF-19 Eldridge Llc, $128K Land Val, $1.16M Tot Val, Unlisted SF, 578 days since logged occupancy.

61 East Broadway, Jun 2019, Yee Shan Benevolent Society, $219K Land Val, $751K Tot Val, 2450 SF, 577 days since logged occupancy.

Manhattan Vacancy

55 Delancey Street, Jun 2019, BCD Delancey Llc, $495K Land Val, $4.22M Tot Val, 800 SF, 2952 days since logged occupancy.

53 Delancey Street, Aug 2019, Dayon Realty Corp, $173K Land Val, $2.08M Tot Val, Unlisted SF, 699 days since logged occupancy.

124 Forsyth Street, Sep 2017, Garlyle Realty Corp, $90K Land Val, $598K Tot Val, Unlisted SF, 3075 days since logged occupancy.

42–44 Allen Street, Oct 2019, Unlisted Owner, Unlisted Land Val, Unlisted Tot Val, Unlisted SF, 1125 days since logged occupancy.

10 Eldridge Street, Jun 2019, 10 Eldridge Llc, $55K Land Val, $170K Tot Val, Unlisted SF, 1704 days since logged occupancy.

66 Delancey Street, Jun 2019, William Gottlieb, $298K Land Val, $1.58 Tot Val, Unlisted SF, 638 days since logged occupancy.

Manhattan Vacancy

96 Orchard Street, Jun 2019, 96 Orchard Inc, $495K Land Val, $2.25M Tot Val, 600 SF, 2922 days since logged occupancy.

70 Canal Street, Oct 2019, Friberg Realty Company Llc, $236K Land Val, $1.09M Tot Val, Unlisted SF, 1826 days since logged occupancy.

23 Orchard Street, Jun 2019, Racson Group Inc, $402K Land Val, $993K Tot Val, Unlisted SF, 577 days since logged occupancy.

302 Broome Street, Nov 2017, Unavailable Owner, $90K Land Val, $2.28M Tot Val, Unlisted SF, 1918 days since logged occupancy.

294 Grand Street, Oct 2019, 294 Grand Realty Llc, $225K Land Val, $878K Tot Val, 4100 SF, 1856 days since logged occupancy.

68 Hester Street, Oct 2019, 37 RE Llc, $128K Land Val, $387K Tot Val, Unlisted SF, 2648 days since logged occupancy.

Manhattan Vacancy

24–26 Orchard Street, Jun 2019, Meitov Corp, $115K Land Val, $337K Tot Val, Unlisted SF, 1704 days since logged occupancy.

179 Canal Street, Oct 2019, Francisco Crespo, $135K Land Val, $1.03M Tot Val, Unlisted SF, 395 days since logged occupancy.

286 Broome Street, Nov 2017, Tin T Chang, $115K Land Val, $2.03M Tot Val, Unlisted SF, 3714 days since logged occupancy.

21 Essex Street, Jul 2020, Halifax Mgmt Corp, $108K Land Val, $1.22M Tot Val, Unlisted SF, 304 days since logged occupancy.

15 Essex Street, Jul 2020, 13–15 Essex Street Llc, $314K Land Val, $3.37M Tot Val, Unlisted SF, 1003 days since logged occupancy.

29 Essex Street, Jul 2020, 29 Essex Street Llc, $265K Land Val, $1.03M Tot Val, Unlisted SF, 1003 days since logged occupancy.

Manhattan Vacancy

29 Ludlow Street, Jul 2020, A
Wong Realty Corp, $115K Land Val,
$1.04M Tot Val, Unlisted SF, 304
days since logged occupancy.

32 Ludlow Street, Jul 2020, 34
Ludlow Realty Llc, $221K Land Val,
$1.34M Tot Val, 600 SF, 1064 days
since logged occupancy.

Manhattan Vacancy

Hudson Yards, Chelsea, Flatiron, Union Square

14% of ground-level units, 29% of retail space was reported vacant in Hudson Yards, Chelsea, Flatiron, Union Square

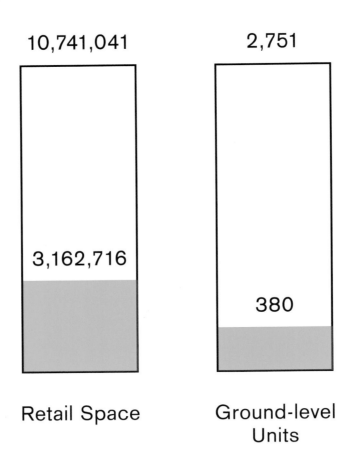

10,741,041

2,751

3,162,716

380

Retail Space

Ground-level Units

Manhattan Vacancy

380 Vacancies in Hudson Yards, Chelsea, Flatiron, Union Square

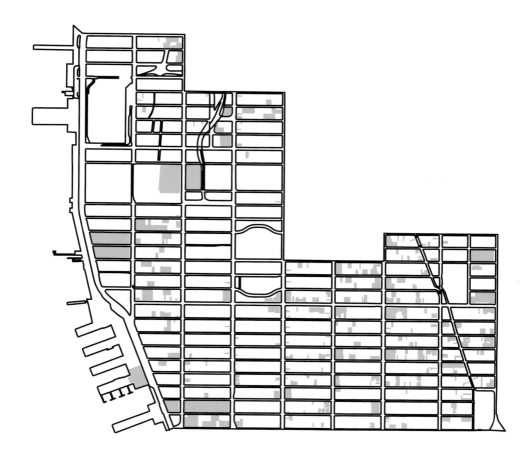

Manhattan Vacancy

Median Gross Rent as Percentage of Household Income

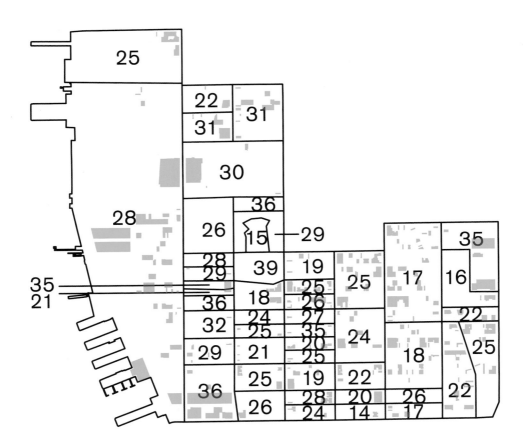

Manhattan Vacancy

Reported Retail Vacancy SF

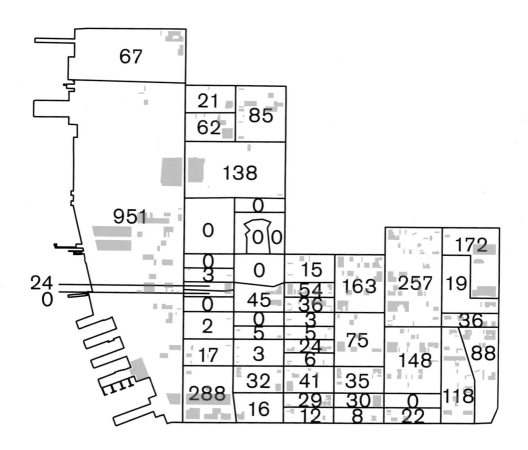

(In thousands)

Manhattan Vacancy

227 10 Avenue, Jun 2019, Unavailable Owner, $323K Land Val, $3.10M Tot Val, 1541 SF, 1704 days since logged occupancy.

117 West 26 Street, Nov 2019, The West Paramont L, $388K Land Val, $1.85M Tot Val, Unlisted SF, 1156 days since logged occupancy.

481 10 Avenue, Oct 2019, 500 West 37th Street Co, $1.18M Land Val, $9.84M Tot Val, Unlisted SF, 3560+ days since logged occupancy.

110 West 27 Street, Jun 2019, Miklos Real Estate, $666K Land Val, $2.42M Tot Val, 3920 SF, 1704 days since logged occupancy.

228 West 18 Street, Jun 2019, Rhumb W 18 Llc, $276K Land Val, $2.47M Tot Val, Unlisted SF, 669 days since logged occupancy.

130 9 Avenue, Oct 2019, Hua Da Inc, $479K Land Val, $1.55M Tot Val, 1500 SF, 1064 days since logged occupancy.

Manhattan Vacancy

238 7 Avenue, Jun 2019, Unavailable Owner, $535K Land Val, $6.64M Tot Val, 2680 SF, 1826 days since logged occupancy.

433 West 18 Street, Oct 2019, Unavailable Owner, $994K Land Val, $21.1M Tot Val, 11040 SF, Unoccupied new construction.

601 West 26 Street, Jun 2019, RXR SI Owner Llc, $14.6M Land Val, $209M Tot Val, Unlisted SF, 3683+ days since logged occupancy.

405 8 Avenue, Jun 2019, West Future Holdco Llc, $242K Land Val, $889K Tot Val, 2150 SF, 2922 days since logged occupancy.

57 West 21 Street, Oct 2019, 57 West Realty Llc, $180K Land Val, $1.28M Tot Val, 2600 SF, 1064 days since logged occupancy.

936 Broadway, Oct 2019, 936 Broadway Condo Assoc, $2.30M Land Val, $11.1M Tot Val, 7107 SF, 760 days since logged occupancy.

Manhattan Vacancy

889 Broadway, Jun 2019, 889 Realty Inc, $774K Land Val, $6.43M Tot Val, 7309 SF, 577 days since logged occupancy.

10 East 16 Street, Sep 2017, Eshanollah Bokhour Ttee, $473K Land Val, $2.31M Tot Val, 4400 SF, 1522 days since logged occupancy.

260 Park Avenue South, Oct 2019, Unavailable Owner, $6.08M Land Val, $32.9M Tot Val, 8925 SF, 1064 days since logged occupancy.

548 West 28 Street, Jun 2019, Mariners Gate Llc, $1.80M Land Val, $12.7M Tot Val, 2265 SF, 2130 days since logged occupancy.

155 West 23 Street, Oct 2019, 155 West 23rd St Prop Llc, $752K Land Val, $6.98M Tot Val, 4267 SF, 3805 days since logged occupancy.

210 7 Avenue, Jun 2019, Errol Rainess, $378K Land Val, $1.22M Tot Val, 1800 SF, 2130 days since logged occupancy.

Manhattan Vacancy

535 West 24 Street, Jun 2019, GTM Associates Llc, $760K Land Val, $6.08M Tot Val, 5163 SF, 973 days since logged occupancy.

550 West 29 Street, Jun 2019, 550 West 29th Street Llc, $1.10M Land Val, $11.0M Tot Val, 5022 SF, 638 days since logged occupancy.

203 10 Avenue, Jun 2019, Highline 22 Llc, $376K Land Val, $3.43M Tot Val, 1733 SF, 669 days since logged occupancy.

19 Union Sq W, Jul 2020, 1641 Park Ave Assocs, $568K Land Val, $2.10M Tot Val, Unlisted SF, 426 days since logged occupancy.

7 East 14 Street, Jun 2019, Victoria Owners Corp, $6.17M Land Val, $55.6M Tot Val, 3277 SF, 1003 days since logged occupancy.

44 Union Square, Jul 2020, Reading Tammany Owner Llc, $1.62M Land Val, $8.48M Tot Val, 8460 SF, 2120 days since logged occupancy.

Manhattan Vacancy

56 West 22 Street, Jul 2020, 56 W 22 Llc, $630K Land Val, $7.13M Tot Val, 4592 SF, 1521 days since logged occupancy.

200 Park Avenue S, Jul 2020, Everett Realty Llc, $8.1M Land Val, $59.7M Tot Val, Unlisted SF, 426 days since logged occupancy.

641 Avenue Of The Amer, Jul 2020, 641 Sixth Fee Own Llc, $7.38M Land Val, $36.8M Tot Val, Unlisted SF, 1095 days since logged occupancy.

600 8 Avenue, Jul 2020, Britex Associates, $585K Land Val, $5.33M Tot Val, Unlisted SF, 669 days since logged occupancy.

603 Avenue Of The Amer, Jul 2020, 595 Realty Llc, $788K Land Val, $1.81M Tot Val, Unlisted SF, 426 days since logged occupancy.

665 Avenue Of The Amer, Jul 2020, Unavailable Owner, $5.81M Land Val, $19.6M Tot Val, Unlisted SF, 426 days since logged occupancy.

Manhattan Vacancy

West Village

10% of ground-level units, 25% of retail space was reported vacant in West Village

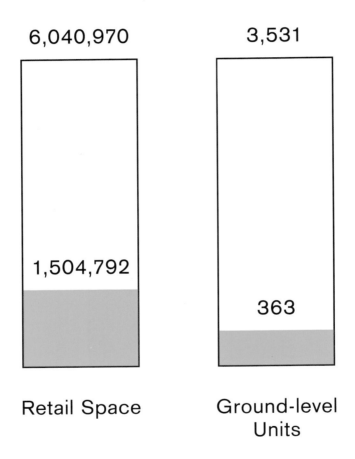

6,040,970

3,531

1,504,792

363

Retail Space

Ground-level Units

Manhattan Vacancy

Median Gross Rent as Percentage of Household Income

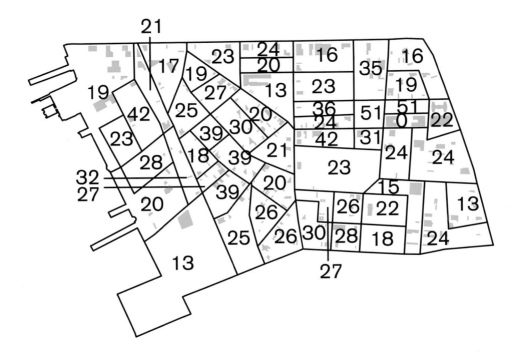

Manhattan Vacancy

Reported Retail Vacancy SF

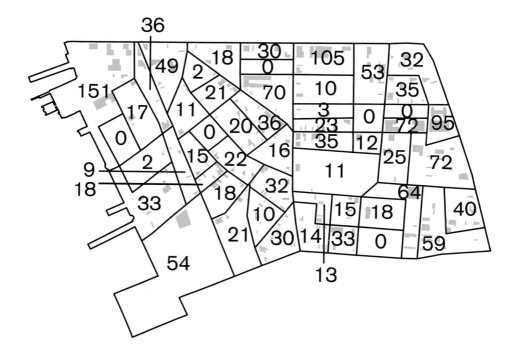

(In thousands)

Manhattan Vacancy

42 East 8 Street, Jun 2019, New York University, $1.13M Land Val, $3.75M Tot Val, Unlisted SF, 638 days since logged occupancy.

374 Bleecker Street, Oct 2019, 376 Bleecker Assoc Llc, $583K Land Val, $1.51M Tot Val, 1550 SF, 760 days since logged occupancy.

585 Hudson Street, Oct 2019, Left Bank APT Corp, $2.26M Land Val, $14.5M Tot Val, 6700 SF, 1064 days since logged occupancy.

266 Bleecker Street, Jun 2019, 266 Bleecker St Llc, $130K Land Val, $.323M Tot Val, 780 SF, 304 days since logged occupancy.

102 MacDougal Street, Jun 2019, Myron Leo Llc, $509K Land Val, $3.31M Tot Val, 1450 SF, 335 days since logged occupancy.

47 7 Avenue South, Jun 2019, Unavailable Owner, $235K Land Val, $2.11M Tot Val, 2665 SF, 638 days since logged occupancy.

Manhattan Vacancy

551 Hudson Street, Oct 2019, 551 Hudson St Property Llc, $635K Land Val, $2.76M Tot Val, 1480 SF, 1826 days since logged occupancy.

378 Avenue Of The Amer, Oct 2019, 378 Sixth Llc, $747K Land Val, $6.86M Tot Val, 3808 SF, 1095 days since logged occupancy.

390 Avenue Of The Amer, Oct 2019, 378 Sixth Llc, $1.21M Land Val, $3.76M Tot Val, 2776 SF, 760 days since logged occupancy.

769 Broadway, Jul 2020, Uniway Partners Lp, $5.14M Land Val, $32.2M Tot Val, Unlisted SF, Temporarily closed due to Covid 19.

134 West Houston Street, Jun 2019, 134–136 W Houston St Llc, $1.1M Land Val, $3.48M Tot Val, 2210 SF, 180 days since logged occupancy.

277 West 4 Street, Oct 2019, Jandale Realty Inc, $116K Land Val, $343K Tot Val, 500 SF, 3805 days since logged occupancy.

Manhattan Vacancy

51 Christopher Street, Jun 2019, Christopher & 7th Rlty Llc, $2.58M Land Val, $8.96M Tot Val, 2200 SF, 577 days since logged occupancy.

30 West 14 Street, Jun 2019, 25 West 13th St Corp, $2.13M Land Val, $17.7M Tot Val, 600 SF, 1704 days since logged occupancy.

33 Carmine Street, Jun 2019, 3133 Ca Llc, $585K Land Val, $3.16M Tot Val, 1000 SF, 577 days since logged occupancy.

61 East 11 Street, Jun 2019, 61 E 11 St Corp, $1.88M Land Val, $12.1M Tot Val, Unlisted SF, 1095 days since logged occupancy.

28 East 10 Street, May 2019, Devonshire House Condo, $1.95M Land Val, $19.0M Tot Val, 375 SF, 1795 days since logged occupancy.

117 7 Avenue S, Jun 2019, 117 Seventh Ave Etc, $1.85M Land Val, $5.17M Tot Val, 2000 SF, 942 days since logged occupancy.

Manhattan Vacancy

20 5 Avenue, Jun 2019, 20 Fifth Avenue Llc, $2.45M Land Val, $19.8M Tot Val, 1100 SF, 669 days since logged occupancy.

1 Astor Place, Jul 2020, Amdar Company Llc, $3.57M Land Val, $28.0M Tot Val, 4800 SF, 396 days since logged occupancy.

233 Bleecker Street, Jul 2020, 233 Bleecker Street Llc, $945K Land Val, $2.31M Tot Val, Unlisted SF, 397 days since logged occupancy.

105 MacDougal Street, Jul 2020, 103–105 MacDougal St Llc, $360K Land Val, $3.62M Tot Val, 6750 SF, 398 days since logged occupancy.

205 Bleecker Street, Jul 2020, Name Not On File, $851K Land Val, $4.05M Tot Val, Unlisted SF, Temporarily closed due to Covid 19.

249 Bleecker Street, Jul 2020, 249 Bleecker Llc, $127K Land Val, $328K Tot Val, 650 SF, 400 days since logged occupancy.

Manhattan Vacancy

267 Bleecker Street, Jul 2020, 265 Bleecker Realty Llc, $281K Land Val, $722K Tot Val, 642 SF, 2531 days since logged occupancy.

33 Greenwich Avenue, Oct 2019, 33 Greenwich Owners Corp, $2.12M Land Val, $21.4M Tot Val, 615 available SF, 699 days since logged occupancy.

Manhattan Vacancy

East Village

Manhattan Vacancy

13% of ground-level units, 31% of retail space was reported vacant in East Village

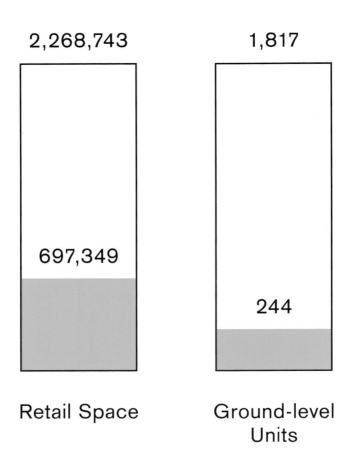

2,268,743

1,817

697,349

244

Retail Space

Ground-level
Units

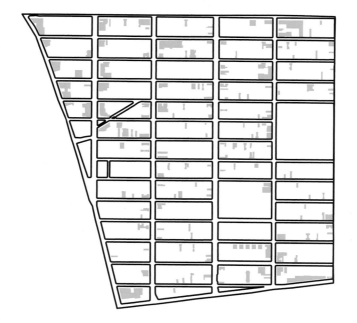

Median Gross Rent as Percentage of Household Income

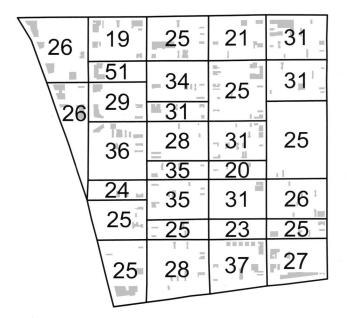

Manhattan Vacancy

Reported Retail Vacancy SF

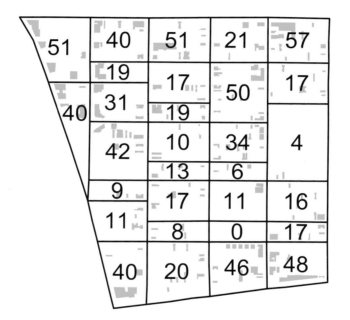

(In thousands)

Manhattan Vacancy

118 2 Avenue, Jun 2019, 118 2nd Ave NY Llc, $540K Land Val, $3.27M Tot Val, 3000 SF, 304 days since logged occupancy.

111 St Marks Place, Jun 2019, St Marks Ev Realty Llc, $185K Land Val, $847K Tot Val, Unlisted SF, 1003 days since logged occupancy.

120 East 7 Street, Oct 2019, Barnes Associates, $235K Land Val, $1.20M Tot Val, 700 SF, 1826 days since logged occupancy.

28 Avenue A, Oct 2019, 28–30 Avenue A Llc, $594K Land Val, $2.62M Tot Val, 5000 SF, 1887 days since logged occupancy.

108 1 Avenue, Jun 2019, 108 1 St Llc, $352K Land Val, $1.68M Tot Val, 1500 SF, 577 days since logged occupancy.

172 East 2 Street, Jul 2019, Village KF 2 Associates Llc, $315K Land Val, $3.19M Tot Val, Unlisted SF, 365 days since logged occupancy.

189 East 3 Street, Oct 2019, 189 East 3 Llc, $197K Land Val, $1.11M Tot Val, 1700 SF, 1826 days since logged occupancy.

11 St Marks Place, Jun 2019, 11 St Marks Assocs Llc, $693K Land Val, $2.46M Tot Val, Unlisted SF, 1003 days since logged occupancy.

58 East 1 Street, Oct 2019, 58 East Partners Llc, $254K Land Val, $1.40M Tot Val, Unlisted SF, 760 days since logged occupancy.

79 3 Avenue, Jun 2019, New York University, $10.6M Land Val, $3.50M Tot Val, 1800 SF, 577 days since logged occupancy.

92 3 Avenue, Oct 2019, 100 Third Corp, $410K Land Val, $4.09M Tot Val, Unlisted SF, 1156 days since logged occupancy.

206 East 14 Street, Jun 2019, Unavailable Owner, $1.86M Land Val, $11.2M Tot Val, Unlisted SF, 1704 days since logged occupancy.

Manhattan Vacancy

181 Avenue A, Jun 2019, Unavailable Owner, $2.27M Land Val, $23.9M Tot Val, 11600 SF, Unoccupied new construction.

93 2 Avenue, Jun 2019, Leeda Realty Llc, $974K Land Val, $2.08M Tot Val, 1300 SF, 823 days since logged occupancy.

91 Avenue A, Jul 2020, Unavailable Owner, $297K Land Val, $3.58M Tot Val, 2900 SF, 2100 days since logged occupancy.

133 2 Avenue, Jul 2020, Unavailable Owner, $1.17M Land Val, $6.31M Tot Val, 1206 SF, 2891 days since logged occupancy.

125 2 Avenue, Jul 2020, Roman Bohdanowycz, $468K Land Val, $1.74M Tot Val, Unlisted SF, 973 days since logged occupancy.

Manhattan Vacancy

Manhattan Vacancy

37% of ground-level units, 62% of retail space was reported vacant in Battery Park City, Lower Manhattan

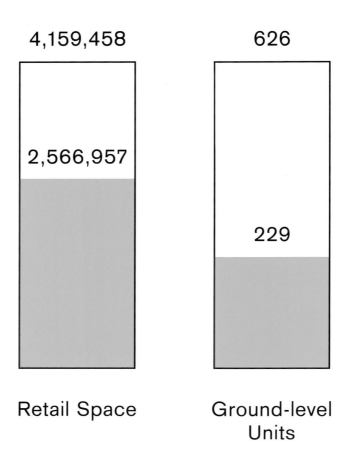

4,159,458

2,566,957

Retail Space

626

229

Ground-level Units

Manhattan Vacancy

229 Vacancies in Battery Park City, Lower Manhattan

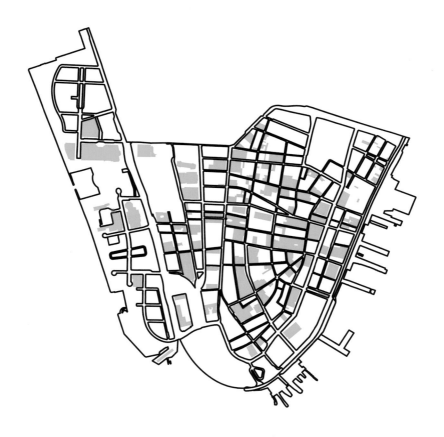

Median Gross Rent as Percentage of Household Income

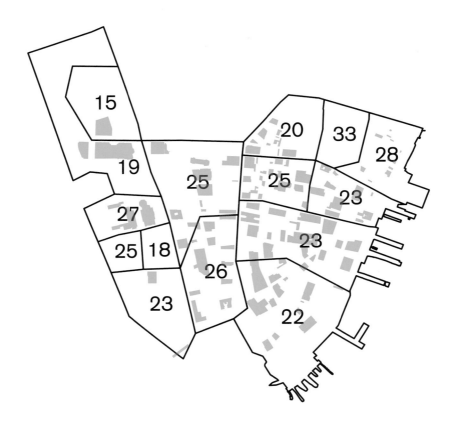

Manhattan Vacancy

Reported Retail Vacancy SF

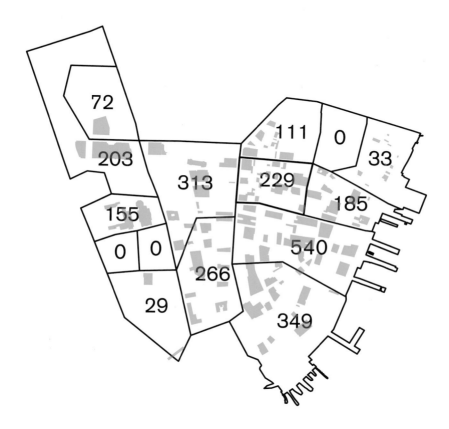

(In thousands)

Manhattan Vacancy

180 Water Street, Oct 2019, EO
180 Water Llc, $12.7M Land Val,
$68.4M Tot Val, 1150 SF, 730 days
since logged occupancy.

229 Front Street, Jun 2019, Yarrow
Two Llc, $272K Land Val, $2.91M
Tot Val, Unlisted SF, 577 days since
logged occupancy.

80 Maiden Lane, Jun 2019, Maple
80 Maiden Minority Owner Llc, $9M
Land Val, $41.2M Tot Val, 3300 SF,
1431 days since logged occupancy.

125 Maiden Lane, Oct 2019, 125
Maiden Lane Condo, $7.92M Land
Val, $33.0M Tot Val, 20684 SF,
730 days since logged occupancy.

160 Water Street, Oct 2019, EO
160 Water Llc, $9.36M Land Val,
$40.1M Tot Val, 9702 SF, 2617
days since logged occupancy.

47 Trinity Place, Jul 2019, EQR-71
Broadway A, Llc, $5.8M Land Val,
$39M Tot Val, Unlisted SF, 1826
days since logged occupancy.

Manhattan Vacancy

120 Wall Street, Oct 2019, 120 Wall Co, $11M Land Val, $50M Tot Val, 42220 SF, 2191+ days since logged occupancy.

45 Nassau Street, Jul 2018, 55 Liberty Owners Corp, $1.57M Land Val, $17.5M Tot Val, 50 SF, 1096 days since logged occupancy.

203 Front Street, Jul 2018, 220 Front St Condo, $285K Land Val, $3.91M Tot Val, Unlisted SF, 303 days since logged occupancy.

82 Beaver Street, Oct 2017, Cocoa Exchange Condo, $1.93M Land Val, $15.5M Tot Val, 4900 SF, 2252 days since logged occupancy.

34 Water Street, Jun 2019, Ph Water Street Llc, $230K Land Val, $615K Tot Val, 2751 SF, 608 days since logged occupancy.

74 Broad Street, Jun 2019, 74 Broad Owners Lp, $639K Land Val, $2.32M Tot Val, 850 SF, 577 days since logged occupancy.

Manhattan Vacancy

7 Maiden Lane, Jul 2019, 176 Broadway Owners Corp, $3.38M Land Val, $18.7M Tot Val, Unlisted SF, 2160 days since logged occupancy.

100 William Street, Jul 2019, John Hancock Life Insurance Co, $10.8M Land Val, $42.4M Tot Val, 12750 SF, 668 days since logged occupancy.

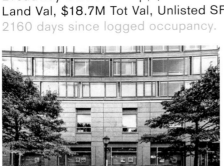

2 River Terrace, Jul 2019, Unavailable Owner, $1.35M Land Val, $75.5M Tot Val, 1340 SF, 638 days since logged occupancy.

120 Broadway, Aug 2017, 120 Broadway Condo Bom, $31.3M Land Val, $174M Tot Val, 11878 SF, 11125 days since logged occupancy.

20 Vesey Street, Jul 2019, Castega 20 Vesey Street Llc, $1.37M Land Val, $5.03M Tot Val, 4500 SF, 273 days since logged occupancy.

90 West Street, Nov 2019, BCRE 90 West Street Llc, $4.50M Land Val, $47.8M Tot Val, 7489 SF, 3075 days since logged occupancy.

Manhattan Vacancy

195 Broadway, Oct 2019, 195 Broadway Ground Own Llc, $12.4M Land Val, $101M Tot Val, 9871 SF, 1826 days since logged occupancy.

111 Broadway, Oct 2019, Trinity Centre Llc, $7.38M Land Val, $39.6M Tot Val, 35666 SF, 1887 days since logged occupancy.

3 Hanover Square, Oct 2019, 3 Hanover Sq Owners Corp, $3.67M Land Val, $24.0M Tot Val, Unlisted SF, 92 days since logged occupancy.

Manhattan Vacancy

8% of ground-level units, 19% of retail space was reported vacant in Upper East Side, Carnegie Hill

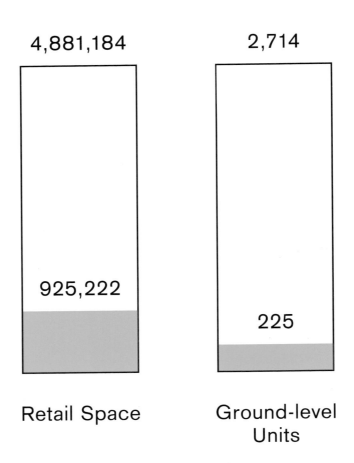

4,881,184

2,714

925,222

225

Retail Space

Ground-level
Units

Manhattan Vacancy

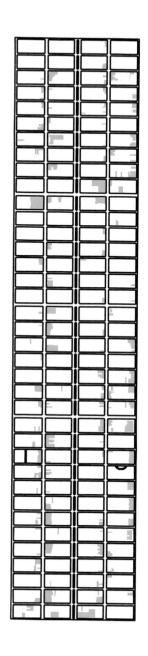

Median Gross Rent as Percentage of Household Income

18	27	20	23
0	22	25	28
28	23	20	24
16	9	44	23
		9	
23	20	25	
		20	
33	0	29	26
9	33	13	26
13	15	0	25
27	32	0	23
0	24	18	18
			0
51	26	51	
			12
30	30	21	22
12	19	41	18

Reported Retail Vacancy SF

0	0	9	13
9	17	14	13
18	25	20	14
0	13	3 / 34	43
42	10	16 / 4	
0	7	9	0
6	11	6	4
3	30	3	5
4	18	19	32
25	28	20	29 / 32
23	21	19	27
9	38	19	30
31	40	52	11

(In thousands)

Manhattan Vacancy

1221 3 Avenue, May 2019, Fraydun Realty Llc, $9.9M Land Val, $37.4M Tot Val, 4083 SF, 911 days since logged occupancy.

817 Madison Avenue, May 2019, L&M 825 Llc Co Fri, $1.54M Land Val, $10.8M Tot Val, 3200 SF, 546 days since logged occupancy.

872 Lexington Avenue, Jun 2019, Blue Water Head Holding, $315K Land Val, $612K Tot Val, Unlisted SF, 3700+ days since logged occupancy.

777 Madison Avenue, May 2019, 777 Madison Condo, $4.96M Land Val, $29.4M Tot Val, 600 SF, 1308 days since logged occupancy.

1022 Lexington Avenue, Jun 2019, 73rd Partners Llc, $842K Land Val, $1.89M Tot Val, Unlisted SF, 669 days since logged occupancy.

857 Lexington Avenue, May 2019, 857 Lex Llc, $603K Land Val, $2.11M Tot Val, 600 SF, 1125 days since logged occupancy.

Manhattan Vacancy

1049 3 Avenue, May 2019,
Unavailable Owner, $10.3M Land
Val, $40.7M Tot Val, 1600 SF, 1330+
days since logged occupancy.

757 Madison Avenue, Nov 2019, 27
East 65th St Owners Corp, $3.10M
Land Val, $19.1M Tot Val, 2600 SF,
1156 days since logged occupancy.

1024 3 Avenue, Jun 2019, 1020
Third Ave Assoc, $603K Land Val,
$2.04M Tot Val, 2800 SF, 1704
days since logged occupancy.

45 East 80 Street, Jun 2019,
Unavailable Owner, $4.64M Land
Val, $22.1M Tot Val, Unlisted SF,
761 days since logged occupancy.

133 East 61 Street, May 2019,
Project 61 Assoc, $309K Land Val,
$2.03M Tot Val, 2700 SF, 577 days
since logged occupancy.

55 East 59 Street, Jun 2019,
Unavailable Owner, $10.4M Land
Val, $61.9M Tot Val, 1704 SF, 997
days since logged occupancy.

Manhattan Vacancy

1186 3 Avenue, May 2019, 169 East 69th St Corp, $2.76M Land Val, $17.1M Tot Val, 973 SF, 1095 days since logged occupancy.

795 Madison Avenue, Nov 2019, EGAT America Ltd, $639K Land Val, $2.05M Tot Val, 1400 SF, 457 days since logged occupancy.

Manhattan Vacancy

17% of ground-level units, 43% of retail space was reported vacant in Turtle Bay, East Midtown

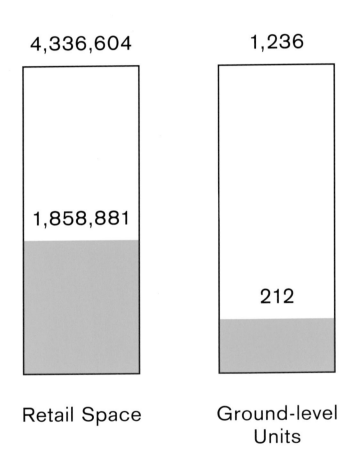

4,336,604

1,236

1,858,881

212

Retail Space

Ground-level
Units

Manhattan Vacancy

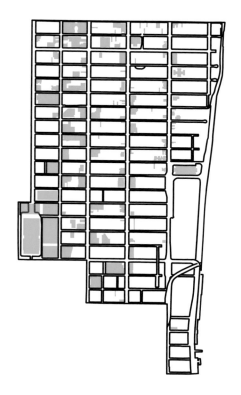

Median Gross Rent as Percentage of Household Income

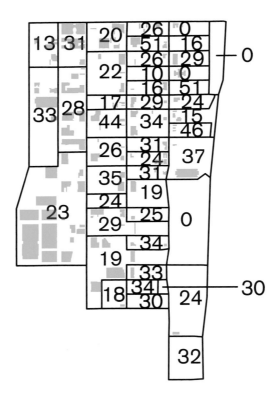

Reported Retail Vacancy SF

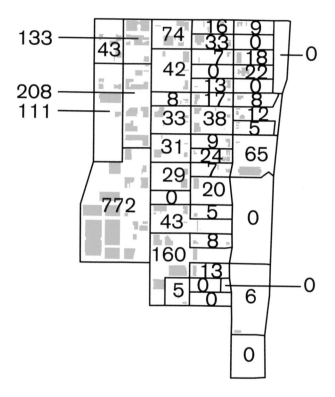

133 — 43

74 16 9
    33 0
42 7   18
    0   22
    13
208 — 8 17 0
111 — 33 38 8
              12
31 9   5
    24 65
29 7
772 0 20
    43 5 0
       8
    160
       13
    5 0   0
       0   6

0

(In thousands)

303 East 56 Street, Jun 2019, JJNK Corp, $432K Land Val, $1.05M Tot Val, 2300 SF, 608 days since logged occupancy.

300 East 42 Street, Jun 2019, 300 East 42nd St Own Llc, $7.92M Land Val, $33.6M Tot Val, Unlisted SF, 2130 days since logged occupancy.

1030 2 Avenue, Jun 2019, 1030 Second Avenue Llc, $270K Land Val, $874K Tot Val, 2060 SF, 669 days since logged occupancy.

526 Lexington Avenue, Nov 2019, 277 Park Ave Llc, $6.62M Land Val, $41.8M Tot Val, Unlisted SF, 3500+ days since logged occupancy.

760 3 Avenue, Jun 2019, 160 East 48th St Own II Llc, $6.93M Land Val, $34.1M Tot Val, Unlisted SF, 577 since logged occupancy.

400 East 54 Street, Nov 2019, Name Not On File, $2.63M Land Val, $34.2M Tot Val, Unlisted SF, 1279 days since logged occupancy.

Manhattan Vacancy

947 1 Avenue, Jun 2019, 947–949 First Avenue Llc, $473K Land Val, $1.77M Tot Val, 1300 SF, 1369 days since logged occupancy.

800 2 Avenue, Jun 2019, 800 Second Ave Condo Assoc, $7.85M Land Val, $40.3M Tot Val, 1300 SF, 669 days since logged occupancy.

1055 2 Avenue, Jun 2019, 1055–1057 Second Avenue Llc, $206K Land Val, $925K Tot Val, 1200 SF, 335 days since logged occupancy.

241 East 58 Street, May 2019, 241 E 58th Realty Llc, $180K Land Val, $2.86M Tot Val, 2200 SF, 972 days since logged occupancy.

849 2 Avenue, Jun 2019, JT Tai & Co Inc, $2.09M Land Val, $6.32M Tot Val, 703 SF, 1857 days since logged occupancy.

993 1 Avenue, Nov 2019, 360 East 55th Street Corp, $2.53M Land Val, $11.7M Tot Val, 500 SF, 1279 days since logged occupancy.

Manhattan Vacancy

401 East 50 Street, Jun 2019, East 50 St Investors Llc, $363K Land Val, $2.23M Tot Val, Unlisted SF, 3560 days since logged occupancy.

947 2 Avenue, Jun 2019, 947 Second Ave Owner Llc, $587K Land Val, $1.46M Tot Val, 2000 SF, 1400 days since logged occupancy.

135 East 57 Street, Aug 2019, Wallace Stratford Ctr, $27.7M Land Val, $89.3M Tot Val, Unlisted SF, 3744 days since logged occupancy.

715 Lexington Avenue, Nov 2019, Vornando Realty Lp, $30.8M Land Val, $17.6M Tot Val, 22524 SF, 720 days since logged occupancy.

Manhattan Vacancy

East Harlem North

12% of ground-level units, 31% of retail space was reported vacant in East Harlem North

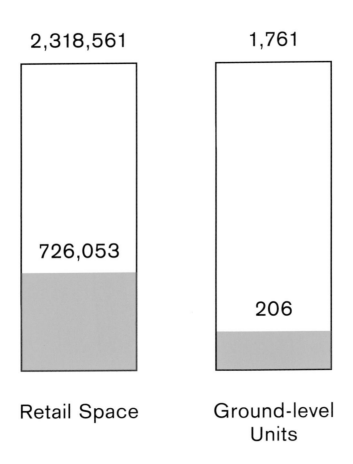

2,318,561

1,761

726,053

206

Retail Space

Ground-level Units

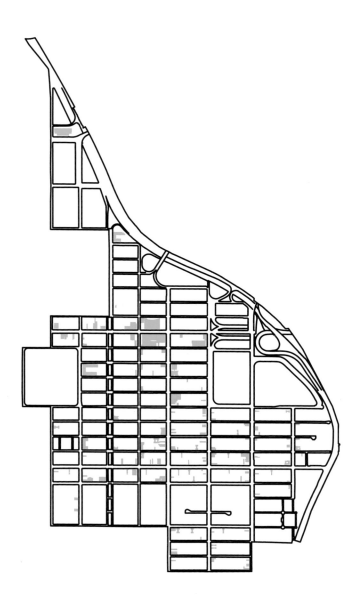

Manhattan Vacancy

Median Gross Rent as Percentage of Household Income

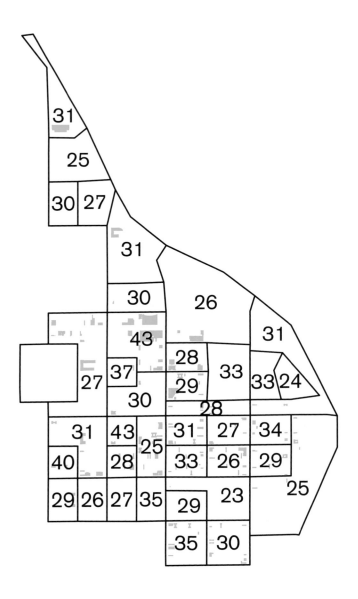

Manhattan Vacancy

Reported Retail Vacancy SF

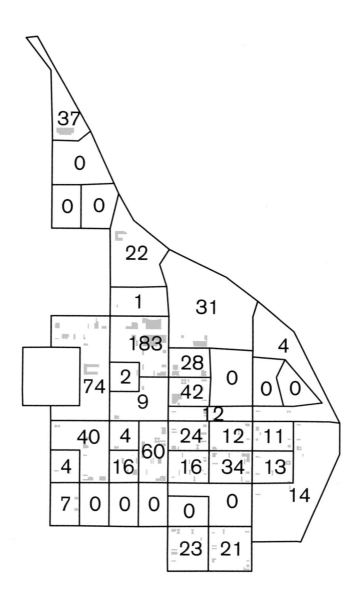

(In thousands)

Manhattan Vacancy

201 East 125 Street, May 2019, 209 W 125 St Rlty Assoc, $1.20M Land Val, $6.31M Tot Val, Unlisted SF, 573 days since logged occupancy.

1879 Lexington Avenue, Jul 2019, Unavailable Owner, $484K Land Val, $5.09M Tot Val, 3500 SF, 3900 days since logged occupancy.

1885 Lexington Avenue, Jul 2019, 1641 Park Ave Assoc, $568K Land Val, $2.10M Tot Val, 3500 SF, 2160 days since logged occupancy.

2006 Lexington Avenue, May 2019, LEX 162 Inc, $200K Land Val, $1.3M Tot Val, Unlisted SF, 1095 days since logged occupancy.

2310 1 Avenue, Jun 2019, Hydrogen USA Llc, $215K Land Val, $342K Tot Val, Unlisted SF, 2130 days since logged occupancy.

2331 2 Avenue, Jul 2019, Pecora Group Dev Llc, $186K Land Val, $539K Tot Val, 1875 SF, 638 days since logged occupancy.

Manhattan Vacancy

2330 2 Avenue, Jul 2019, Hope
East of Fifth Hdfc, $131K Land Val,
$207K Tot Val, Unlisted SF, 638
days since logged occupancy.

2127 1 Avenue, Jun 2019, 2127
First Ave Hdfc, $132K Land Val,
$428K Tot Val, Unlisted SF, 638
days since logged occupancy.

2267–2269 1 Avenue, Jun 2019,
JJP Rental Property Inc, $144K
Land Val, $449K Tot Val, 3677 SF,
850 days since logged occupancy.

2027 Lexington Avenue, Jul 2019,
Milton Boron, $225K Land Val,
$1.84M Tot Val, Unlisted SF, 638
days since logged occupancy.

1936 Madison Avenue, May 2019,
124 Madison Assoc Lpc, $110K Land
Val, $1.67M Tot Val, Unlisted SF, 273
days since logged occupancy.

Manhattan Vacancy

Manhattan Vacancy

11% of ground-level units, 31% of retail space was reported vacant in Clinton

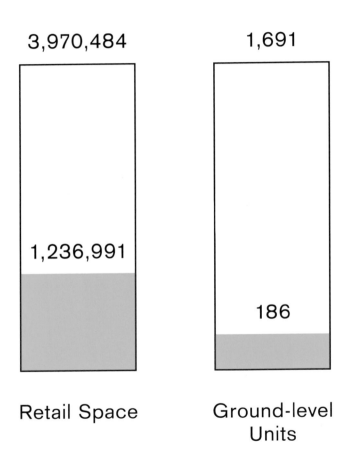

3,970,484

1,691

1,236,991

186

Retail Space

Ground-level
Units

Manhattan Vacancy

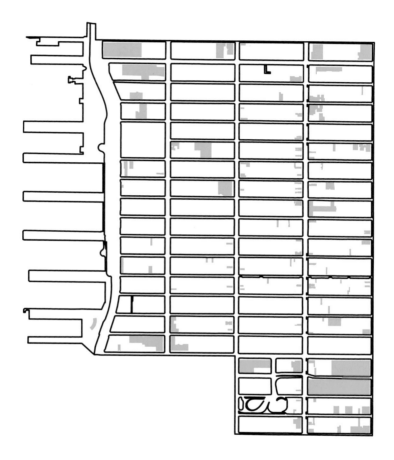

Manhattan Vacancy

Median Gross Rent as Percentage of Household Income

31	28	31
	19	12
	21	26
		29
23	28	21
	23	32
		39
27	23	32
		51
	38	37
27	28	45
	36	
	35	39
	28	
	26	24

Manhattan Vacancy

Reported Retail Vacancy SF

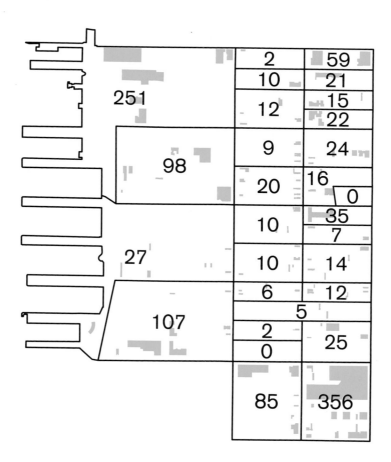

(In thousands)

Manhattan Vacancy

525 West 52 Street, Jun 2019, Apple Industrial Condo, $5.12M Land Val, $70.9M Tot Val, Unlisted SF, Unoccupied new construction.

572 11 Avenue, Jun 2019, Mezuyon Owner Llc, $1.18M Land Val, $29.8M Tot Val, 25000 SF, Unoccupied new construction.

803 9 Avenue, May 2019, 801–803 Llc, $680K Land Val, $1.86M Tot Val, 900 SF, 273 days since logged occupancy.

790 9 Avenue, Jun 2019, 790 Ninth Successor Llc, $129K Land Val, $1.50M Tot Val, 600 SF, 304 days since logged occupancy.

735–737 9 Avenue, Aug 2019, 735–739 Ninth Avenue Rlty Corp, $675K Land Val, $3.70M Tot Val, 2000 SF, 1187 days since logged occupancy.

642 10 Avenue, Aug 2019, Spi Maui Llc, $190K Land Val, $2.10M Tot Val, 1100 SF, 122 days since logged occupancy.

Manhattan Vacancy

177 9 Avenue, Jun 2019, Chelsea West 21st Street Llc, $5.33M Land Val, $28.1M Tot Val, Unlisted SF, 669 days since logged occupancy.

723 11 Avenue, Jun 2019, 723 Eleventh Ave Llc, $226K Land Val, $1.21M Tot Val, 2000 SF, 335 days since logged occupancy.

639 11 Avenue, Jun 2019, Samruve Operating Corp, $653K Land Val, $5.15M Tot Val, 18743 SF, Unoccupied new construction.

534 West 42 Street, Jun 2019, Unavailable Owner, $19K Land Val, $2.30M Tot Val, 189 SF, 3683 days since logged occupancy.

829 9 Avenue, May 2019, Four Hand Realty Llc, $221K Land Val, $1.87M Tot Val, 500 SF, 395 days since logged occupancy.

821 9 Avenue, May 2019, Joe G & Sons Llc, $206K Land Val, $825K Tot Val, 2300 SF, 2830 days since logged occupancy.

Manhattan Vacancy

707 11 Avenue, Oct 2019, 707
11 Owner Llc, $1.37M Land Val,
$12.1M Tot Val, 2068 SF, 3075
days since logged occupancy.

Manhattan Vacancy

Central Harlem North

185

Manhattan Vacancy

6% of ground-level units, 40% of retail space was reported vacant in Central Harlem North

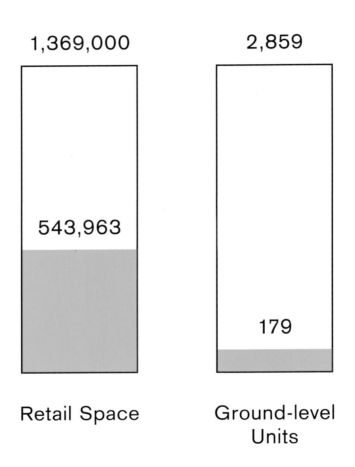

1,369,000

2,859

543,963

179

Retail Space

Ground-level Units

Manhattan Vacancy

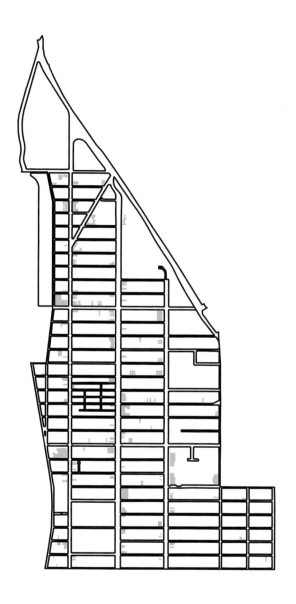

Median Gross Rent as Percentage of Household Income

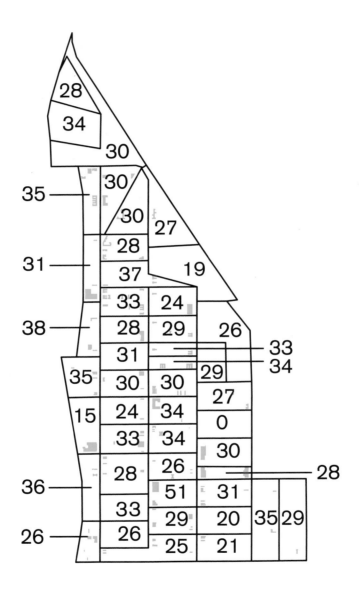

Reported Retail Vacancy SF

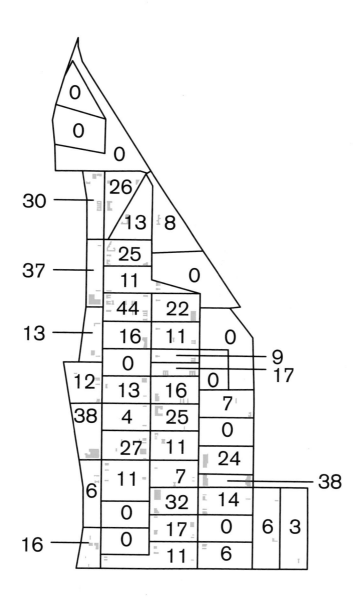

(In thousands)

Manhattan Vacancy

453–457 Lenox Avenue, May 2019, 453 Lenox Ave Corp, $35K Land Val, $153K Tot Val, Unlisted SF, 577 days since logged occupancy.

685 Lenox Avenue, Nov 2019, Lenox by the Bridge Llc, $607K Land Val, $1.30M Tot Val, Unlisted SF, 1979 days since logged occupancy.

621 Lenox Avenue, Oct 2017, NYCHPD, $90K Land Val, $1.08M Tot Val, Unlisted SF, 3105 days since logged occupancy.

567 Lenox Avenue, May 2019, 561 Lenox Ave Llc, $281K Land Val, $3.26M Tot Val, Unlisted SF, 304 days since logged occupancy.

2816 Frederick Douglass Bl, Aug 2019, Dunbar Own Llc, $923K Land Val, $13.5M Tot Val, Unlisted SF, 3774 days since logged occupancy.

430 Lenox Avenue, Nov 2019, 430 Lenox Ave Hdfc, $128K Land Val, $239K Tot Val, Unlisted SF, 3900+ days since logged occupancy.

Manhattan Vacancy

367 Lenox Avenue, May 2019, Monroe H&C Llc, $126K Land Val, $619K Tot Val, Unlisted SF, 1826 days since logged occupancy.

2494 Frederick Douglass Bl, Nov 2019, AFF WHGA MIN11E Lp, $345K Land Val, $533K Tot Val, Unlisted SF, 761 days since logged occupancy.

2726 Frederick Douglass Bl, Apr 2019, 2726 Realty, $55K Land Val, $1.08M Tot Val, Unlisted SF, 547 days since logged occupancy.

2798 Frederick Douglass Bl, Nov 2019, 2798 8th Ave Apts Corp, $46K Land Val, $745K Tot Val, 1200 SF, 92 days since logged occupancy.

2180 5 Avenue, Nov 2019, Lenox Terr Dev Assoc, $509K Land Val, $1.04M Tot Val, Unlisted SF, 3045+ days since logged occupancy.

2168 5 Avenue, Nov 2019, Lenox Terr Dev Assoc, $509K Land Val, $1.04M Tot Val, Unlisted SF, 3045+ days since logged occupancy.

Manhattan Vacancy

488 Lenox Avenue, Nov 2019, Lenox Trrc Dev Assoc, $581K Land Val, $2.22M Tot Val, Unlisted SF, 761 days since logged occupancy.

2730 F. Doug. Bl, Nov 2019, Harlem Shangri-La Housing Dev. Fund, $158K Land Val, $2.06M Tot Val, 1279 days since logged occupancy.

56 Macombs Place, Aug 2019, NYCHA, $2.66M Land Val, $8.65M Tot Val, Unlisted SF, 3652 days since logged occupancy.

2627 Adam C Powell Bl, May 2018, NYCHA, $2.62M Land Val, $6.37M Tot Val, Unlisted SF, 1430 days since logged occupancy.

Manhattan Vacancy

Upper West Side

Manhattan Vacancy

5% of ground-level units, 39% of retail space was reported vacant in Upper West Side

2,963,235

3,373

1,160,604

166

Retail Space

Ground-level Units

Manhattan Vacancy

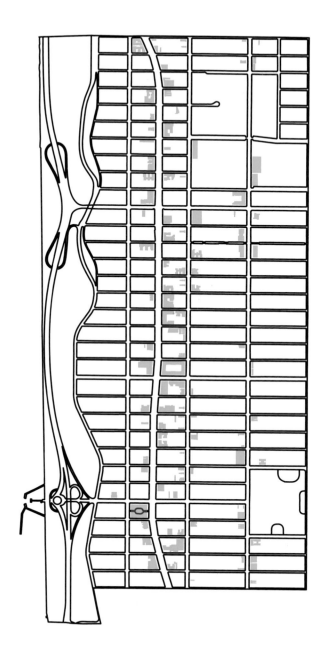

Manhattan Vacancy

Median Gross Rent as Percentage of Household Income

Manhattan Vacancy

Reported Retail Vacancy SF

(In thousands)

Manhattan Vacancy

888 Amsterdam Avenue, Jun 2019, Hudson Realty Assoc Llc, $450K Land Val, $3.59M Tot Val, Unlisted SF, 608 days since logged occupancy.

772 Amsterdam Avenue, Jul 2019, Brusco Equities Llc, $324K Land Val, $1.27M Tot Val, Unlisted SF, 1673 days since logged occupancy.

2284 Broadway, Jun 2019, 221 W 82 St Owners Corp, $3.78M Land Val, $19.2M Tot Val, 1172 SF, 608 days since logged occupancy.

328 Columbus Avenue, Jun 2019, Greystone Properties, $576K Land Val, $4.75M Tot Val, 2650 SF, 608 days since logged occupancy.

330 Columbus Avenue, Jun 2019, Greystone Properties, $576K Land Val, $4.75M Tot Val, 3350 SF, 1126 days since logged occupancy.

251 West 86 Street, Jul 2019, The Boulevard Condominium, $19.5M Land Val, $76.1M Tot Val, 12290 SF, 638 days since logged occupancy.

Manhattan Vacancy

2700 Broadway, May 2019, The 2700 Broadway Condo, $2.01M Land Val, $16.1M Tot Val, 5264 SF, 577 days since logged occupancy.

2642 Broadway, May 2019, 2640 Rlty Corp, $259K Land Val, $1.44M Tot Val, 750 SF, 1338 days since logged occupancy.

1272 Amsterdam Avenue, May 2019, Amsterdam Ave Investor Llc, $51K Land Val, $1.74M Tot Val, 2250 SF, 577 days since logged occupancy.

110 West 79 Street, Jun 2019, NYC 79 Lacoya Llc, $245K Land Val, $.442M Tot Val, 1250 SF, 1796 days since logged occupancy.

252 West 79 Street, Jul 2019, Unavailable Owner, $7.40M Land Val, $67.3M Tot Val, 1870 SF, 607 days since logged occupancy.

522–526 Amsterdam Avenue, Jul 2019, Cleo Realty Assoc, $2.25M Land Val, $7.80M Tot Val, 2175 SF, 686 days since logged occupancy.

Manhattan Vacancy

2575 Broadway, Jul 2019, The Columzia Poiudo, $3.64M Land Val, $48.5M Tot Val, 14151 SF, 638 days since logged occupancy.

2831 Broadway, May 2019, 2825 Broadway Llc, $1.05M Land Val, $7.04M Tot Val, 2500 SF, 1338 days since logged occupancy.

2234 Broadway, May 2019, 2228–2236 Broadway Llc, $7.49M Land Val, $18.8M Tot Val, 7184 SF, 850 days since logged occupancy.

434 Amsterdam Avenue, Sep 2019, 200 West 81st Street Co, $770K Land Val, $2.02M Tot Val, 1500 SF, 700 days since logged occupancy.

Manhattan Vacancy

Manhattan Vacancy

13% of ground-level units, 39% of retail space was reported vacant in Lower East Side

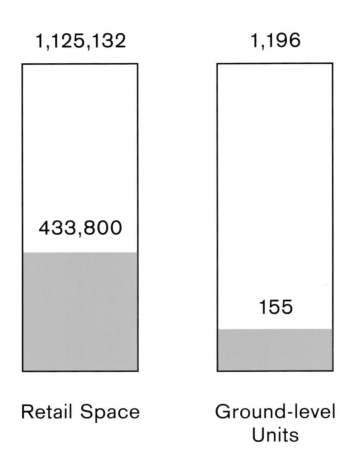

1,125,132

1,196

433,800

155

Retail Space

Ground-level Units

Manhattan Vacancy

155 Vacancies in Lower East Side

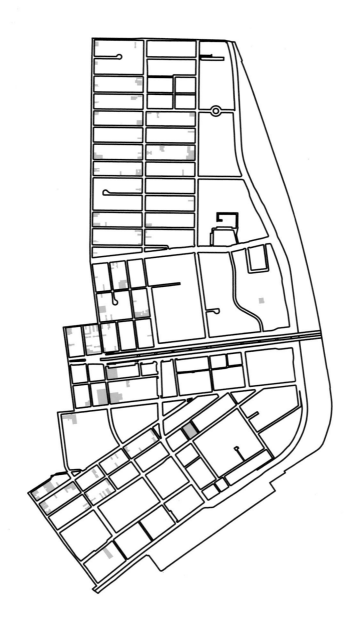

Manhattan Vacancy

Median Gross Rent as Percentage of Household Income

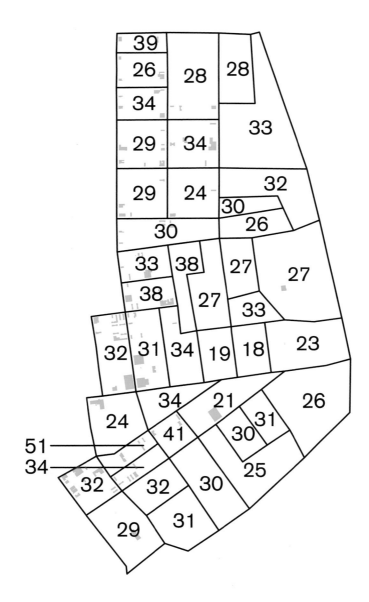

Reported Retail Vacancy SF

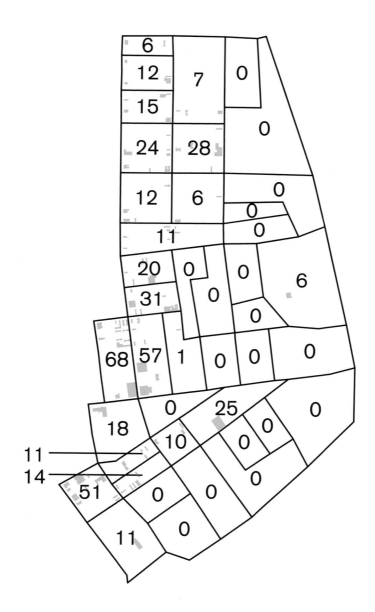

(In thousands)

Manhattan Vacancy

324 Grand Street, Oct 2019, Empire 326 Grand Llc, $1.34M Land Val, $3.12M Tot Val, 1800 SF, 2099 days since logged occupancy.

163 Ludlow Street, Jun 2019, 167 Ludlow Owner Llc, $32K Land Val, $1.68M Tot Val, Unlisted SF, 2526 days since logged occupancy.

10 Montgomery Street, Oct 2019, 201 Clinton St Rlty Inc, $90K Land Val, $782K Tot Val, Unlisted SF, 1948 days since logged occupancy.

37 Clinton Street, Jun 2019, 37–39 Clinton Llc, $282K Land Val, $1.85M Tot Val, 1000 SF, 335 days since logged occupancy.

124 Ridge Street, Oct 2019, 124 Ridge Llc, $342K Land Val, $1.71M Tot Val, Unlisted SF, 1948 days since logged occupancy.

187 Stanton Street, Oct 2019, Unavailable Owner, $225K Land Val, $698K Tot Val, Unlisted SF, 2252 days since logged occupancy.

Manhattan Vacancy

210 Rivington Street, Oct 2019, 210 Rivington AS Rlty Llc, $241K Land Val, $1.98M Tot Val, Unlisted SF, 699 days since logged occupancy.

92 Orchard Street, Jun 2019, 92 Orchard Realty Llc, $276K Land Val, $2.15M Tot Val, Unlisted SF, 577 days since logged occupancy.

561 Grand Street, Nov 2019, East River Housing Corp, $1.53M Land Val, $4.03M Tot Val, Unlisted SF, 791 days since logged occupancy.

198 Rivington Street, Oct 2019, 106 Ridge St Ground Own Llc, $406K Land Val, $3.07M Tot Val, 3500 SF, 2252 days since logged occupancy.

183 Stanton Street, Oct 2019, Unavailable Owner, $225K Land Val, $698K Tot Val, 400 SF, 1187 days since logged occupancy.

25 Clinton Street, Jun 2019, 25 Clinton Street Assoc, $254K Land Val, $1.63M Tot Val, Unlisted SF, 3713 days since logged occupancy.

Manhattan Vacancy

198 Stanton Street, Oct 2019, 196 Stanton St Condo, $416K Land Val, $10.9M Tot Val, Unlisted SF, 3835 days since logged occupancy.

20 Clinton Street, Jun 2019, Unavailable Owner, $281K Land Val, $5.65M Tot Val, 3500 SF, 1704 days since logged occupancy.

108 Ridge Street, Oct 2019, 106 Ridge St Ground Own Llc, $406K Land Val, $3.07M Tot Val, Unlisted SF, 1217 days since logged occupancy.

154 Stanton Street, Jun 2019, Y&K 155 Llc, $151K Land Val, $473K Tot Val, Unlisted SF, 1734 days since logged occupancy.

Manhattan Vacancy

Central Harlem South

7% of ground-level units, 42% of retail space was reported vacant in Central Harlem South

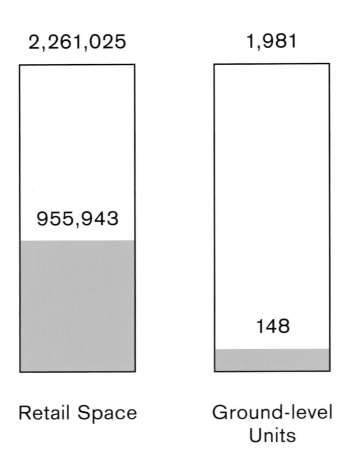

2,261,025

1,981

955,943

148

Retail Space

Ground-level Units

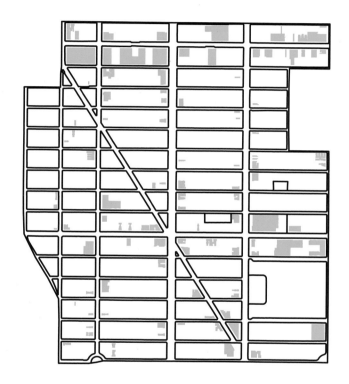

Median Gross Rent as Percentage of Household Income

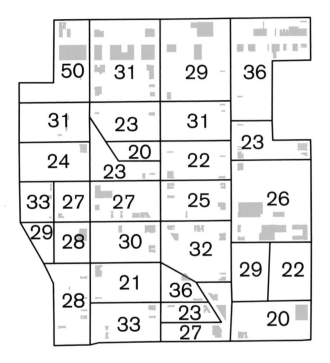

Reported Retail Vacancy SF

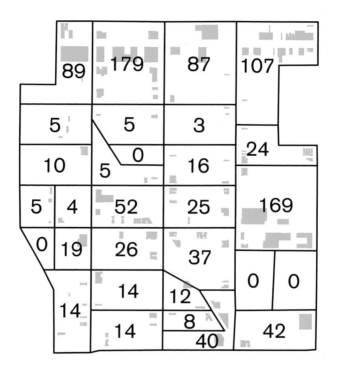

(In thousands)

1 West 125 Street, Jul 2019, Three West 125th Street De Llc, $735K Land Val, $3.87M Tot Val, 3600 SF, 365 days since logged occupancy.

26 East 125 Street, Jul 2019, 26 East 125 Street Llc, $43K Land Val, $561K Tot Val, 3150 SF, 2129 days since logged occupancy.

317 Lenox Avenue, May 2019, Harlem Center Condo, $1.60M Land Val, $37.0M Tot Val, 17432 SF, 1095 days since logged occupancy.

69 East 125 Street, Jul 2019, 69 East 125th St Owner Llc, $194K Land Val, $6.16M Tot Val, 3500 SF, 638 days since logged occupancy.

275 St Nicholas Avenue, May 2019, 281 St Nicholas Partners Llc, $250K Land Val, $3.02M Tot Val, 5250 SF, 2099 days since logged occupancy.

61 Lenox Avenue, Jul 2019, Unavailable Owner, $144K Land Val, $1.81M Tot Val, 1467 SF, 638 days since logged occupancy.

Manhattan Vacancy

2070 Adam Clayton Bl, May 2019, Adc/Ennis Francis II Hdfc Inc, $141K Land Val, $5.16M Tot Val, 3864+ days since logged occupancy.

2051–2057 Frederick Douglass Bl, May 2019, FDB 111 St Llc, $338K Land Val, $2.92M Tot Val, 2450 SF, 942 days since logged occupancy.

110 Lenox Avenue, May 2019, NYCHPD, $39K Land Val, $756K Tot Val, Unlisted SF, 1703 days since logged occupancy.

56 West 22 Street, May 2019, 56 W 22 Llc, $630K Land Val, $7.13M Tot Val, 2411 SF, 3600 days since logged occupancy.

254 West 125 Street, May 2019, 252 West 125th St, $518K Land Val, $3.10M Tot Val, 4256 SF, 1673 days since logged occupancy.

111 West 110 Street, Sep 2019, 111 Central Pk N Condo, $357K Land Val, $12.2M Tot Val, 1502 SF, 3805 days since logged occupancy.

Manhattan Vacancy

2154 2 Avenue, Jul 2019, 2154 2nd Llc, $157K Land Val, $480K Tot Val, Unlisted SF, 365 days since logged occupancy.

2164 Frederick Douglass Bl, May 2019, 2162–68 8 Ave Rlty Llc, $72K Land Val, $2.40M Tot Val, Unlisted SF, 273 days since logged occupancy.

1970 Adam C Powell Bl, May 2019, Harlem Prop Llc, $80K Land Val, $1.16M Tot Val, 2500 SF, 577 days since logged occupancy.

1967 Adam C Powell Bl, May 2019, Unavailable Owner, $273K Land Val, $3.99M Tot Val, Unlisted SF, 2891 days since logged occupancy.

1955 Adam C Powell Bl, Jul 2019, Unavailable Owner, $26K Land Val, $1.64M Tot Val, Unlisted SF, 1156 days since logged occupancy.

1941 Adam C Powell Bl, Jul 2019, Manhattan Powell Lp, $21K Land Val, $468K Tot Val, Unlisted SF, 638 days since logged occupancy.

Manhattan Vacancy

1890 Adam C Powell Bl, May 2019, Unavailable Owner, $270K Land Val, $3.58M Tot Val, 1730 SF, 546 days since logged occupancy.

67 Lenox Avenue, Jul 2019, 65–67 Lenox Llc, $74K Land Val, $548K Tot Val, Unlisted SF, 1399 days since logged occupancy.

285 West 110 Street, May 2019, Unavailable Owner, $1.22M Land Val, $13.8M Tot Val, Unlisted SF, 577 days since logged occupancy.

123 West 112 Street, May 2019, MPLP 6 HDFC, $90K Land Val, $1M Tot Val, Unlisted SF, 2464 days since logged occupancy.

Manhattan Vacancy

Washington Heights South

Manhattan Vacancy

11% of ground-level units, 47% of retail space was reported vacant in Washington Heights South

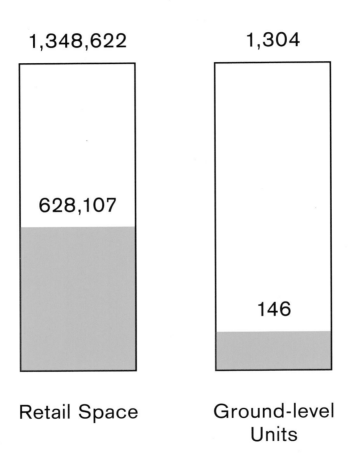

1,348,622

628,107

Retail Space

1,304

146

Ground-level Units

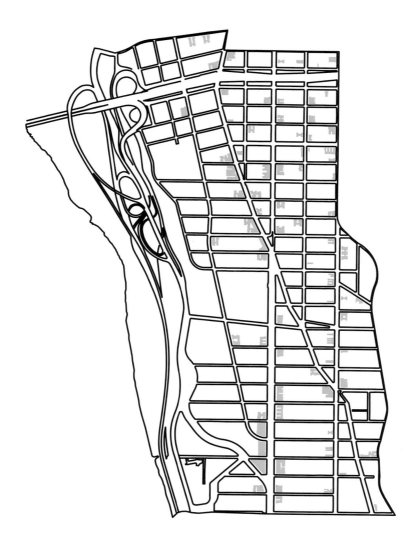

Median Gross Rent as Percentage of Household Income

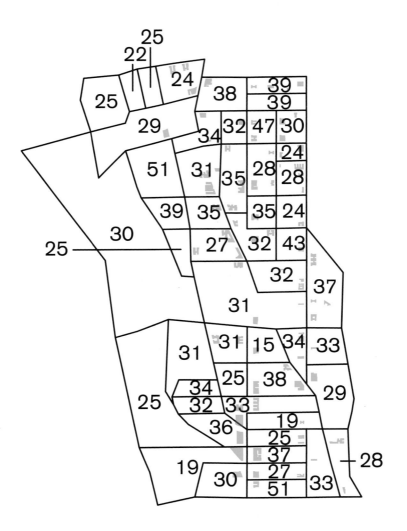

Reported Retail Vacancy SF

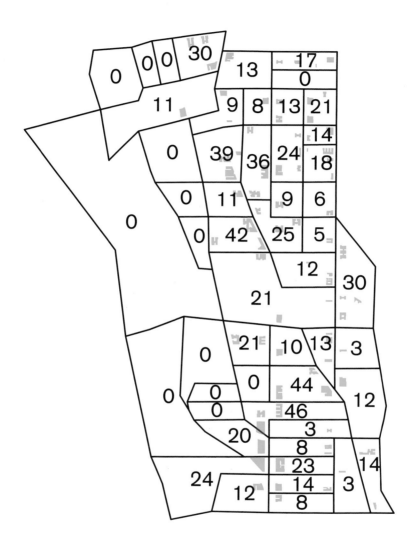

(In thousands)

Manhattan Vacancy

4066 Broadway, Nov 2019, 4060 Sky Llc, $197K Land Val, $1.63M Tot Val, Unlisted SF, 2252 days since logged occupancy.

4081–4083 Broadway, Aug 2019, Mrs Realty Llc, $369K Land Val, $3.14M Tot Val, Unlisted SF, 720 days since logged occupancy.

4103 Broadway, Nov 2019, Broadway Towers NYC Llc, $161K Land Val, $2.88M Tot Val, 2410 SF, 3106 days since logged occupancy.

2308 Amsterdam Avenue, Nov 2019, Mauray Realty USA Llc, $199K Land Val, $959K Tot Val, 3211 SF, 3000+ days since logged occupancy.

4186 Broadway, Aug 2019, Riviera International Llc, $81K Land Val, $862K Tot Val, 2500 SF, 669 days since logged occupancy.

2170–2172 Amsterdam Avenue, Nov 2019, NYCHPD, $23K Land Val, $663K Tot Val, 4400 SF, 3000+ days since logged occupancy.

Manhattan Vacancy

550 West 174 Street, Aug 2019, Atsiki Realty Llc, $186K Land Val, $1.21M Tot Val, Unlisted SF, 395 days since logged occupancy.

1326 St Nicholas Avenue, Nov 2019, HP Washington Port HD, $219K Land Val, $3.23M Tot Val, Unlisted SF, 761 days since logged occupancy.

2106 Amsterdam Avenue, Nov 2019, Amsterdam 1 Llc, $24K Land Val, $617K Tot Val, Unlisted SF, 791 days since logged occupancy.

528 West 162 Street, Nov 2019, 528 W 162 Llc, $225K Land Val, $1.40M Tot Val, 30000 SF, 3045 days since logged occupancy.

4126 Broadway, Aug 2019, 4126 Realty Corp, $89K Land Val, $381K Tot Val, 1000 SF, 1187 days since logged occupancy.

4211 Broadway, Oct 2019, Port Authority of NY and NJ, $2.26M Land Val, $33.9M Tot Val, 2180 SF, 1248 days since logged occupancy.

Manhattan Vacancy

3781 Broadway, Nov 2019, 3781 Broadway Llc, $540K Land Val, $6.67M Tot Val, Unlisted SF, 761 days since logged occupancy.

3789 Broadway, Nov 2019, 3781 Broadway Llc, $540K Land Val, $6.67M Tot Val, 805 SF, 1126 days since logged occupancy.

1345 St Nicholas Avenue, Nov 2019, 1341 Realty Group Llc, $212K Land Val, $1.20M Tot Val, 595 SF, 761 days since logged occupancy.

Manhattan Vacancy

11% of ground-level units, 35% of retail space was reported vacant in Murray Hill, Kips Bay

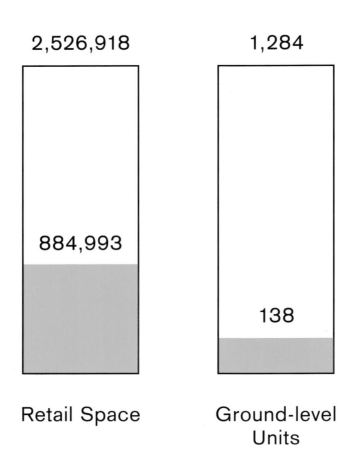

2,526,918

1,284

884,993

138

Retail Space

Ground-level
Units

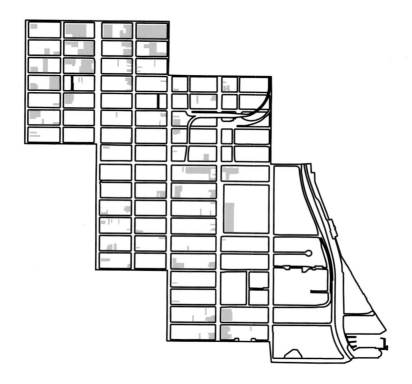

Median Gross Rent as Percentage of Household Income

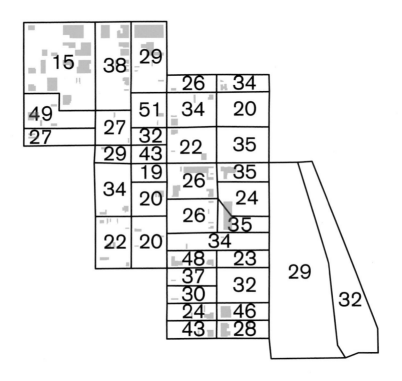

Reported Retail Vacancy SF

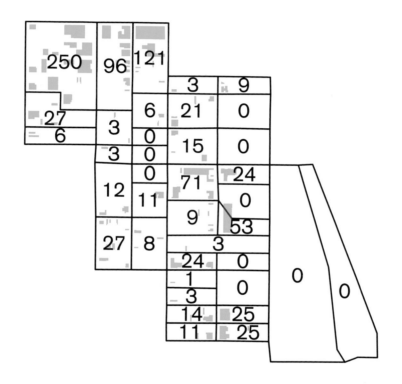

(In thousands)

Manhattan Vacancy

200 East 23 Street, Oct 2019, Unavailable Owner, $2.52M Land Val, $35.8M Tot Val, Unlisted SF, 791 days since logged occupancy.

184 Lexington Avenue, Jun 2019, Trico Equities Co, $2.73M Land Val, $17.8M Tot Val, 2200 SF, 638 days since logged occupancy.

445 5 Avenue, Jun 2019, Fifth Ave Condo BHS Mgmnt, $8.37M Land Val, $31.2M Tot Val, 18317 SF, 304 days since logged occupancy.

440 3 Avenue, Nov 2019, LTG Property Holdings Inc, $103K Land Val, $1.33M Tot Val, Unlisted SF, 153 days since logged occupancy.

141 Lexington Avenue, Jun 2019, Marbilla Llc, $248K Land Val, $1.27M Tot Val, 1400 SF, 1704 days since logged occupancy.

606 2 Avenue, Jun 2019, HKAL 34th Street Lp, $6.98M Land Val, $46.1M Tot Val, 1500 SF, 304 days since logged occupancy.

Manhattan Vacancy

405 3 Avenue, Jun 2019,
Chesapeake Owners Corp, $2.45M
Land Val, $26.2M Tot Val, 1442 SF,
2130 days since logged occupancy.

650 1 Avenue, Jun 2019, Jericho
Office Llc, $363K Land Val, $2.23M
Tot Val, Unlisted SF, 2830 days
since logged occupancy.

106 Lexington Avenue, Jun 2019,
Igratz Realty Inc, $495K Land Val,
$2.12M Tot Val, Unlisted SF, 1095
days since logged occupancy.

361 3 Avenue, Oct 2019, Eleanor
Wong Chew Trustee, $909K Land
Val, $2.43M Tot Val, Unlisted SF,
122 days since logged occupancy.

237 East 34 Street, Oct 2019,
Theater House Apts Llc, $4.75M
Land Val, $16.6M Tot Val, 6000 SF,
791 days since logged occupancy.

314 East 34 Street, Oct 2019,
Bashi Rafael Llc, $380K Land Val,
$1.88M Tot Val, 1800 SF, 1125
days since logged occupancy.

Manhattan Vacancy

423 2 Avenue, Jun 2019, Tracy
Tenants Corp, $1.01M Land Val,
$13.3M Tot Val, 2950 SF, 1003
days since logged occupancy.

Lenox Hill, Roosevelt Island

Manhattan Vacancy

8% of ground-level units, 31% of retail
space was reported vacant in Lenox Hill,
Roosevelt Island

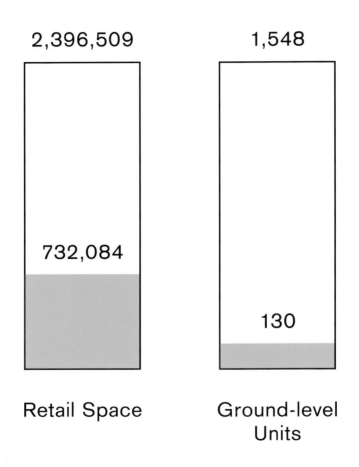

2,396,509

732,084

Retail Space

1,548

130

Ground-level
Units

Manhattan Vacancy

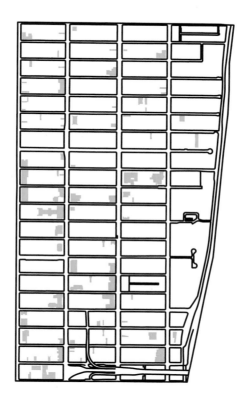

Median Gross Rent as Percentage of Household Income

0	51	30	32
32	51	25	16
38	51	33	
33	32	28	29
	20		
25	42	24	
		20	23
25	0	29	13
20	20	28	35
17	29	15	
35			
31	27	21	
18			
20	34	33	
14	39	29	
28	27	28	
19	19		
23	31	27	21

Reported Retail Vacancy SF

13	4	0	0
2	2	13	
6	14	0	0
24	0	15	0
	2		
7	12	9	
		2	10
14	2	0	0
22	0	54	0
34	25	10	
42			
14	9	4	
9			
0	29	0	
0	32	0	
26	24	2	
14	5		
75	14	40	7

(In thousands)

1373 1 Avenue, May 2019, 1373 First Avenue Assoc Llc, $549K Land Val, $1.20M Tot Val, 1100 SF, 577 days since logged occupancy.

1365 1 Avenue, May 2019, 1365 Empire Llc, $180K Land Val, $1.53M Tot Val, Unlisted SF, 1308 days since logged occupancy.

1427 2 Avenue, May 2019, 255 East 74th Street Condo, $3.53M Land Val, $45.3M Tot Val, 985 SF, 273 days since logged occupancy.

1306 2 Avenue, May 2019, 2nd Ave Holding 1 Llc, $383K Land Val, $1.33M Tot Val, 500 SF, 304 days since logged occupancy.

1122 1 Avenue, May 2019, 1122 First Avenue Llc, $253K Land Val, $768K Tot Val, 1980 SF, 911 days since logged occupancy.

1155 2 Avenue, Jun 2019, SP 1143 Second Llc, $2.93M Land Val, $8.97M Tot Val, 1350 SF, 608 days since logged occupancy.

Manhattan Vacancy

1164 2 Avenue, Jun 2019,
Unavailable Owner, $798K Land
Val, $10.6M Tot Val, 2730 SF,
Unoccupied new construction.

1433 1 Avenue, May 2019, Betty
Weg, $155K Land Val, $1.37M
Tot Val, 950 SF, 2586 days since
logged occupancy.

1177 2 Avenue, Jun 2019, 253
East 62nd Street, $384K Land
Val, $3.21M Tot Val, 985 SF,
Unoccupied new construction.

348 East 62 Street, Nov 2019, 348
East 62nd Llc, $274K Land Val,
$1.46M Tot Val, 1500 SF, 2010
days since logged occupancy.

1245 2 Avenue, Jun 2019,
Manhattan House Condo, $13.7M
Land Val, $119M Tot Val, 800 SF,
335 days since logged occupancy.

1261 2 Avenue, Jun 2019,
Townhouse Company II Llc, $27.2M
Land Val, $68.8M Tot Val, 3600 SF,
3713 days since logged occupancy.

Manhattan Vacancy

1300 3 Avenue, May 2019, 196 Owners Corp, $3.48M Land Val, $18.4M Tot Val, 3180 SF, 638 days since logged occupancy.

1475 2 Avenue, May 2019, Mhg Family Limited Pa, $896K Land Val, $3.71M Tot Val, 2351 SF, 911 days since logged occupancy.

1509 2 Avenue, May 2019, El Kam Realty Co, $749K Land Val, $1.51M Tot Val, Unlisted SF, 1673 days since logged occupancy.

Manhattan Vacancy

11% of ground-level units, 32% of retail space was reported vacant in East Harlem South

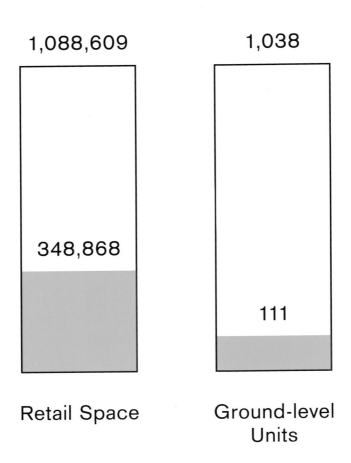

1,088,609

1,038

348,868

111

Retail Space

Ground-level Units

Manhattan Vacancy

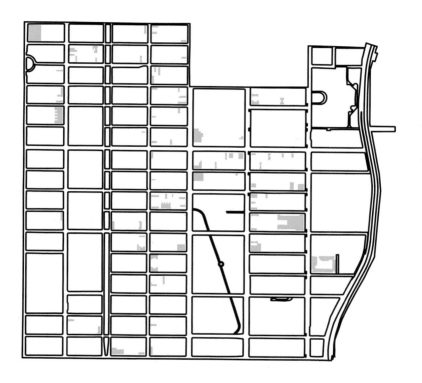

Median Gross Rent as Percentage of Household Income

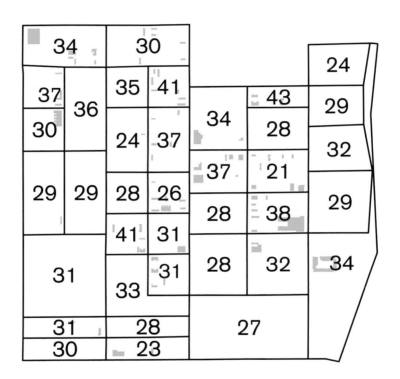

Reported Retail Vacancy SF

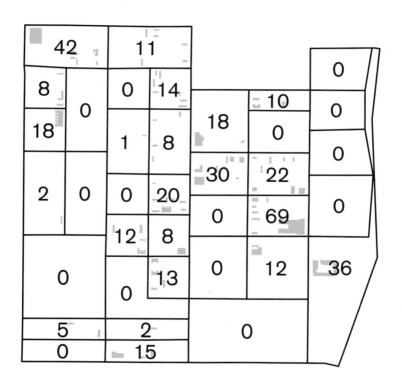

(In thousands)

Manhattan Vacancy

1992 3 Avenue, Jun 2019, 1992
Third Realty Llc, $119K Land Val,
$1.63M Tot Val, 1200 SF, 1126
days since logged occupancy.

333 East 101 Street, Jun 2019,
Aspen 2016 Llc, $684K Land Val,
$18.2M Tot Val, 1600 SF, 608 days
since logged occupancy.

1773 Lexington Avenue, Jul 2019,
Caritas Dev L, $32K Land Val,
$858K Tot Val, Unlisted SF, 1156
days since logged occupancy.

1630 Madison Avenue, Jun 2019,
Unavailable Owner, $61K Land Val,
$1.39M Tot Val, 1635 SF, 1734
days since logged occupancy.

176 East 101 Street, Jun 2019,
Lott Legacy Apts Hdfc, $26K Land
Val, $568K Tot Val, 1000 SF, 3683
days since logged occupancy.

141 East 96 Street, Jun 2019,
Pelas Realty Corp, $130K Land Val,
$267K Tot Val, Unlisted SF, 396
days since logged occupancy.

Manhattan Vacancy

154 Tito Puente Way, Jul 2019, Samsar Llc, $164K Land Val, $544K Tot Val, Unlisted SF, 3743 days since logged occupancy.

22 East 108 Street, Jun 2019, Hope East of Fifth Hdfc, $140K Land Val, $317K Tot Val, Unlisted SF, 335 days since logged occupancy.

347 East 109 Street, Jun 2019, Narinder Pal Singh, $140K Land Val, $290K Tot Val, 800 SF, 2099 days since logged occupancy.

1905 3 Avenue, Jun 2019, Third Ave Enterprises, $113K Land Val, $1.13M Tot Val, Unlisted SF, 304 days since logged occupancy.

1557 Lexington Avenue, Jul 2019, 1557 Lex Ave Llc, $314K Land Val, $836K Tot Val, Unlisted SF, 1369 days since logged occupancy.

1638 Lexington Avenue, Jul 2019, Lexington NY Rlty Llc, $81K Land Val, $1.10M Tot Val, Unlisted SF, 2526 days since logged occupancy.

Manhattan Vacancy

1631 Lexington Avenue, Jul 2019,
Metro Properties Llc, $45K Land
Val, $735K Tot Val, Unlisted SF,
638 days since logged occupancy.

12% of ground-level units, 56% of retail space was reported vacant in Washington Heights North

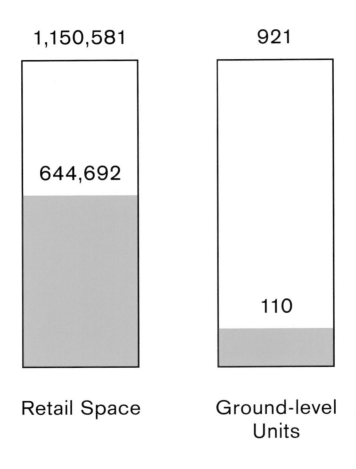

1,150,581

921

644,692

110

Retail Space

Ground-level Units

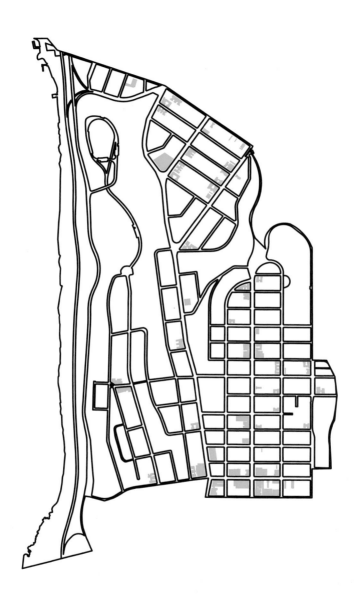

Median Gross Rent as Percentage of Household Income

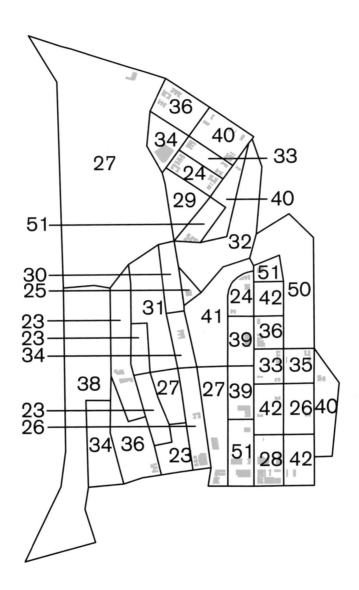

Manhattan Vacancy

Reported Retail Vacancy SF

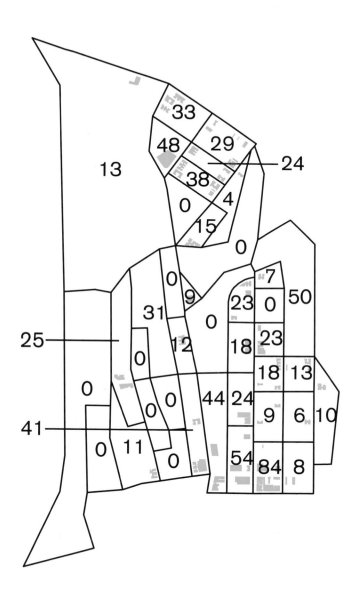

(In thousands)

Manhattan Vacancy

1495 St Nicholas Avenue, Oct 2019, The Luna Properties Llc, $363K Land Val, $2.46M Tot Val, Unlisted SF, 1248 days since logged occupancy.

4292 Broadway, Nov 2019, Regent Associates, $797K Land Val, $6.12M Tot Val, 20000 SF, 1279 days since logged occupancy.

4300 Broadway, Nov 2019, 4300 Broadway Lp, $282K Land Val, $2.46M Tot Val, Unlisted SF, 2010 days since logged occupancy.

617 West 181 Street, Aug 2019, NYC Housing Authority, $900K Land Val, $2.45M Tot Val, 3000 SF, 1187 days since logged occupancy.

1563 St Nicholas Avenue, Aug 2019, 188 St Nick Assoc Llc, $207K Land Val, $1.85M Tot Val, Unlisted SF, 457 days since logged occupancy.

1569 St Nicholas Avenue, Aug 2019, 188 St Nick Assoc, $279K Land Val, $2.10M Tot Val, Unlisted SF, 669 days since logged occupancy.

Manhattan Vacancy

1564 St Nicholas Avenue, Oct 2019, 1562–68 St Nic Ave Llc, $303K Land Val, $1.64M Tot Val, 3700 SF, 1248 days since logged occupancy.

1588 St Nicholas Avenue, Oct 2019, 1588 Llc, $113K Land Val, $633K Tot Val, Unlisted SF, 2952 days since logged occupancy.

4421 Broadway, Nov 2019, 4423–29 Broadway Llc, $100K Land Val, $921K Tot Val, Unlisted SF, 1887 days since logged occupancy.

1487 St Nicholas Avenue, Oct 2019, Randi Mgmt Co Llc, $308K Land Val, $2.84M Tot Val, 900 SF, 212 days since logged occupancy.

720 West 181 Street, Aug 2019, Viaveb Llc, $251K Land Val, $2.98M Tot Val, 2200 SF, 1034 days since logged occupancy.

1431 St Nicholas Avenue, Aug 2019, Regent Associates, $320K Land Val, $1.63M Tot Val, 3500 SF, 457 days since logged occupancy.

Manhattan Vacancy

1 Nagle Avenue, Oct 2019, Granite Realty Llc, $342K Land Val, $4.18M Tot Val, 3000 SF, 1979 days since logged occupancy.

1570 St Nicholas Avenue, Oct 2019, 1570 St Nick Assoc Lp, $191K Land Val, $2.41M Tot Val, Unlisted SF, 1248 days since logged occupancy.

4746 Broadway, Oct 2019, First Street Development Llc, $284K Land Val, $2.95M Tot Val, 2810 SF, 457 days since logged occupancy.

Manhattan Vacancy

Manhattan Vacancy

6% of ground-level units, 28% of retail space was reported vacant in Yorkville

1,749,752

1,670

484,630

106

Retail Space

Ground-level Units

Manhattan Vacancy

106 Vacancies in Yorkville

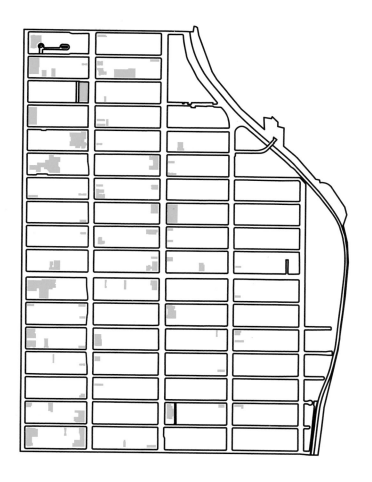

Manhattan Vacancy

Median Gross Rent as Percentage of Household Income

22	37	
22	27	32
18	30	
17	30	36
32		19
51	26	28
35	29	22
34	33	23
24	25	27
19	22	27
26	30	39
27	20	40
22	25	36
27		24
28	36	28
22	45	27
38	26	19

34
19
25
23
29
35
24
32

Reported Retail Vacancy SF

0	3				
40	32	0			
17	2				
14	6	0			
29		6	0		
36	12	4			
5	14	0			
2	8	21	0		
2	11	3		1	
10	11	8			
41	11	0	2		
6	0	13	0		
23	10	3	6	0	
6					
2	2	0	0		
19	0	13	2		
36	5	0			

(In thousands)

1720 2 Avenue, Jul 2019, Dovom, $2.03M Land Val, $6.13M Tot Val, Unlisted SF, 638 days since logged occupancy.

1660 1 Avenue, May 2019, 1660 1St Llc, $608K Land Val, $1.96M Tot Val, Unlisted SF, 638 days since logged occupancy.

1633 2 Avenue, May 2019, VDK Realty Corp, $180K Land Val, $1.47M Tot Val, Unlisted SF, 273 days since logged occupancy.

1711 1 Avenue, May 2019, Unavailable Owner, $2.09M Land Val, $12.2M Tot Val, 1140 SF, 304 days since logged occupancy.

357 East 86 Street, Jun 2019, First NY Llc, $500K Land Val, $2.93M Tot Val, Unlisted SF, 1369 days since logged occupancy.

1647 1 Avenue, May 2019, First NY Llc, $608K Land Val, $1.82M Tot Val, 2250 SF, 1765 days since logged occupancy.

Manhattan Vacancy

500 East 81 Street, May 2019, WMF 502 East 81st Llc, $774K Land Val, $2.39M Tot Val, Unlisted SF, 1673 days since logged occupancy.

1590 York Avenue, Nov 2019, Goodwood Realty, $729K Land Val, $2.32M Tot Val, 1500 SF, 457 days since logged occupancy.

401 East 90 Street, Jun 2019, 401 East 90th Street Llc, $170K Land Val, $2.14M Tot Val, Unlisted SF, 2099 days since logged occupancy.

1589 2 Avenue, May 2019, Jomel Associates Inc, $1.16M Land Val, $2.36M Tot Val, Unlisted SF, 638 days since logged occupancy.

163 East 87 Street, May 2019, LGF Enterprises, $234K Land Val, $1.42M Tot Val, 320 SF, 577 days since logged occupancy.

1710 1 Avenue, May 2019, 1700 First Avenue, $4.77M Land Val, $18.3M Tot Val, 760 SF, 577 days since logged occupancy.

Manhattan Vacancy

Hamilton Heights

Manhattan Vacancy

6% of ground-level units, 48% of retail space was reported vacant in Hamilton Heights

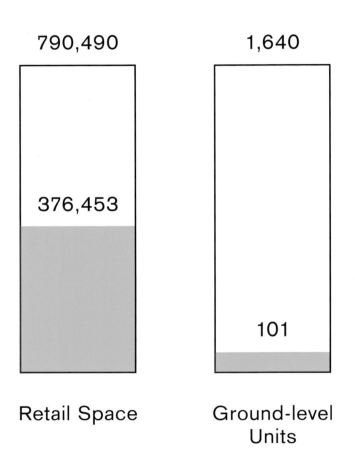

790,490

1,640

376,453

101

Retail Space

Ground-level
Units

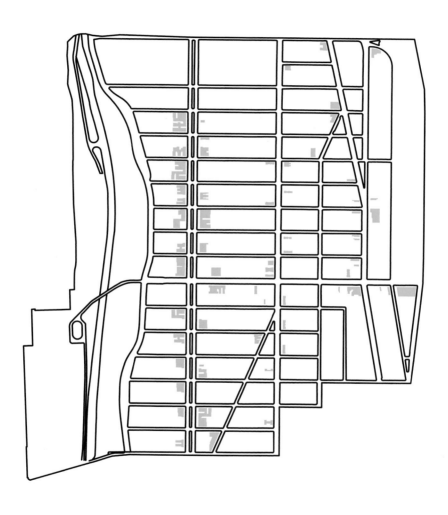

Median Gross Rent as Percentage of Household Income

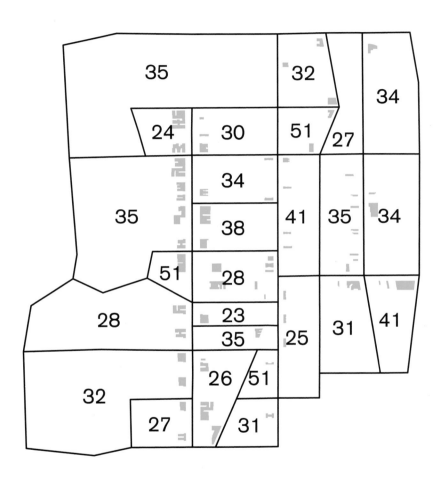

Reported Retail Vacancy SF

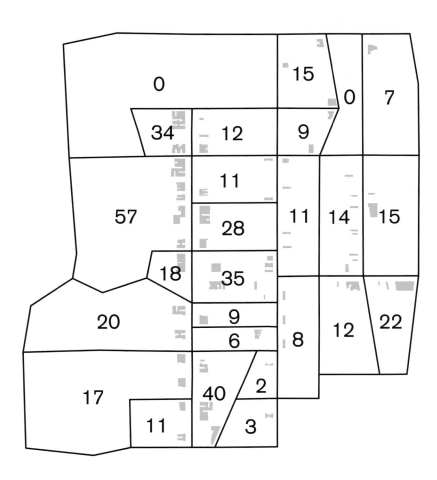

(In thousands)

Manhattan Vacancy

140 Hamilton Place, Oct 2017, Hmtn Hts Cluster Assoc Lp, $28K Land Val, $1.07M Tot Val, Unlisted SF, 1188 days since logged occupancy.

1707 Amsterdam Avenue, Nov 2019, 1697 Amsterdam Assoc Llc, $48K Land Val, $909K Tot Val, Unlisted SF, 761 days since logged occupancy.

3451 Broadway, Nov 2019, Pole Realty Llc C/o L, $203K Land Val, $2.15M Tot Val, 3700 SF, 92 days since logged occupancy.

1726 Amsterdam Avenue, Aug 2019, 1726 Amsterdam Llc, $286K Land Val, $736K Tot Val, Unlisted SF, 2922 days since logged occupancy.

3560 Broadway, Nov 2019, 146 Upper Bdwy Holdings Llc, $104K Land Val, $1.83M Tot Val, 27960 SF, 3866 days since logged occupancy.

470 Convent Avenue, Nov 2019, 470 Convent Ave Hdfc, $128K Land Val, $1.12M Tot Val, 2839 SF, 3866 days since logged occupancy.

Manhattan Vacancy

1774 Amsterdam Avenue, Aug 2019, 500 W 148 Llc, $169K Land Val, $1.49M Tot Val, 750 SF, 669 days since logged occupancy.

30 Hamilton Place, Nov 2019, RLSA Rlty Corp, $698K Land Val, $3.41M Tot Val, Unlisted SF, 3866+ days since logged occupancy.

1624 Amsterdam Avenue, Dec 2017, Unavailable Owner, $60K Land Val, $1.42M Tot Val, Unlisted SF, 3166+ days since logged occupancy.

609 West 141 Street, Oct 2017, NYCHPD, $76K Land Val, $572K Tot Val, Unlisted SF, 2284 days since logged occupancy.

600 West 142 Street, Oct 2017, 142 Bdwy Assoc, $225K Land Val, $1.79M Tot Val, Unlisted SF, 1887 days since logged occupancy.

532 West 145 Street, Nov 2019, 540 West 145 Llc, $108K Land Val, $2.68M Tot Val, 5950 SF, 2648 days since logged occupancy.

Manhattan Vacancy

Lincoln Square

Manhattan Vacancy

8% of ground-level units, 37% of retail space
was reported vacant in Lincoln Square

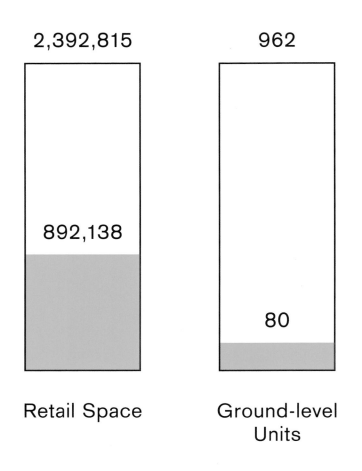

2,392,815

892,138

Retail Space

962

80

Ground-level
Units

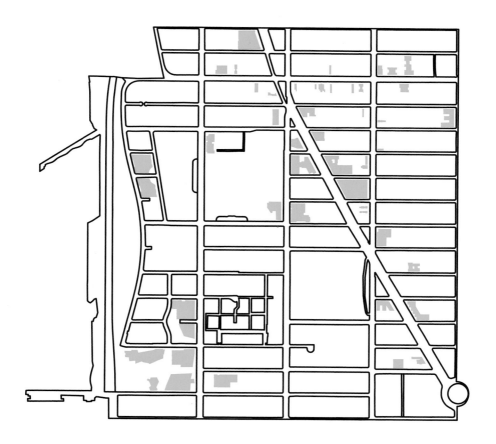

Median Gross Rent as Percentage of Household Income

Manhattan Vacancy

Reported Retail Vacancy SF

0	41	0	0
	14	2	27
0	6	16	8
0	12	15	22
0		22	1
36	0	37	73	0
31	55	
0	36	0
	0		23
		14	10
209	0		0
	0		19
		0	27
	30	0	0

(In thousands)

279   Manhattan Vacancy

146 West 72 Street, Nov 2017,
140–154 W 72 Rlty Llc, $2.74M
Land Val, $9.41M Tot Val, 1300 SF,
61 days since logged occupancy.

156 Columbus Avenue, May 2019,
148–154 Columbus Rlty Llc, $391K
Land Val, $2.23M Tot Val, 1609 SF,
1338 days since logged occupancy.

217 Columbus Avenue, May 2019,
SG 211–217 Col Ave Llc, $4.19M
Land Val, $7.88M Tot Val, 12122 SF,
972 days since logged occupancy.

150 Amsterdam Avenue, May 2019,
Unavailable Owner, $10.8M Land
Val, $64.3M Tot Val, 1562 SF, 1338
days since logged occupancy.

21 West End Avenue, Jul 2019,
Unavailable Owner, $37.4M Land
Val, $145M Tot Val, 900 SF,
Unoccupied new construction.

2062 Broadway, Jun 2019, South
Pierre Associates Llc, $5.08M Land
Val, $22M Tot Val, 1075 SF, 608
days since logged occupancy.

Manhattan Vacancy

2011 Broadway, Jul 2019, Dorchester Tower Condo, $23.6M Land Val, $104M Tot Val, Unlisted SF, 607 days since logged occupancy.

265 Columbus Avenue, May 2019, Partnership 92 West Lp, $1.57M Land Val, $6.86M Tot Val, 488 SF, 3652 days since logged occupancy.

37 West End Avenue, Jun 2019, Brodcom West Dev Co Llc, $18.1M Land Val, $86.7M Tot Val, 950 SF, 2892 days since logged occupancy.

1 West End Avenue, Jun 2019, Unavailable Owner, $32.4M Land Val, $142M Tot Val, 2624 SF, Unoccupied new construction.

1865 Broadway, Jun 2019, Unlisted Owner, Unlisted Land Val, Unlisted Tot Val, 21000 SF, Unoccupied new construction.

2028 Broadway, Jun 2019, Ormonde Equities Llc, $5.22M Land Val, $24.9M Tot Val, Unlisted SF, 2130 days since logged occupancy.

Manhattan Vacancy

25 Central Park West, Jun 2019,
Century Condominium, $26.8M
Land Val, $113M Tot Val, 3100 SF,
1857 days since logged occupancy.

Manhattan Vacancy

Gramercy

Manhattan Vacancy

9% of ground-level units, 27% of retail space was reported vacant in Gramercy

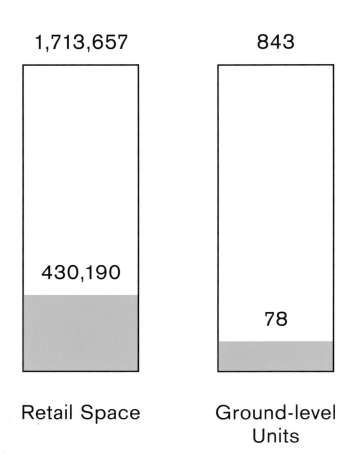

1,713,657   843

430,190

78

Retail Space   Ground-level
Units

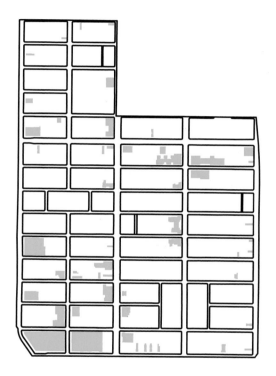

Median Gross Rent as Percentage of Household Income

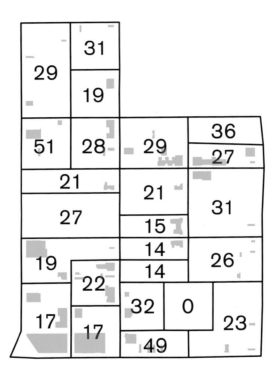

Reported Retail Vacancy SF

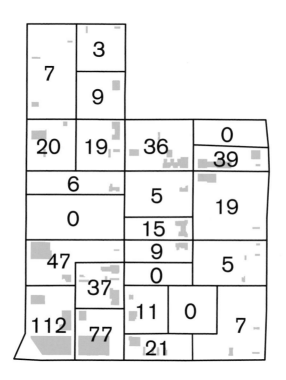

(In thousands)

Manhattan Vacancy

157 3 Avenue, Oct 2019, 200 E 16 St Housing Corp, $1.04M Land Val, $16.4M Tot Val, Unlisted SF, 1156 days since logged occupancy.

214 3 Avenue, Oct 2019, 214 3rd Avenue Llc, $116K Land Val, $203K Tot Val, 1093 SF, 760 days since logged occupancy.

190 3 Avenue, Jun 2019, Saul S Katz Trust, $410K Land Val, $1.21M Tot Val, 6670 SF, 577 days since logged occupancy.

79 Irving Place, Jun 2019, Irving Pl Realty Llc, $477K Land Val, $3.60M Tot Val, Unlisted SF, 638 days since logged occupancy.

295 3 Avenue, Oct 2019, 293 Third Avenue Llc, $281K Land Val, $480K Tot Val, 1300 SF, 1948 days since logged occupancy.

359 2 Avenue, Jun 2019, SD Second Ave Prop Llc, $316K Land Val, $491K Tot Val, Unlisted SF, 577 days since logged occupancy.

Manhattan Vacancy

127 East 17 Street, Jun 2019, 130 E 18 Owners Corp, $2.73M Land Val, $20.6M Tot Val, Unlisted SF, 1704 days since logged occupancy.

38 Union Sq E, Jul 2020, 101 East 16th Realty Llc, $2.75M Land Val, $13.2M Tot Val, Unlisted SF, 1034 days since logged occupancy.

335 2 Avenue, Jun 2019, 245 E 19 Realty Llc, $2.53M Land Val, $29.3M Tot Val, Unlisted SF, 669 days since logged occupancy.

111 East 18 Street, Jun 2019, 225 Fourth Llc, $24.6M Land Val, $83.7M Tot Val, 10000 SF, 577 days since logged occupancy.

321 East 22 Street, Jun 2019, 5531 – 321 E 22 St Manhattan Llc, $1.76M Land Val, $11.5M Tot Val, Unlisted SF, 577 days since logged occupancy.

380 2 Avenue, Jun 2019, Andrew Mogelof Trustee, $4.64M Land Val, $23.1M Tot Val, 2532 SF, 304 days since logged occupancy.

Manhattan Vacancy

234 3 Avenue, Oct 2019, 32 Gramercy Pk Owners Corp, $2.31M Land Val, $24.3M Tot Val, 1200 SF, 1156 days since logged occupancy.

328 East 14 Street, Jun 2019, Golden Realty Co, $522K Land Val, $3.26M Tot Val, Unlisted SF, 1003 days since logged occupancy.

329 East 14 Street, Jun 2019, 329 East 14th Street Llc, $90K Land Val, $1.48M Tot Val, Unlisted SF, 577 days since logged occupancy.

233 East 14 Street, Jun 2019, Berliza Corporation, $1.34M Land Val, $2.88M Tot Val, Unlisted SF, 1003 days since logged occupancy.

227 East 14 Street, Jun 2019, 227–229 E 14th St Hdfc, $104K Land Val, $1.12M Tot Val, 850 SF, 577 days since logged occupancy.

207 East 14 Street, Jun 2019, 207 East 14th St Rlty, $180K Land Val, $2.15M Tot Val, 1100 SF, 638 days since logged occupancy.

Manhattan Vacancy

8.3% of ground-level units, 51% of retail space was reported vacant in Marble Hill, Inwood

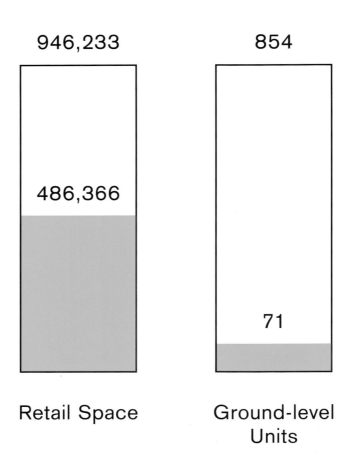

946,233

854

486,366

71

Retail Space

Ground-level
Units

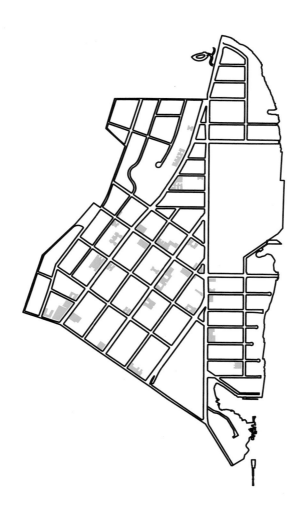

Manhattan Vacancy

Median Gross Rent as Percentage of Household Income

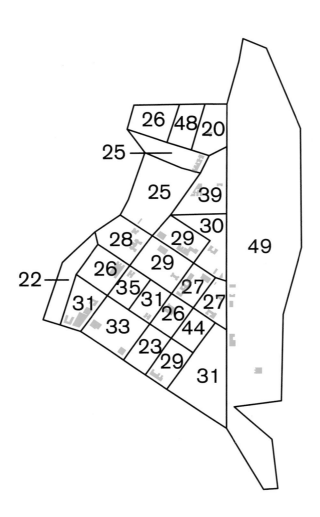

Reported Retail Vacancy SF

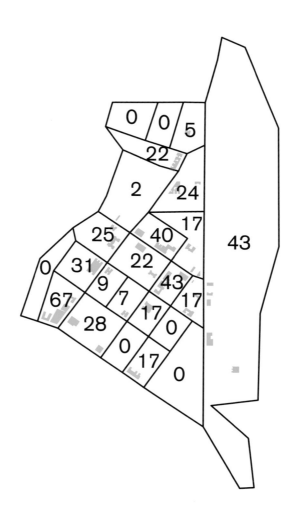

(In thousands)

Manhattan Vacancy

101 Dyckman Street, Jul 2019,
Dyckman 101 Llc, $244K Land Val,
$3.93M Tot Val, Unlisted SF, 638
days since logged occupancy.

154 Dyckman Street, Oct 2019,
Silpar Realty Inc, $90K Land Val,
$1.37M Tot Val, 950 SF, 1248 days
since logged occupancy.

200 Dyckman Street, Oct 2019,
Cherry Lane Assets Llc, $410K Land
Val, $3.87M Tot Val, Unlisted SF,
426 days since logged occupancy.

4771 Broadway, Oct 2019, 4761
Broadway Assoc Llc, $527K Land
Val, $7.41M Tot Val, 600 SF, 760
days since logged occupancy.

207 Sherman Avenue, Oct 2019,
207 Sherman Assoc, $192K Land
Val, $2.68M Tot Val, Unlisted SF,
2252 days since logged occupancy.

5025 Broadway, Oct 2019, Inwood
Ventura Ii Ll, $195K Land Val,
$2.58M Tot Val, 1366 SF, 518 days
since logged occupancy.

Manhattan Vacancy

565 West 207 Street, Oct 2019, 565 Realty Assoc Llc, $333K Land Val, $1.47M Tot Val, 2400 SF, 1248 days since logged occupancy.

4770 Broadway, Jul 2019, 4768 Broadway Llc, $752K Land Val, $3.20M Tot Val, 1350 SF, 365 days since logged occupancy.

5008 Broadway, Oct 2019, 5008 Broadway Llc, $79K Land Val, $2.65M Tot Val, 1687 SF, 1856 days since logged occupancy.

4925 Broadway, Oct 2019, MN Urban 207 Llc, $237K Land Val, $3.95M Tot Val, 500 SF, 2617 days since logged occupancy.

4867 Broadway, Oct 2019, Hawthorne Gardens, $549K Land Val, $7.49M Tot Val, Unlisted SF, 426 days since logged occupancy.

179 Sherman Avenue, Aug 2019, MMLERY Llc, $132K Land Val, $2.29M Tot Val, 835 SF, 457 days since logged occupancy.

Manhattan Vacancy

173 Sherman Avenue, Aug 2019,
165 Sherman Ave Llc, $292K Land
Val, $3.20M Tot Val, Unlisted SF,
1187 days since logged occupancy.

135 Post Avenue, Aug 2019,
Benvento One Llc, $42K Land Val,
$230K Tot Val, Unlisted SF, 1826
days since logged occupancy.

263 Sherman Avenue, Jul 2019,
HRS Equities, $241K Land Val,
$2.32M Tot Val, Unlisted SF, 365
days since logged occupancy.

3855 10 Avenue, Oct 2019, 449
West 206th St Heights Assoc
Llc, $37K Land Val, $1.46M Tot
Val, Unlisted SF, 1095 days since
logged occupancy.

Manhattan Vacancy

5% of ground-level units, 21% of retail space was reported vacant in Morningside Heights

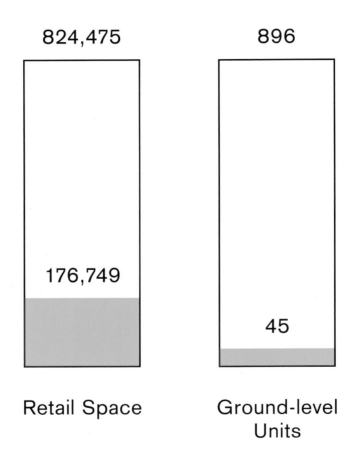

824,475

896

176,749

45

Retail Space

Ground-level
Units

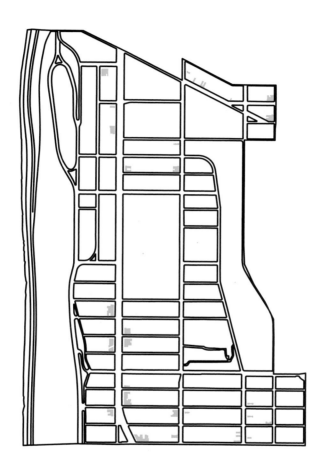

Median Gross Rent as Percentage of Household Income

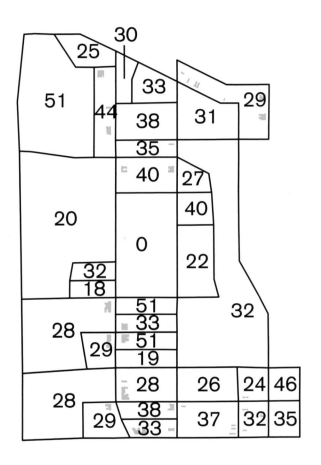

Reported Retail Vacancy SF

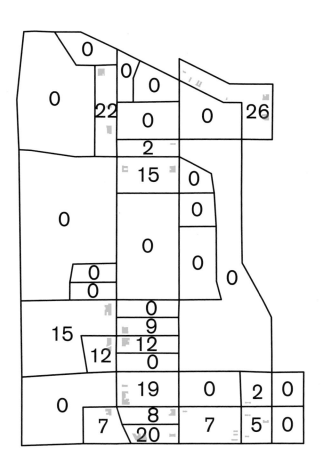

(In thousands)

Manhattan Vacancy

2872 Broadway, Jun 2019, Trustees of Columbia University, $1.06M Land Val, $7.36M Tot Val, 4557 SF, 608 days since logged occupancy.

2818 Broadway, May 2019, 2810 Broadway Llc, $545K Land Val, $4.44M Tot Val, 2120 SF, 577 days since logged occupancy.

52 Tiemann Place, Nov 2019, 200 Claremont Hdfc, $289K Land Val, $2.71M Tot Val, Unlisted SF, 1279 days since logged occupancy.

970 Amsterdam Avenue, Jun 2019, 200 W 108th St Housing, $585K Land Val, $8.85M Tot Val, Unlisted SF, 608 days since logged occupancy.

70 West 106 Street, Jul 2019, Sai Niwas Llc, $135K Land Val, $.93M Tot Val, Unlisted SF, 638 days since logged occupancy.

712 West 125 Street, Nov 2019, Columbia Waterfront, $470K Land Val, $1.24M Tot Val, 1500 SF, 1126 days since logged occupancy.

Manhattan Vacancy

2875 Broadway, Jun 2019, 600
W 112th St Llc, $819K Land Val,
$6.19M Tot Val, 8863 SF, 973 days
since logged occupancy.

2851 Broadway, Jul 2019,
Broadway 111 St Condo, $2M Land
Val, $16M Tot Val, Unlisted SF, 638
days since logged occupancy.

Manhattan Vacancy

Manhattanville

Manhattan Vacancy

7% of ground-level units, 33% of retail space was reported vacant in Manhattanville

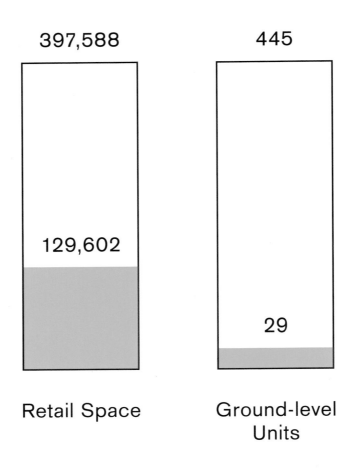

397,588

445

129,602

29

Retail Space

Ground-level Units

Manhattan Vacancy

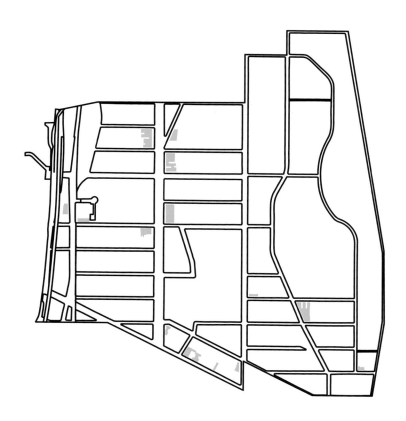

Manhattan Vacancy

Median Gross Rent as Percentage of Household Income

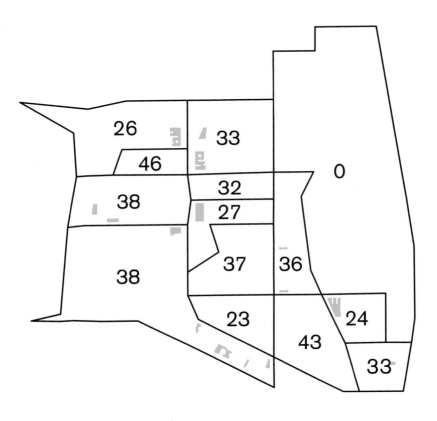

26

33

46

0

32

38

27

37

36

38

23

24

43

33

Manhattan Vacancy

Reported Retail Vacancy SF

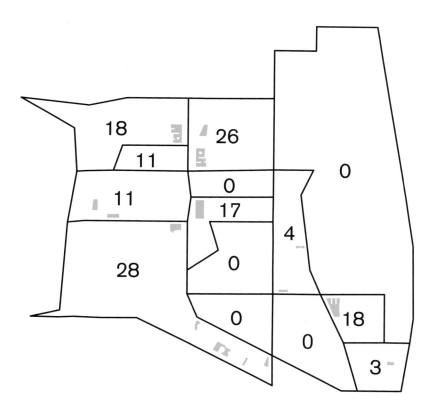

(In thousands)

Manhattan Vacancy

1341 Amsterdam Avenue, Nov 2017,
Ben Hur Ams Llc, $45K Land Val,
$279K Tot Val, Unlisted SF, 1157 days
since logged occupancy.

3405 Broadway, Nov 2019, 3405
Broadway Hdfc, $26K Land Val,
$820K Tot Val, 735 SF, 720 days
since logged occupancy.

1348 Amsterdam Avenue, Nov 2017,
Bahar Realty Assoc, $113K Land
Val, $605K Tot Val, Unlisted SF,
1553 days since logged occupancy.

3344 Broadway, Nov 2019, 817
West End Co, $486K Land Val,
$2.88M Tot Val, 1100 SF, 3045
days since logged occupancy.

3210 Broadway, Nov 2019, West
126th Investors Llc, $113K Land
Val, $1.61M Tot Val, 2513 SF, 761
days since logged occupancy.

1411 Amsterdam Avenue, Nov 2017,
1411 Amsterdam Ave, $52K Land
Val, $683K Tot Val, Unlisted SF, 549
days since logged occupancy.

Manhattan Vacancy

3300 Broadway, Nov 2019, Trustees of Columbia Univ in the City of NY, $468K Land Val, $3.36M Tot Val, Unlisted SF, 3866+ days since logged occupancy.

3360 Broadway, Nov 2019, 3350 Bw 136 Inc, $303K Land Val, $2.95M Tot Val, Unlisted SF, 488 days since logged occupancy.

Stuyvesant Town, Cooper Village

5% of ground-level units, 45% of retail space was reported vacant in Stuyvesant Town, Cooper Village

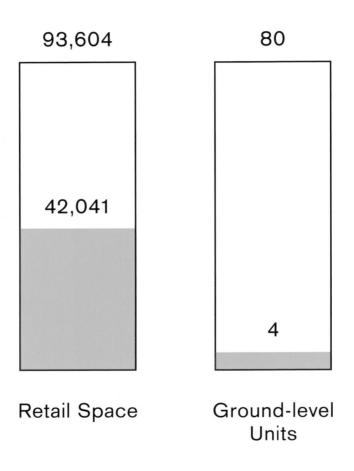

93,604

42,041

Retail Space

80

4

Ground-level
Units

4 Vacancies in Stuyvesant Town, Cooper Village

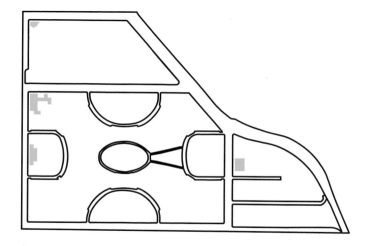

Median Gross Rent as Percentage of Household Income

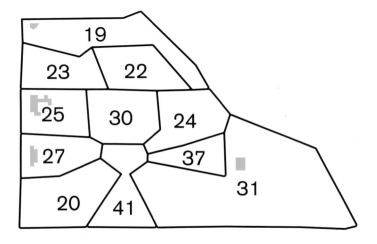

Reported Retail Vacancy SF

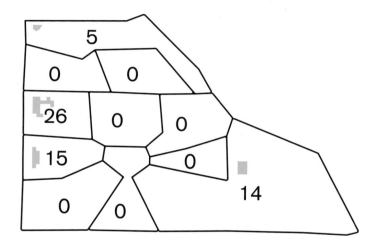

(In thousands)

Manhattan Vacancy

532 East 14 Street, Oct 2019, Unavailable Owner, $3.00M Land Val, $30.1M Tot Val, 1600 SF, Unoccupied new construction.

536 East 14 Street, Oct 2019, Betty Lily Corp, $.071M Land Val, $.682M Tot Val, 600 SF, 760 days since logged occupancy.

315 1 Avenue, Jun 2019, 315 1St Avenue Llc, $.432M Land Val, $1.56M Tot Val, 900 SF, 577 days since logged occupancy.

Manhattan Vacancy

Covid

19

While the coronavirus has increased vacancy rates by shifting how we must live and work, these trends existed long before it. The amount of vacant space was growing before and is likely to continue after. Covid 19 is an accelerant, not a primary cause. Still, the figures are stark. Many businesses have been forced to close. Temporarily for some, permanently for others. Unemployment remains at an all-time high. People of color have been disproportionately affected because of systemic healthcare and social inequities. E-commerce companies and online digital communication platforms have had enormous profits.[1]

Between March and July 2020, with offices implementing work-from-home strategies, thousands fled New York City, moving to larger houses with more green space and less noise.[2] The people who left were those that could afford to. As the demand for suburban, single-family houses grew, New York City rental prices decreased, although much less drastically in neighborhoods hardest hit by the pandemic, predominantly Black, Hispanic, and immigrant communities.[3] Today, the country-wide shutdown in response to the virus has made the future uncertain; we are still witnessing the effects of Covid 19 play out in real time.

1. They are physically expanding. In August 2020, Facebook leased all the office space in the James A. Farley Building in Manhattan. 730,000 square feet. It now owns over 2.2 million square feet in the city. Amazon has bought at least nine new warehouses in the city, including one in Queens that is over a million square feet.

2. The coronavirus created many conditions that have caused migration historically: economic advantages and disadvantages, changes in employment, few social, educational, leisure activities, expensive cost of housing. More than a third of jobs in the US are now done at home. These jobs that are able to be done remotely typically pay more than jobs that cannot be done at home. See Jonathan Dingel and Brent Neiman, "How Many Jobs Can Be Done at Home?", *University of Chicago Booth School of Business*, June 19, 2020.

3. Stefanos Chen, Vivian Marino, and C. J. Hughes, "The Real Estate Collapse of 2020," *New York Times*, December 29, 2020.

Covid 19

Covid 19

Business Closures

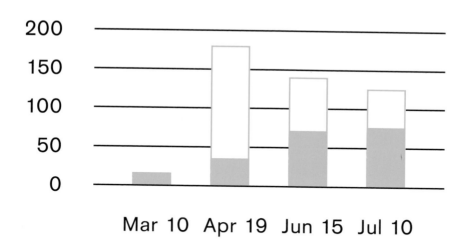

Temporary ■ Permanent

Permanent and Temporary Closures in the US in thousands, (Yelp)

Covid 19

US National Unemployment

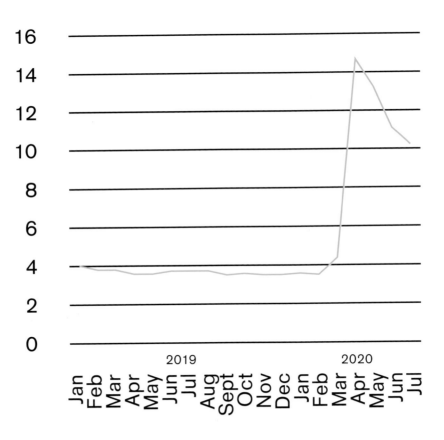

Percentage, US National Unemployment Rate

Covid 19

Between February and May 2020, the unemployment rate grew 14.9%

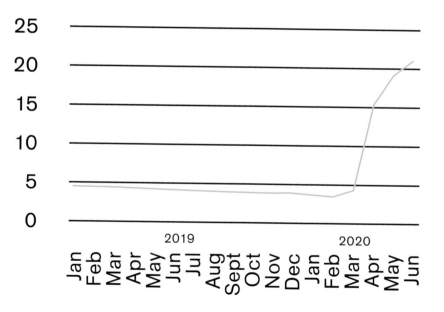

Percentage, New York City Unemployment Rate

Covid 19

Housing

Active eviction cases in New York City increased by 26% between July and December

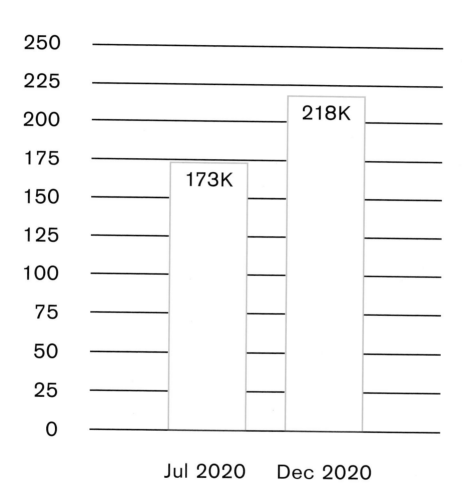

(Eviction Crisis Monitor, Right to Counsel NYC Coalition)

Covid 19

Households in New York State that fell behind on rent payments

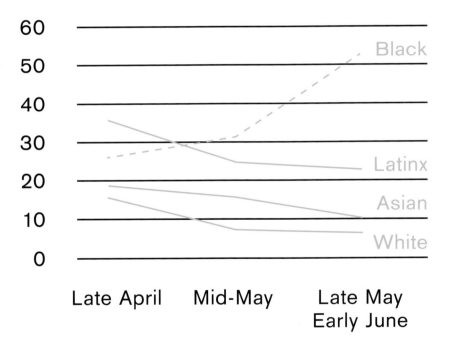

Percentage, (Race and Evictions in New York City, Community Service Society)

Covid 19

New York City 2020–2024 Capital Budget

In June 2020, due to Covid 19, the de Blasio Administration proposed a 2.3 billion dollar reduction in New York City's Capital Commitment Plan for fiscal years 2020–2024, which will delay funding for 20,000 affordable housing units. This cut generally maintains funding for projects with higher income affordable housing, but decreases financing for lower income affordable housing.

New York City Council, *A Capital Mistake for NYC* (New York: New York City Council, 2020).

Covid 19

2020–2024 Capital Budget, 2020 and 2021 cuts to affordable housing

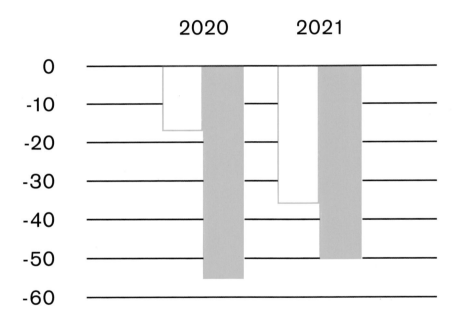

2020   2021

New Construction   Preservation

Percentage, (A Capital Mistake for NYC)

81,000 mail forwarding requests were filed in New York City in April, 60% to areas outside the city

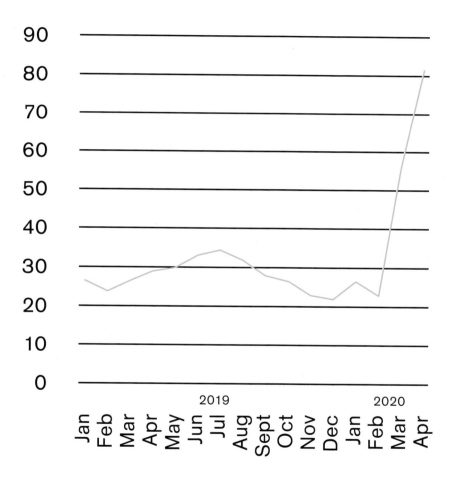

Mail-forwarding requests from New York City in thousands,
(US Postal Service)

333

Covid 19

Change of household waste collected between April 2020 and April 2019

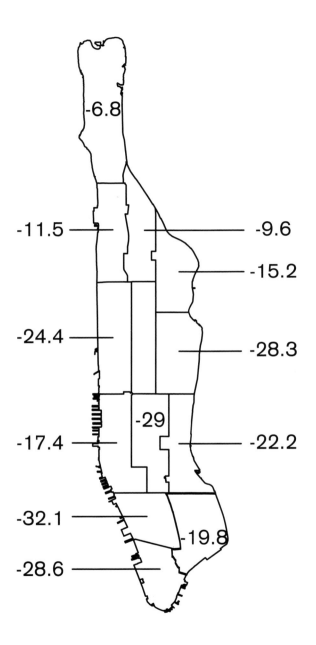

-6.8

-11.5

-9.6

-15.2

-24.4

-28.3

-29

-17.4

-22.2

-32.1

-19.8

-28.6

Percentage, (New York City Department of Sanitation)

Covid 19

Open Streets

Begun in May 2020, the Open Streets program opens miles of roads in New York City for pedestrian use by fully and partially closing blocks to cars. It is widely popular, with support for the program to continue even after the coronavirus. Manhattan has the lowest number of hours that Open Streets are open, compared to the other boroughs.

New York City Open Streets, Full-Block Closures

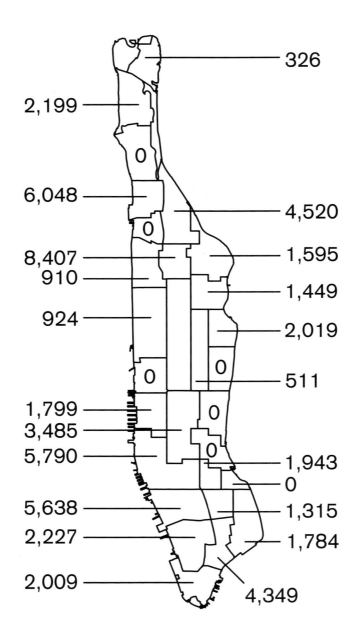

326

2,199

0

6,048

4,520

0

8,407

1,595

910

1,449

924

2,019

0 0

511

1,799

0

3,485

5,790

0

1,943

0

5,638

1,315

2,227

1,784

2,009

4,349

Feet of Open Streets, (New York City Department of Transportation)

Covid 19

Protected Bike Lanes

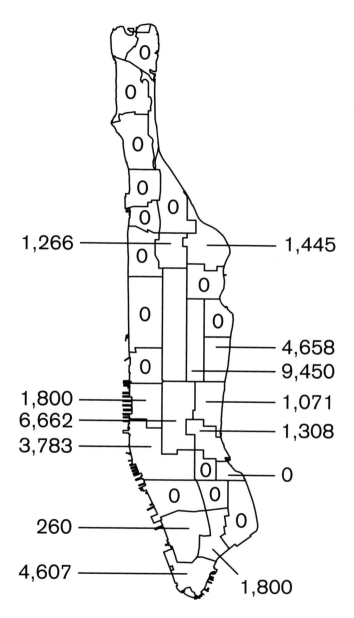

Feet of protected bike lanes added through the Open Street program,
(New York City Department of Transportation)

Covid 19

Houselessness

Covid 19 has exacerbated problems of a long-strained system for those experiencing homelessness: lack of public programs and mental health resources, unemployment, and the scarcity of quality, low-cost housing. On June 1, the mortality rate of sheltered houseless New Yorkers was 61% higher than the city's rate.

The New York City Department of Homeless Services began relocating those in shelters into hotels around the city, which were closed during the lockdown. Nearly 9,500 people were relocated according to the *New York Times*.[1] Beginning in early May 2020, for the first time in Metropolitan Transportation Authority history, the subway system shut down for nightly cleaning. In February 2021, the MTA began removing benches, which were already anti-homeless public furniture, designed to prevent people from sleeping on the public seating. The closures and removal of furniture displace people who often sleep in train cars and raise pressure on homeless shelters, which are already operating at unprecedented levels due to the virus.

A Department of Homeless Services study in 2017 found that approximately 2 in 3 of single adults experiencing homelessness had some kind of disability that may require special accommodation to ensure they have access to shelters. Shelters that are already high-risk sites for spreading the coronavirus because the majority are shared dormitories, with shared bathrooms and dining areas. Social distancing is nearly impossible.

1. Daniel E. Slotnik, "What Happened When Homeless Men Moved Into a Liberal Neighborhood," *New York Times*, August 18, 2020.

Covid 19

Vacancy as an Opportunity

New York City faces a severe shortage in afford-able housing units. Around 582,000 households in New York City are severely burdened due to cost and/or crowding, or have already spent a year or more in a homeless shelter due to the shortage of affordable housing. The current plan for affordable housing, Housing New York 2.0, aims to build or preserve 300,000 units by 2026. Regulations require affordable housing in most new construction, yet it is still out of reach for many. In 2018, the odds of winning the city's affordable housing lottery was 1 in 592, 0.17 percent. Affordability is relative, based on income and rent burden, or 30 percent of annual income. For example, "middle" income affordable housing is classified as affordable for a single person making between 95,520 and 131,340 dollars. Despite this crisis, only 25 percent of planned housing under the plan is directed toward the 88 percent of households at the lowest end of the economic spectrum. Who need affordable housing the most.

Along with housing, public services and resources are unequally distributed in neighbor-hoods around the city. Vacancies offer opportu-nities for social services such as health services, community centers, community gardens, daycare and pre-kindergarten locations, and public librar-ies, increasing social wellbeing and addressing issues such as homelessness and food insecurity.

Vacancy as an Opportunity

New Housing Units Completed in New York City

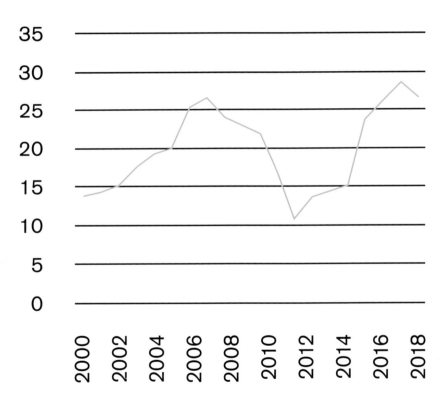

In thousands, (New York City Department of City Planning)

Vacancy as an Opportunity

New Housing Units Completed in Manhattan

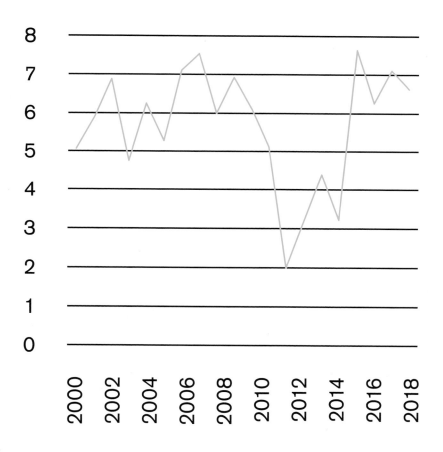

In thousands, (New York City Department of City Planning)

Vacancy as an Opportunity

Demolition and Residential Building Permits in New York City

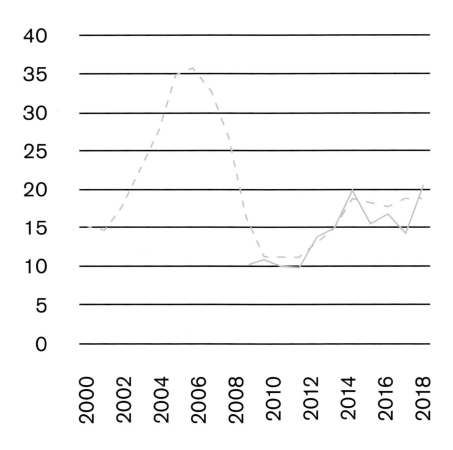

Residential Permits --- Demolished

In hundreds, (New York City Department of City Planning)

Vacancy as an Opportunity

Demolition and Residential Building Permits in Manhattan

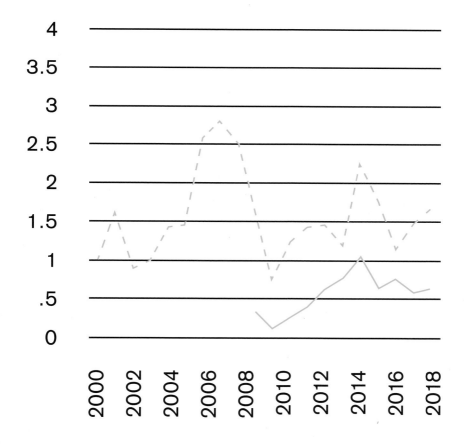

4			
3.5			
3			
2.5			
2			
1.5			
1			
.5			
0			

2000 2002 2004 2006 2008 2010 2012 2014 2016 2018

—— Residential Permits --- Demolished

In hundreds, (New York City Department of City Planning)

Vacancy as an Opportunity

Affordable Units

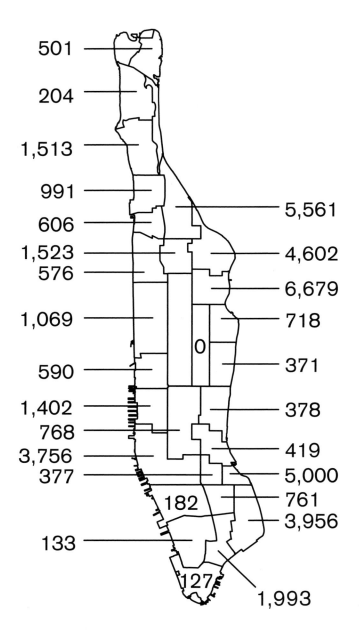

501
204
1,513
991
606
1,523
576
1,069
590
1,402
768
3,756
377
133

5,561
4,602
6,679
718
0
371
378
419
5,000
761
3,956
182
127
1,993

(Housing New York, Department of Housing Preservation and Development)

Vacancy as an Opportunity

Buildings with Affordable Units

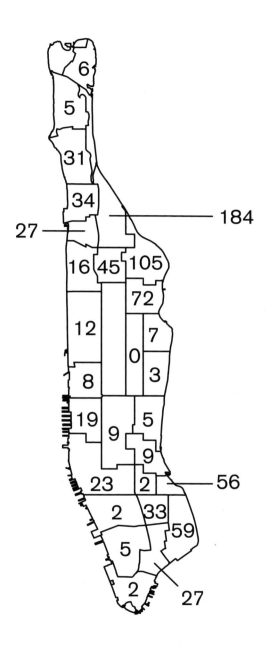

(Housing New York, Department of Housing Preservation and Development)

Vacancy as an Opportunity

Affordable Units, Extremely Low Income Units

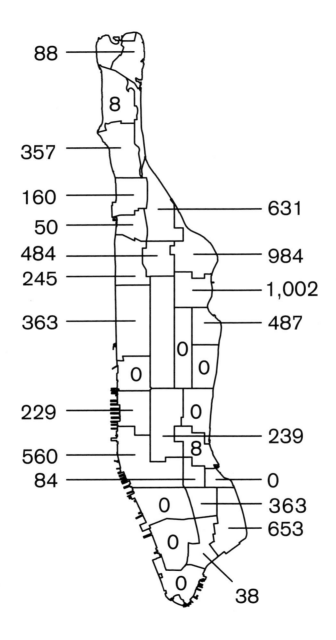

(Housing New York, Department of Housing Preservation and Development)

Affordable Units, Low Income Units

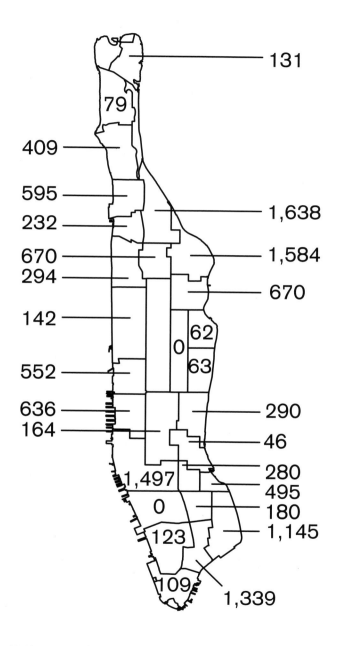

131

79

409

595

232

1,638

670

1,584

294

670

142

62

0

552

63

636

290

164

46

280

1,497

495

0

180

123

1,145

109

1,339

(Housing New York, Department of Housing Preservation and Development)

Vacancy as an Opportunity

Affordable Units, Moderate Income

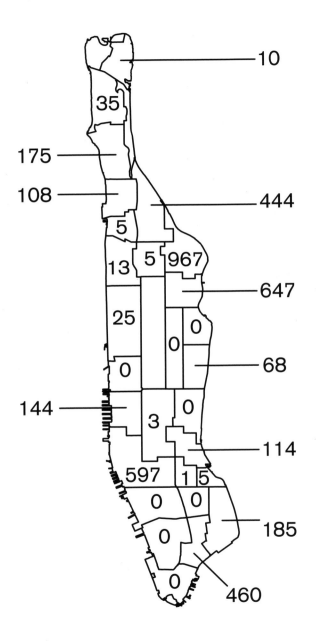

(Housing New York, Department of Housing Preservation and Development)

Vacancy as an Opportunity

Affordable Units, Middle Income

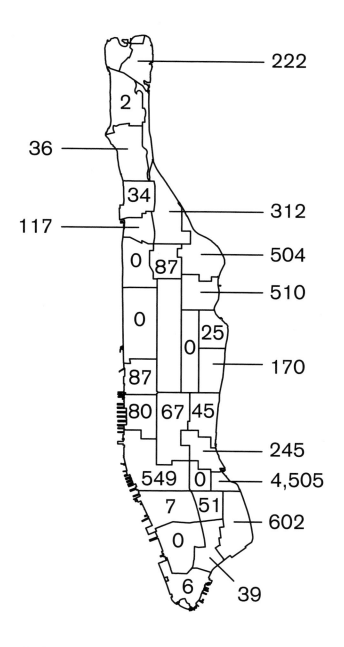

(Housing New York, Department of Housing Preservation and Development)

Vacancy as an Opportunity

The odds of winning the New York City affordable housing lottery was 0.17% in 2018

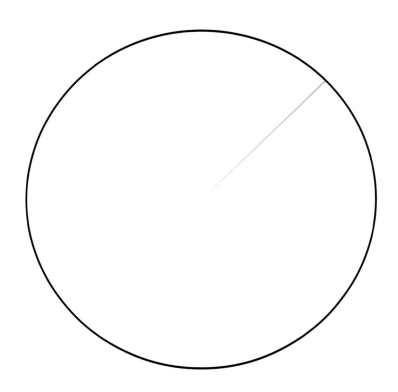

New York City Housing Connect is the city's system of finding and applying to affordable housing within the boroughs, (Julie Satow, "Better Than the Powerball," *New York Times*, January 11, 2019.)

Vacancy as an Opportunity

Vacancy as an Opportunity

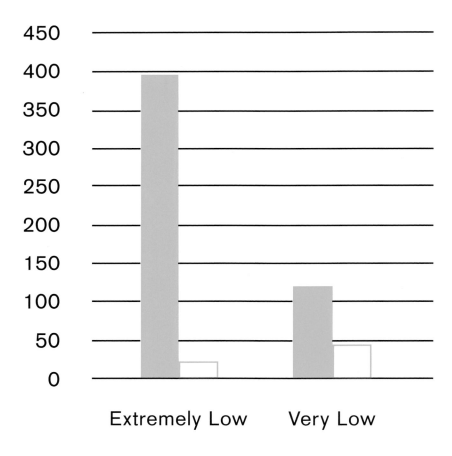

Needed affordable units versus the planned Housing New York units by AMI, in thousands, (*NYC For All: The Housing We Need*, New York City Comptroller, November 2018.)

Vacancy as an Opportunity

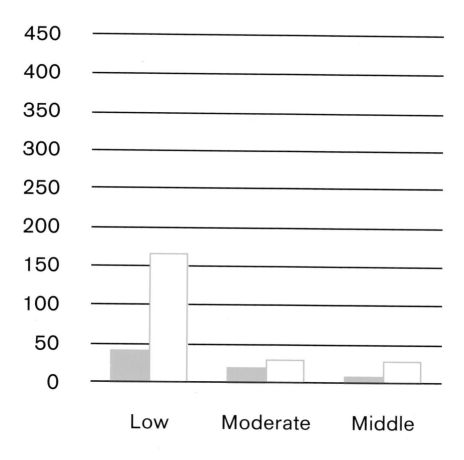

450		
400		
350		
300		
250		
200		
150		
100		
50		
0		

Low   Moderate   Middle

■ Need   □ HNY Goal

Extremely Low Income <$28,170; Very Low Income <$46,950; Low
<$75,120; Moderate <$112,680; Middle <$154,935

357   Vacancy as an Opportunity

Housing Policies

Vacancy as an Opportunity

Federal Housing Assistance Funding

Federal housing assistance includes Section 8, public housing, homelessness assistance, Section 521, HOME, Native American housing, HOPWA, as well as Section 202 and 811.

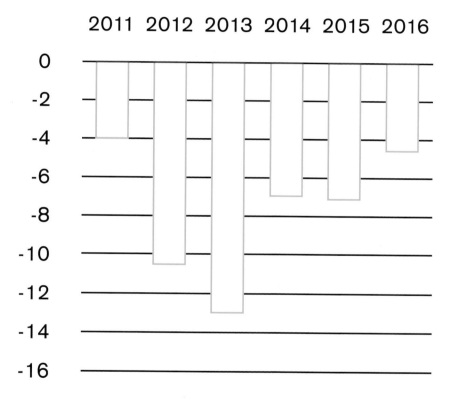

Percent reduction compared to 2010 discretionary housing funding, (Center on Budget and Policy Priorities)

Vacancy as an Opportunity

Tax Credits and Exemptions

Tax Exemption Programs provide exemptions and abatements in order to incentivize affordable, rent-stabilized units. Recently, they are losing popularity among building owners. For them, raising rent is more financially desirable than these tax exemptions. Between 2002 and 2017, the number of rent-stabilized units has decreased 10 percent, and the number of rent-controlled apartments has decreased by 37 percent. Of the 966,000 rent-stabilized units, only 20,000 were available for rent in 2017.[1]

Moon Wha Lee, *Selected Findings of the 2002 New York City Housing and Vacancy Survey* (New York: New York City Department of Housing Preservation and Development, 2003); Elyzabeth Gaumer, *Selected Initial Findings of the 2017 New York City Housing and Vacancy Survey* (New York: New York City Department of Housing Preservation and Development, 2018.)

Vacancy as an Opportunity

There are 20% fewer units newly receiving 421-a tax exemptions in 2019 than 2018

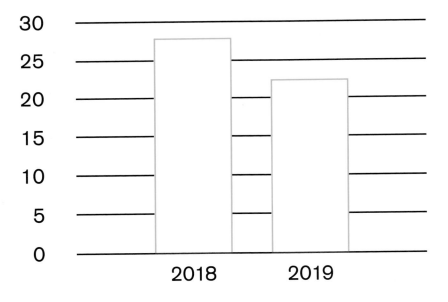

To receive the 421-a(17) program tax exemption, the building owner is required to rent at least 20% of the units to households whose income is below 100% AMI and at least 5% of the units to households whose income is below 130% AMI.

Vacancy as an Opportunity

18.5% of units newly receiving 421-a Exemption in 2019 were in Manhattan

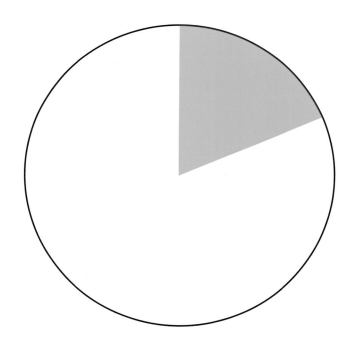

Vacancy as an Opportunity

There were 55% fewer units newly receiving J-51 tax abatements and exemptions in 2019 than 2018

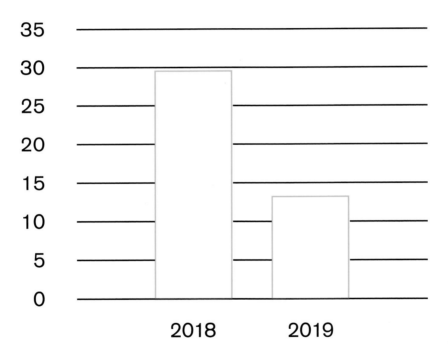

The J-51 Tax Incentive program is a tax exemption and abatement for repairing residential units or multi-family housing conversions.

Vacancy as an Opportunity

3% of Units Newly Receiving J-51 Tax Abatements and Exemptions in 2019 were in Manhattan

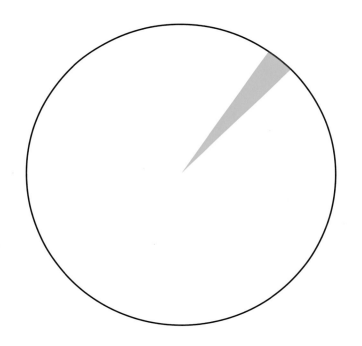

Vacancy as an Opportunity

Houselessness

Vacancy as an Opportunity

The primary cause of homelessness, particularly among families, is lack of affordable housing

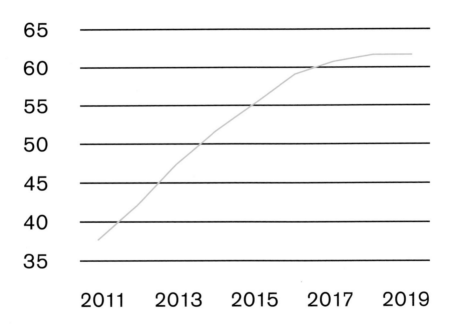

65				
60				
55				
50				
45				
40				
35				
	2011	2013	2015	2017	2019

People Sleeping in Shelters Each Night in thousands, (Coalition for the Homeless)

Vacancy as an Opportunity

440 days was the average length of stay for a family in a Department of Homeless Services Shelter in 2019

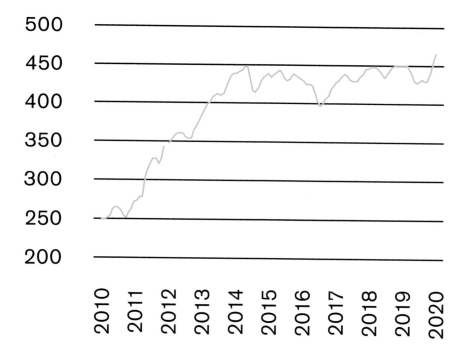

500
450
400
350
300
250
200

2010 2011 2012 2013 2014 2015 2016 2017 2018 2019 2020

(Coalition for the Homeless)

Vacancy as an Opportunity

Families in DHS Shelters

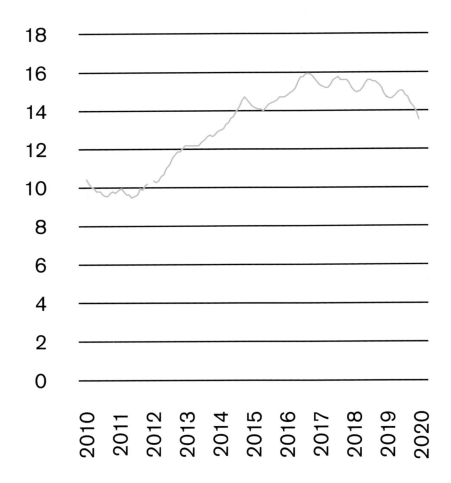

18
16
14
12
10
8
6
4
2
0

2010 2011 2012 2013 2014 2015 2016 2017 2018 2019 2020

In thousands, (Coalition for the Homeless)

Vacancy as an Opportunity

35.3% of individuals in DHS shelters were children in 2019

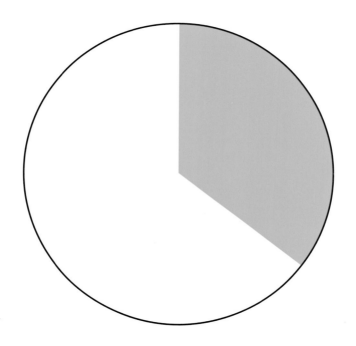

(Coalition for the Homeless)

Vacancy as an Opportunity

86% of homeless single adults in family shelters identify as Black, Hispanic, or Latino

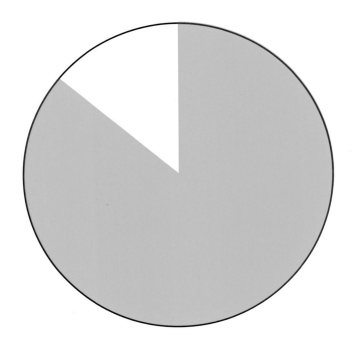

(Coalition for the Homeless)

Vacancy as an Opportunity

93% of heads-of-household in family shelters identify as Black, Hispanic, or Latino

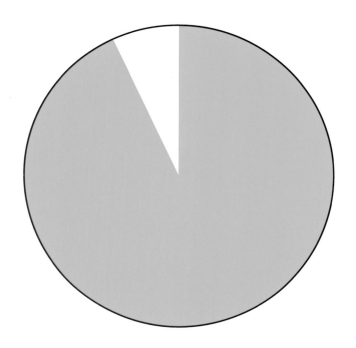

(Coalition for the Homeless)

Vacancy as an Opportunity

53% of New York City's overall population identify as Black, Hispanic, or Latino

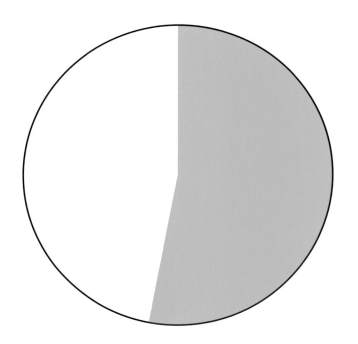

(Coalition for the Homeless)

Vacancy as an Opportunity

Food Insecurity

Vacancy as an Opportunity

In February 2020, prior to Covid 19, 74 percent of surveyed food pantries and soup kitchens reported an increase in the overall number of visitors compared to 2019. 75 percent reported an increase in the number of visitors between February and April 2020. The average number of people served has doubled compared to before the coronavirus, increasing from an average of 2,000 people served per month to an average of 4,050 in April.

More than 1.2 million New York City residents, or 14.4 percent, are food insecure. This is 12 percent higher than the national rate. 67 percent of Manhattan-based organizations reported serving clients coming from the Bronx in addition to Manhattan residents.

US: United States Department of Agriculture, 2020; New York State and New York City: Map the Meals Gap, 2020; Feeding America, 2020. This data is released one year after it is collected.

Vacancy as an Opportunity

Food Retail

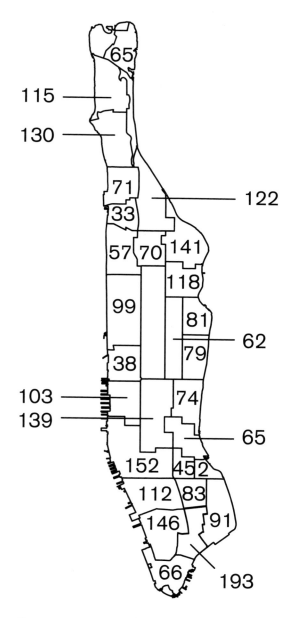

Delis, Bodegas, Grocery stores, and Fresh Food Markets, (New York State Department of Agriculture and Markets)

Vacancy as an Opportunity

Supermarkets over 5,000 SF

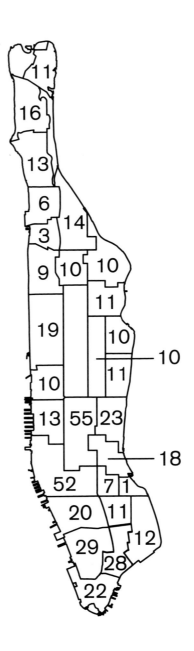

(New York State Department of Agriculture and Markets)

Vacancy as an Opportunity

Percent of Population with Poorly Controlled Diabetes

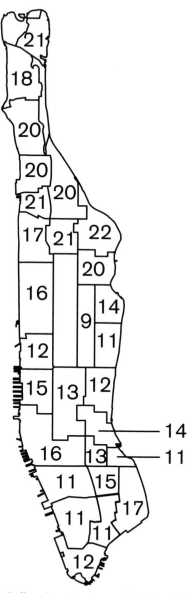

Poorly controlled diabetes is defined as having consistently high blood glucose levels, heightening the risk of health complications, (New York City A1C Registry)

Vacancy as an Opportunity

Food Pantries and Soup Kitchens

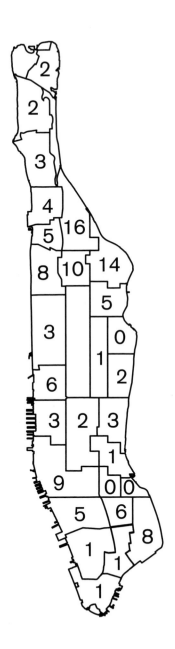

(Food Bank for New York City)

Vacancy as an Opportunity

Social Services

Vacancy as an Opportunity

Mental Health Service Facilities

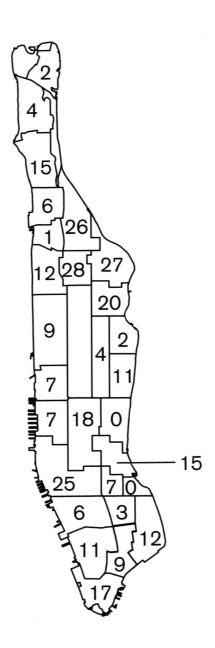

(New York City Department of Health and Mental Hygiene)

Vacancy as an Opportunity

Chemical Dependency Services

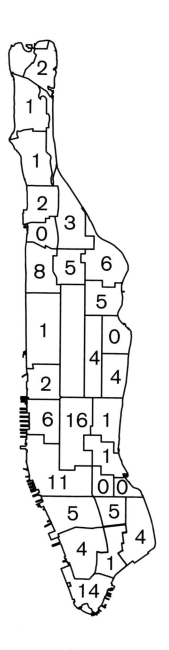

(New York City Department of Health and Mental Hygiene)

Vacancy as an Opportunity

Hospitals and Clinics

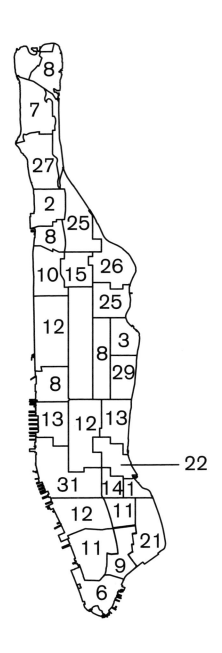

(New York City Department of Health and Mental Hygiene)

Vacancy as an Opportunity

Community Centers

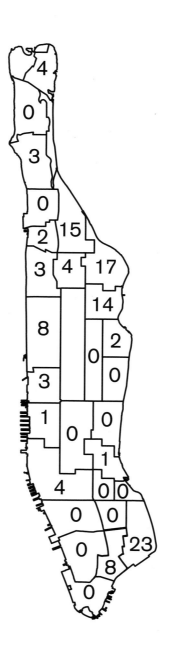

(New York City Housing Authority)

Vacancy as an Opportunity

Community Gardens

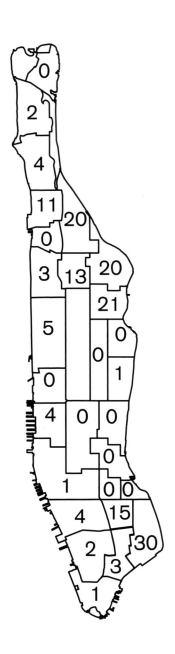

(Open Accessible Space Information System)

Vacancy as an Opportunity

Day Care and Pre-Kindergarten

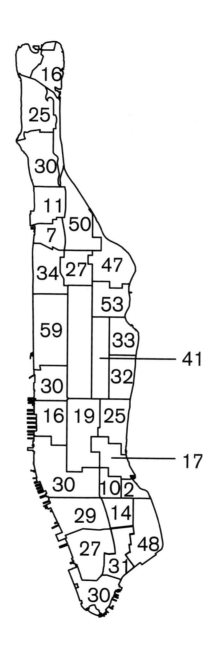

(Department of Information Technology & Telecommunications)

Vacancy as an Opportunity

Adult Literacy Centers

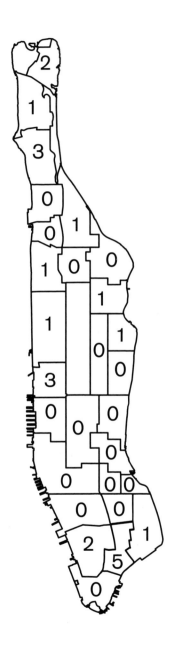

(New York City Department of Youth and Community Development)

Vacancy as an Opportunity

Public Libraries

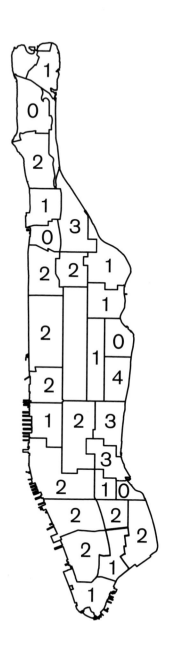

Vacancy as an Opportunity

Case   Studies

The following case studies propose alternative uses for ground-level vacancies dispersed throughout Manhattan. Each are local modifications based on the physical building contexts and conditions needed for adaptive reuse. It should be noted that the current zoning laws would not allow these proposals in many cases. We assume that these zoning regulations will need to change in order to promote new uses of vacant spaces, similar to when zoning laws changed in the 1950s and '60s to allow for lofts in Lower Manhattan.

The current zoning laws and policy have produced mega-developments such as Hudson Yards, constructed between 2012 and 2019, with another upcoming phase immediately to its west. At 18 million square feet in total, including a mall with 1 million square feet of retail space, it is the largest and most expensive private real estate development in US history. The Sunnyside Yard project in Queens, another megaproject, will focus on providing affordable housing, although the 140-acre development is still in the proposal phase and will take years to complete. But New York City faces an affordable housing crisis now.

Our case studies capitalize on the estimated 31 million square feet of space that is available already, nearly twice the size of Hudson Yards.

Case Studies

Unlike Hudson Yards, this model of development is meant to be an aggregate of many individual developers and property owners, not a single large-scale development by one large company in one place. Promoting the redevelopment of vacant spaces dispersed throughout the city, developed by smaller developers or individual property owners, allows for greater economic and cultural diversity.

These case studies show a range of possibilities, from more traditional living arrangements, to live and work hybrids, to communal living, to social programs like community spaces, libraries, health and education services. In many cases, we introduced porches or garden buffers for added light and air access, and provide a little privacy from the street, common design challenges in New York City. Each case study is unique and meant to promote accessible social services and housing, both of which are desperately needed now. The total of these case studies accounts for less than 1 percent of the estimated vacant retail space in Manhattan.

512 7 Avenue

This is at the base of a tall building in Midtown, Midtown South. 17-stories-tall, constructed in 1921, and located on 7th Avenue (this section is commonly referred to as Fashion Avenue) in the city's "Garment District," named because of the historic density of the fashion-related industries. The surrounding buildings are a similar height. There is a FedEx and a restaurant on the block, and across the street there is a parking garage, cafe, and jewelry store. The street is busy and does not have any bike lanes. The sidewalk is extended into a lane normally for street parking using cement barriers.

There are 0 community gardens and 0 community centers nearby, so a community center is added. Possible funding from the 450 million dollars in NYPD capital funds reinvested in community services by de Blasio. A place for everyone. A space that was once commercial, run by a corporation, now a space for living, run by a non-profit. Spaces like this will be needed as additional housing is introduced and the community grows. A room with a large communal table is surrounded by a bathroom, kitchen, and private rooms. A patio buffers everything from the hectic street and sidewalk.

May 2019, 500 Seventh Avenue, $3.29M Land Val, $66.0M Tot Val, Unlisted SF, 1673 days since logged occupancy.

Case Studies

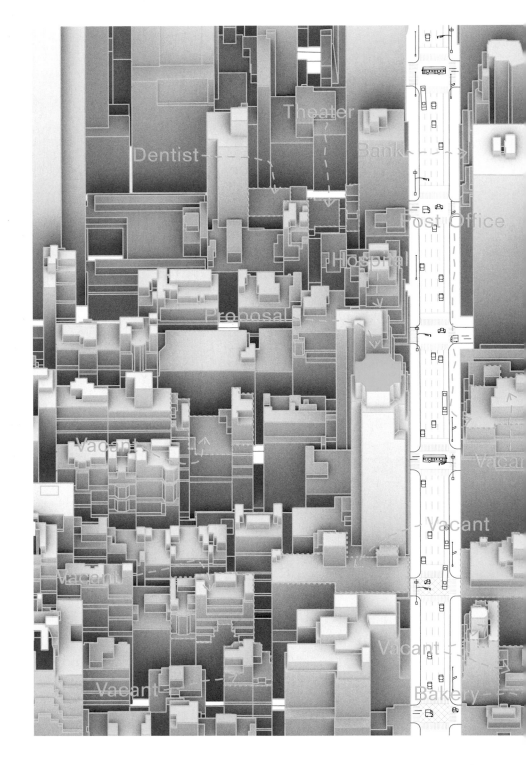

396

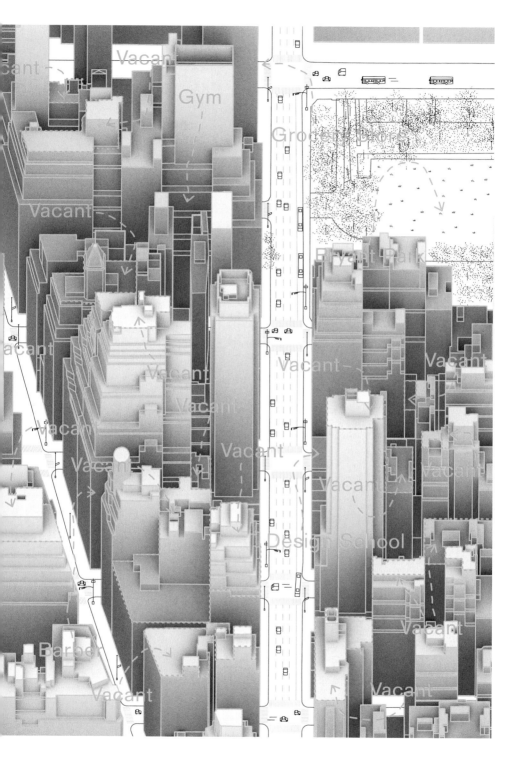

397   Case Studies

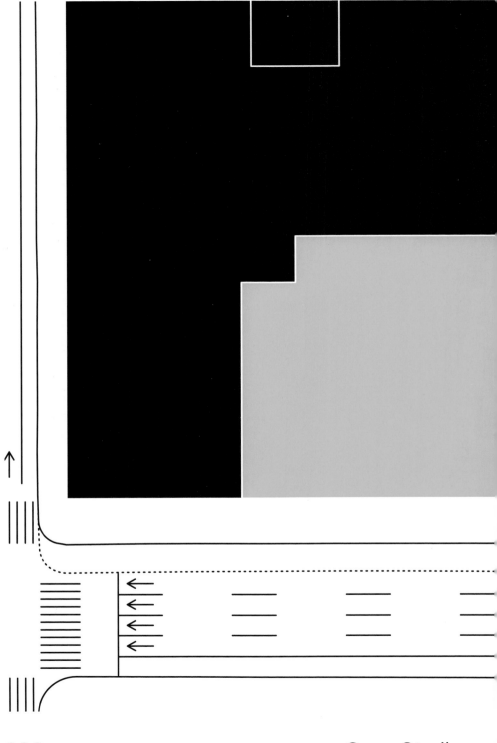

398

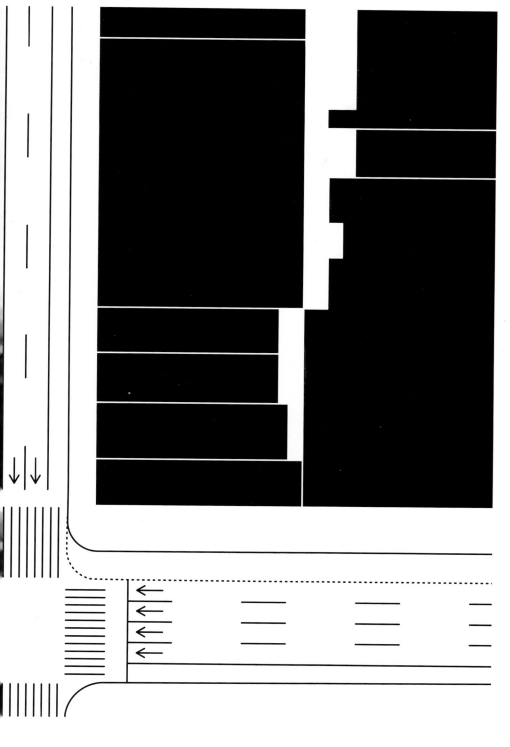

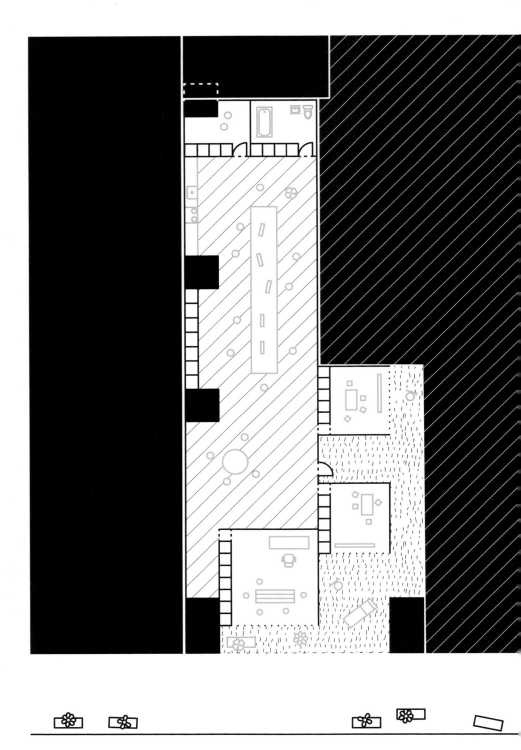

400   Case Studies

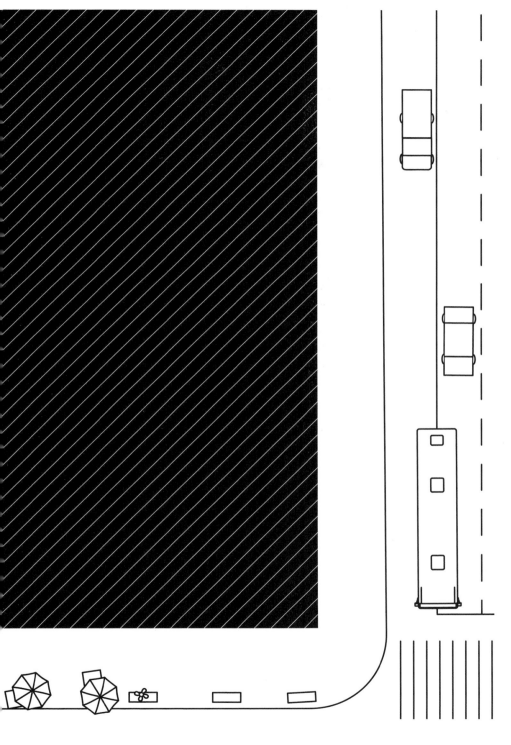

401

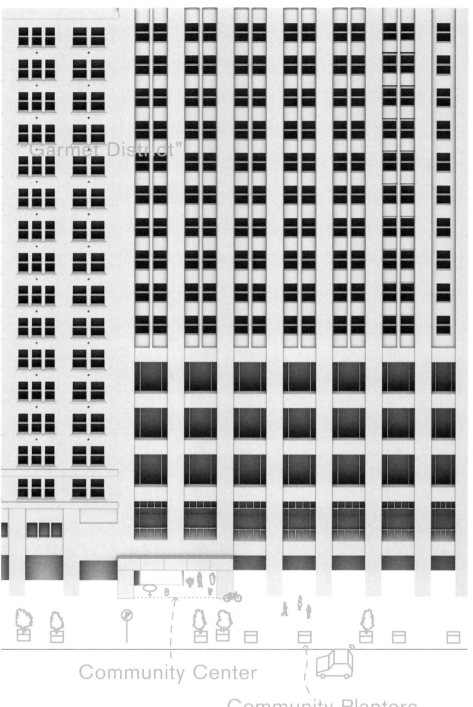

"Garmet District"

Community Center

Community Planters

Case Studies

Common Room

735–737 9 Avenue

A single story and 5-story building connected at their base, 2 adjacent vacancies on 9th Avenue combined into 1. A playground is on the same block. An Amish market next door, and a Duane Reade on the block. Across the street, there are retail stores selling home goods and pet supplies. Most of the nearby buildings are 5 stories and made of brick. Hell's Kitchen is known for its variety of restaurants and off-broadway theaters. 24 percent of renters pay 50 percent or more of income on rent. There is 1 library in the neighborhood.

The Hell's Kitchen Neighborhood Coalition says the neighborhood needs more social services, so a community library is added, along with housing for 3. The library pads the housing from the busy street, while a yard in the back allows light and air to enter. A community book club can meet there. There can be poetry readings. There can be accessible WiFi. The library can organize a farmer's market on West 50th Street on Saturdays.

Aug 2019, 735–739 Ninth Avenue Realty Corp, $675K Land Val, $3.7M Tot Val, 2000 SF, 1187 days since logged occupancy.

405   Case Studies

Vacant

PS 111

Vacant

Church

Vacant

Vacant

Gutenberg Playground

Barber

Clinton
Community Garden

Vacar

Hell's Kitchen
Playground

Va

Vacant

Case Studies

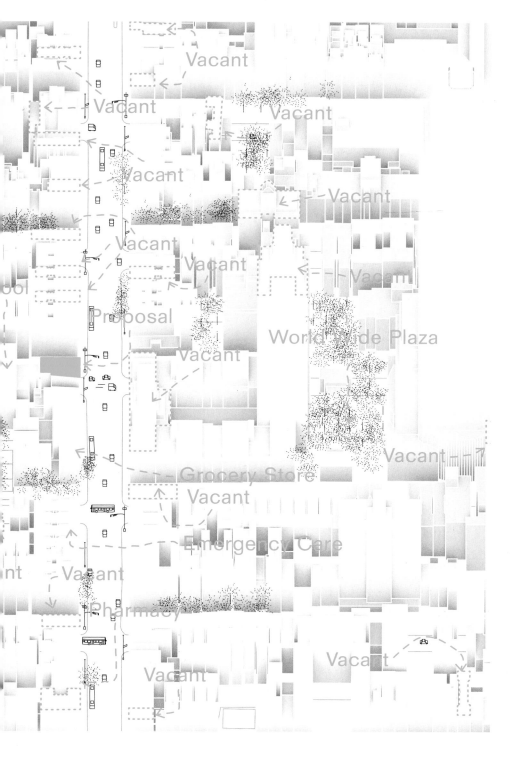

Vacant

Vacant

Vacant

Vacant

Vacant

Vacant

Vacant

Vacant

ool

Proposal

World Wide Plaza

Vacant

Vacant

Grocery Store

Vacant

Emergency Care

nt   Vacant

Pharmacy

Vacant

Vacant

Vacant

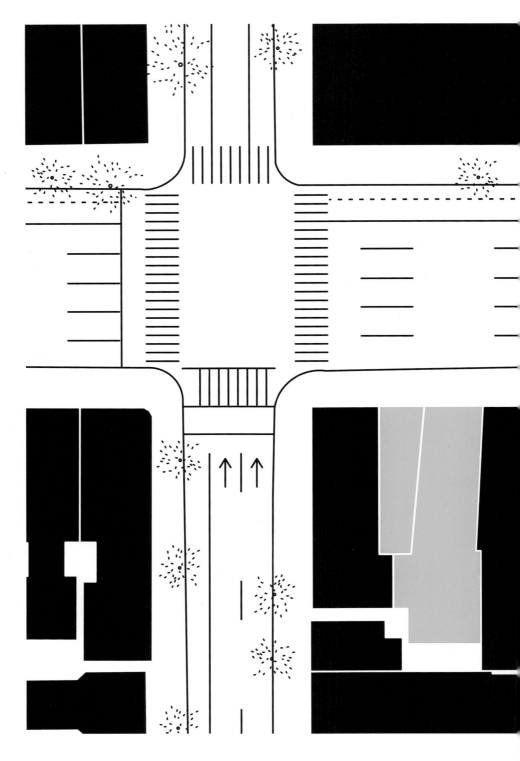

408 Case Studies

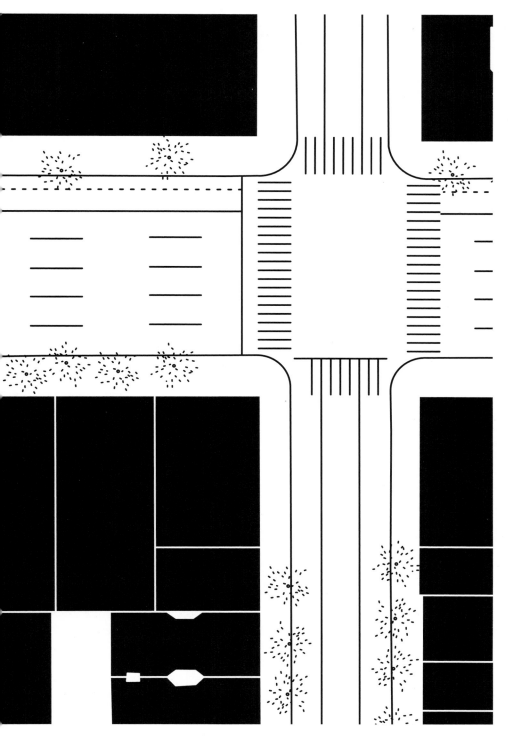

409 Case Studies

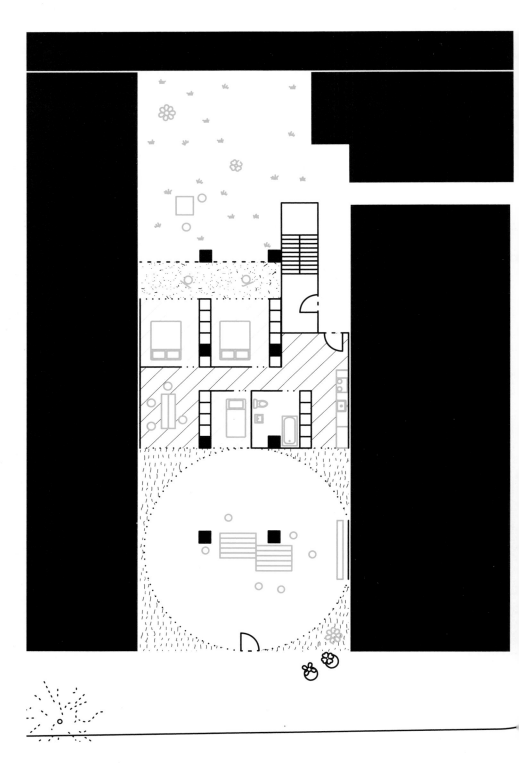

Case Studies

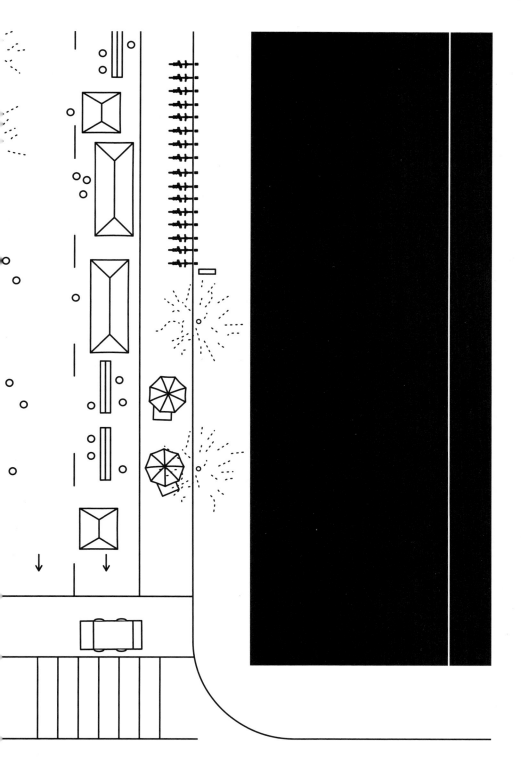

411   Case Studies

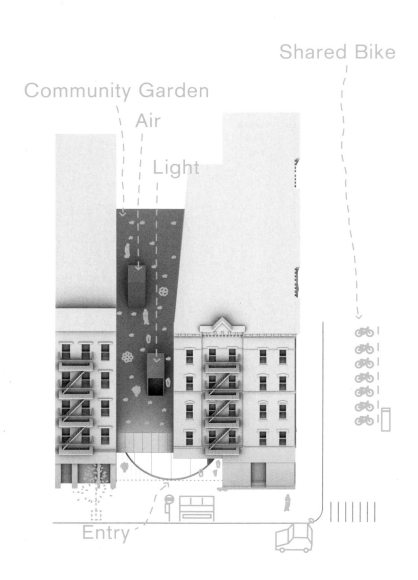

Shared Bike

Community Garden

Air

Light

Entry

Case Studies

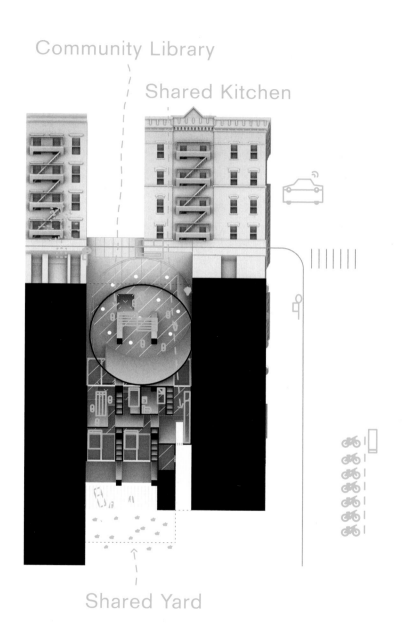

Community Library

Shared Kitchen

Shared Yard

413   Case Studies

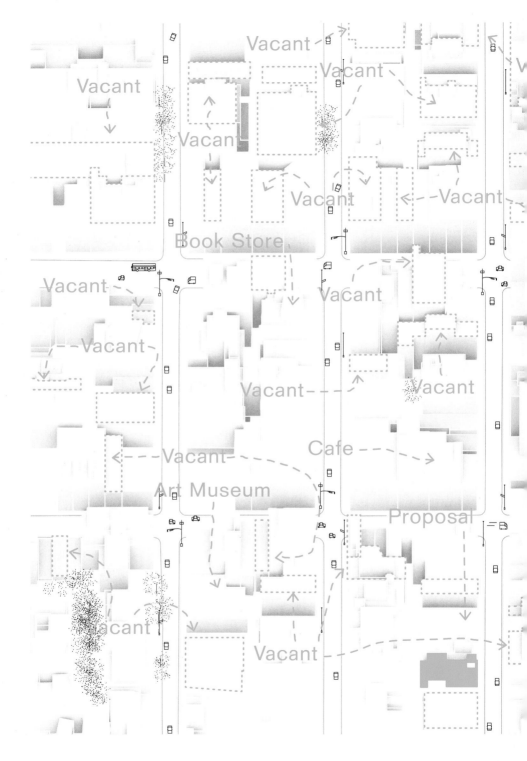

Vacant

Vacant

Vacant

Vacant

Vacant

Vacant

Book Store

Vacant

Vacant

Vacant

Vacant

Vacant

Cafe

Vacant

Art Museum

Proposal

Vacant

Vacant

Case Studies

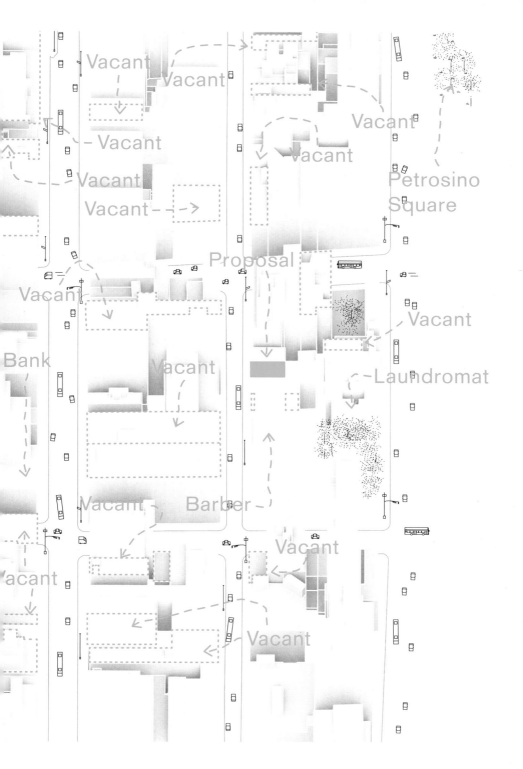

Vacant
Vacant
Vacant
Vacant
Vacant
Vacant
Vacant
Petrosino
Square
Proposal
Vacant
Vacant
Laundromat
Bank
Vacant
Vacant
Barber
Vacant
acant
Vacant

415   Case Studies

37 Crosby Street

Part of the Soho-Historic Cast Iron District Extension. Built in 1900, 7-stories tall, on a quiet street. The cobbled street in front was directly paved over with asphalt. There are 3 clothing retailers along the block. SoHo was once known for its lofted spaces and art galleries, but is now better known for its density of boutique retail. The neighborhood has one of the highest vacancy rates in Manhattan, with 534 reported vacancies, or 35 percent of the total retail space. It is one of the most expensive places to live in Manhattan. The median household income is 130,000 dollars, and the median gross rent is 2,200 dollars.

There are only 133 units of affordable housing here, so housing is added. It can be used by the City's Department of Homeless Services to help secure permanent housing for one of the thousands of families that stays in a shelter each night. It has as much indoor space as outdoor, to maximize light and air quality. Engaging the street in the front and alley in the back. They can host barbecues on the weekends during the summer in their backyard.

Jun 2019, Flagstaff1 Llc, $170K Land Val, $2.45M Tot Val, 2250 SF, 577 days since logged occupancy.

417   Case Studies

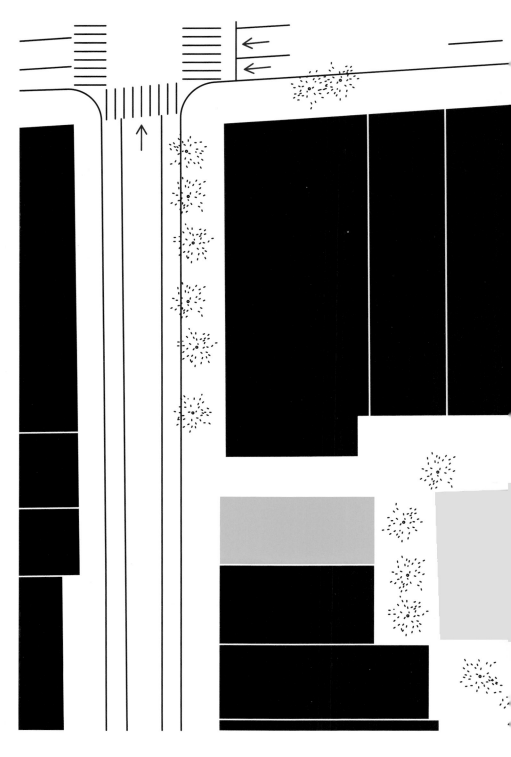

Case Studies

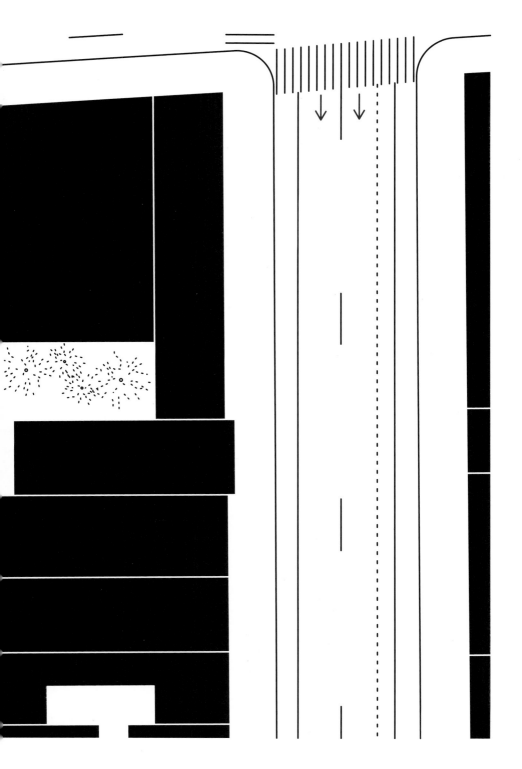

Case Studies

Case Studies

421   Case Studies

"Cast Iron District"

Shared Garden

Case Studies

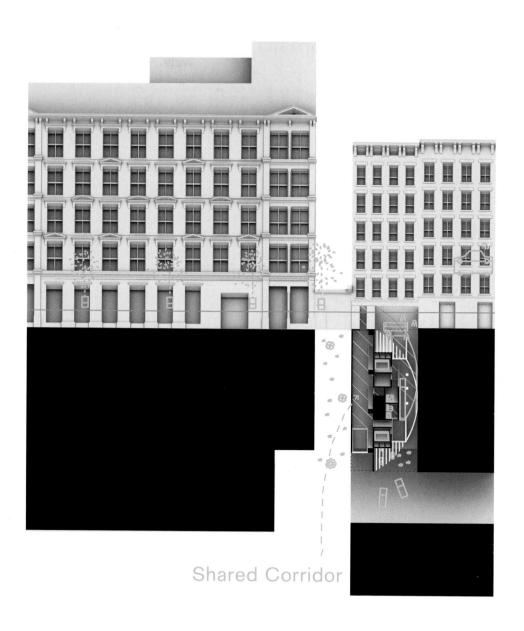

Shared Corridor

423   Case Studies

15 Mercer Street

Another in SoHo, TriBeCa, Civic Center, Little Italy. See also 37 Crosby Street. Inside the Soho-Historic Cast Iron District. Built using cast iron in 1886, designed by architect Samuel A. Warner. On a narrow cobbled street. The steps in front are frequently sat on. There are 4 other vacancies on the block, along with clothing retailers, art galleries, and a lighting store. It is worth restating that there are only 133 units of affordable housing spread between 5 buildings, and 534 reported vacancies. 45 percent of households make more than 150,000 dollars, and 17 percent make less than 35,000 dollars.

There should be more affordable housing, so collective housing for 10 was added. Reusing an existing space instead of building new developments. 2 volumes are split by a patio and circulation space to the upstairs units.

Jun 2019, 15 Mercer Condominium, $286K Land Val, $8.97M Tot Val, 6798 SF, 638 days since logged occupancy.

Case Studies

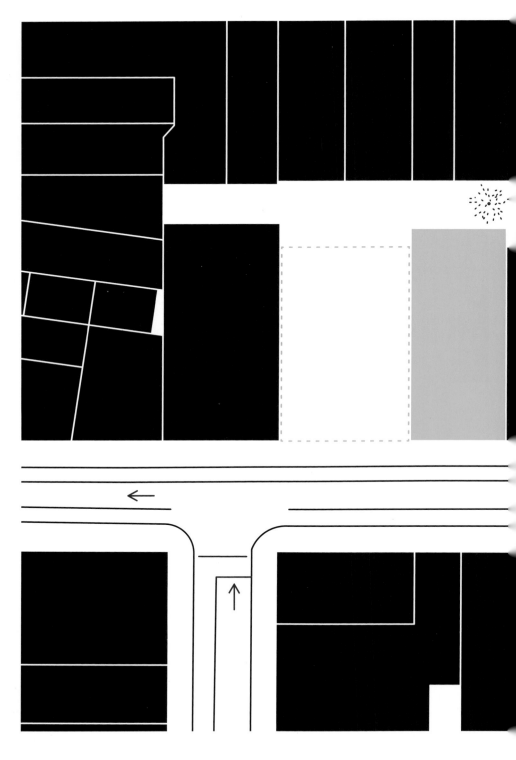

426   Case Studies

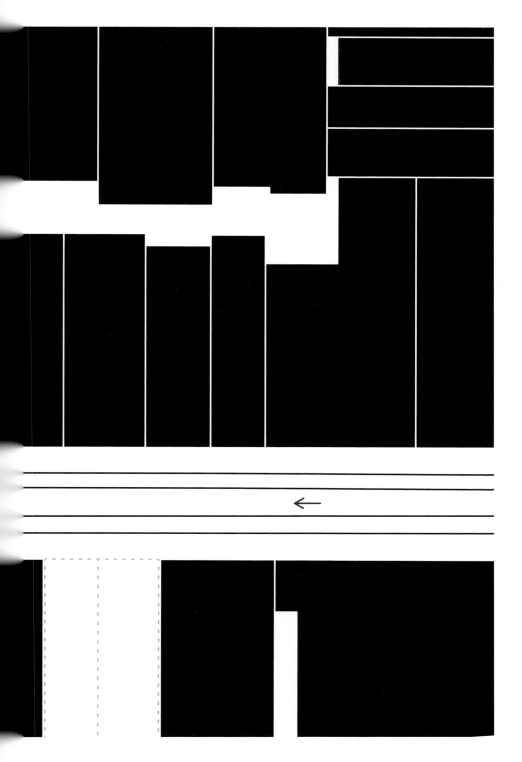

427   Case Studies

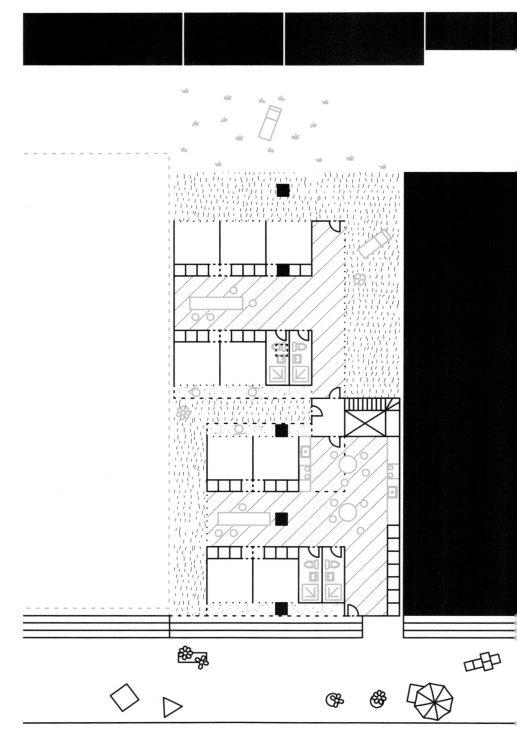

Case Studies

Case Studies

"Cast Iron District"

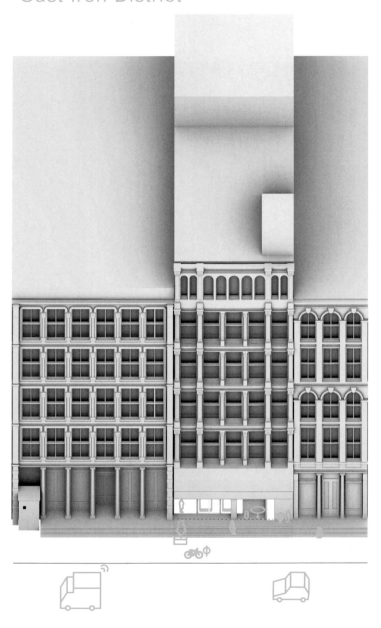

Case Studies

Communal Living

431   Case Studies

947 2 Avenue

Every building on the block is 4 stories tall. Every block around them has buildings that are 18 or more. There are 7 restaurants and 2 cafes on the block, and 2 restaurants and a health center across 2nd Avenue, a busy 1-way street with a bicycle path and bus-only lane. The median household income is 136,000 dollars and median gross rent is 2,500 dollars in Turtle Bay. 22 percent of renters are severely rent burdened, paying more than 50 percent on rent. There are 0 community gardens. Of the nearly 38 thousand units of housing, only 378 are affordable housing – 0 for extremely low income, 43 very low, 290 low, 0 moderate, 45 medium.

1 bedroom and 1 office are added. Patios in the front and back allow light and air to permeate the spaces. One small lot isn't nearly enough to solve the housing crisis, but if all of the available vacant spaces in this area were transformed into housing, we could provide an additional 1.86 million square feet of housing.

Jun 2019, 947 Second Avenue Owner Llc, $587K Land Val, $1.46M Tot Val, 2000 SF, 1400 days since logged occupancy.

433   Case Studies

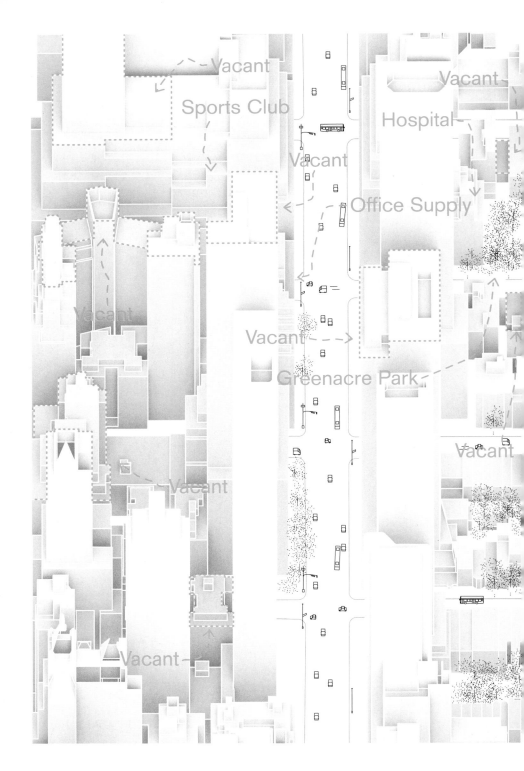

Case Studies

Vacant

Vacant

Vacant

Vacant

Church

Vacant

School

Proposal

Vacant

Vacant

Vacant

...ate of Ukraine

Vacant

Emergency Care

Pharmacy

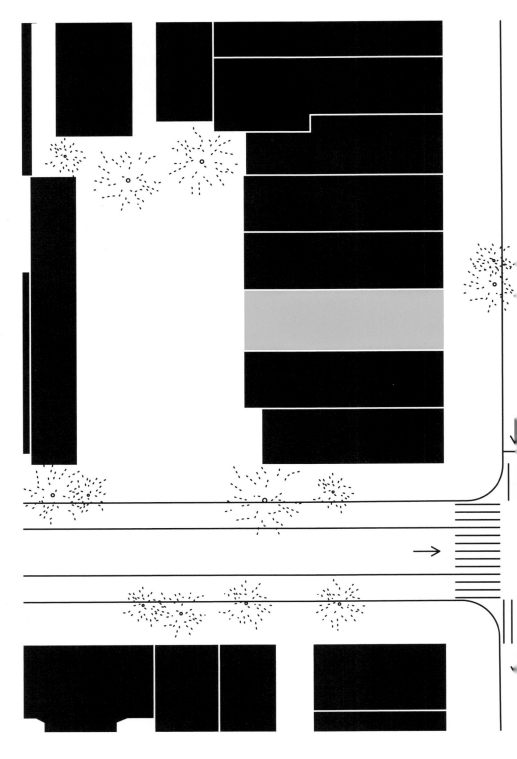

Case Studies

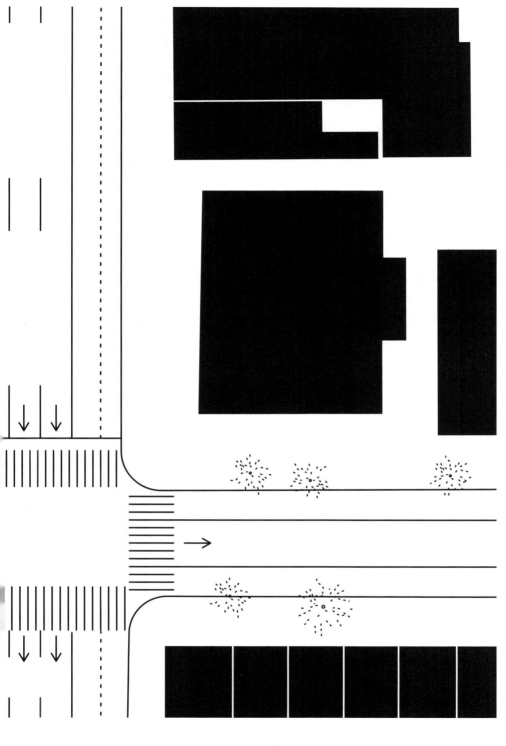

437   Case Studies

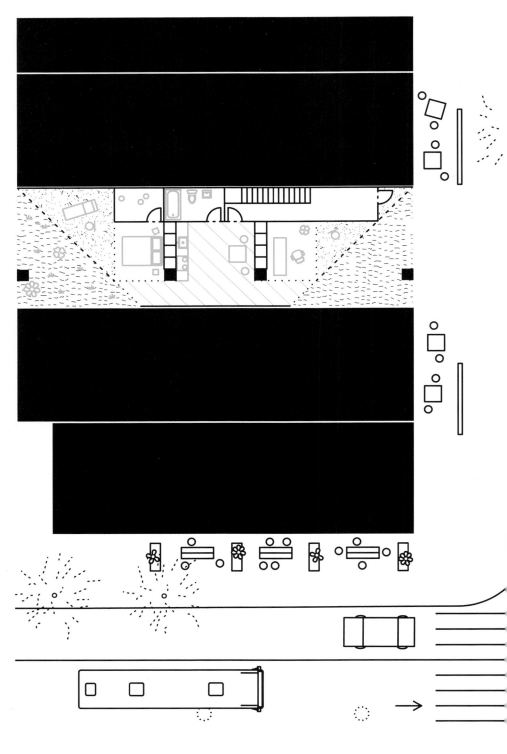

438

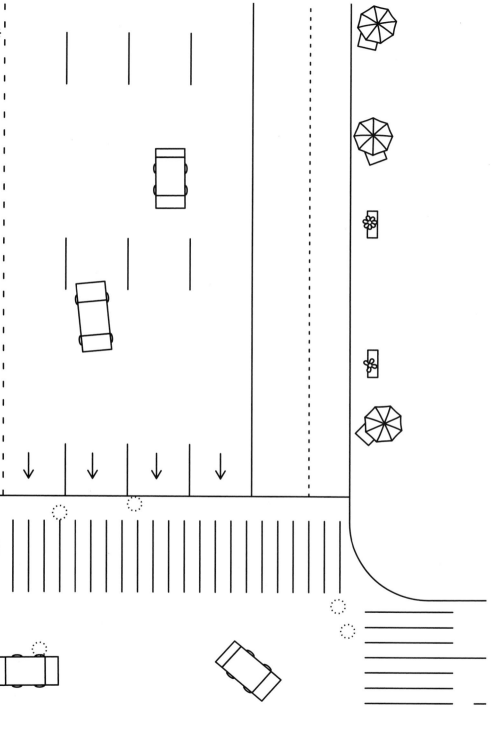

439   Case Studies

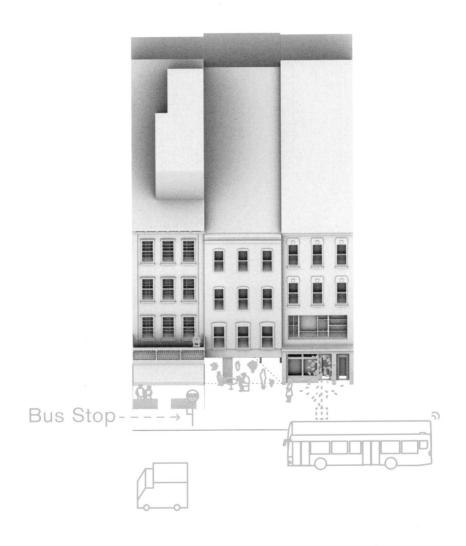

Bus Stop- - - - →

Case Studies

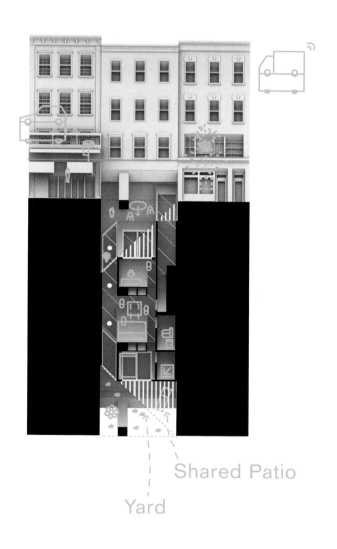

Shared Patio

Yard

Case Studies

238 7 Avenue

On the corner of 7th Avenue and West 24 Street. Half of the block is 4 stories tall, the other half, including this building, is 11 or more. A bicycle shop, fitness center, and 2 restaurants are on the block. Across West 24 Street, there is a grocery store and Citi Bike station, although neither 24th or 7th have bike lanes. Across 7 Avenue, there is a FedEx, tanning salon, and cafe. In Hudson Yards, Chelsea, Flatiron, Union Square, there are a total of 4 community centers. The closest one is a 15-minute walk. 39 percent of households make more than 150,000 dollars; 21 percent make less than 35,000.

The economic inequality is extreme, so collective housing and a community room are added in the corner retail vacancy. 4 bedrooms share a common kitchen space and 2 bathrooms. A patio separates the bedrooms from the sidewalk. A ground-level place for work and leisure, a space for living.

Jun 2019, Unavailable Owner, $535K Land Val, $6.64M Tot Val, 2680 SF,
1826 days since logged occupancy

443   Case Studies

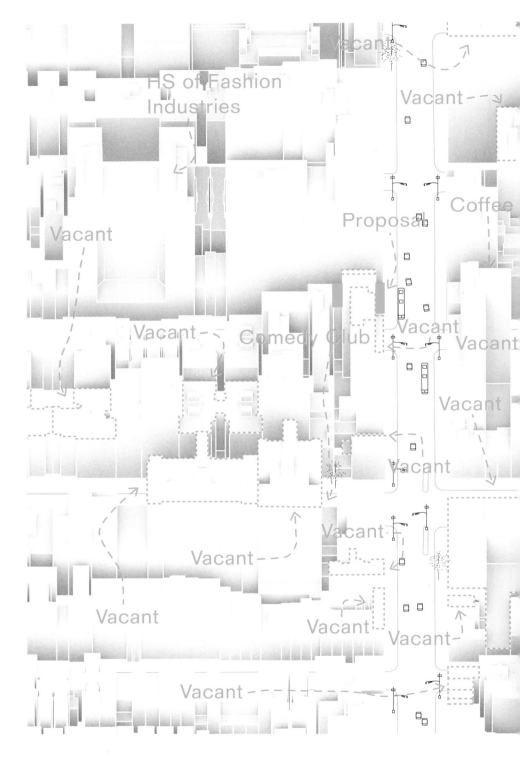

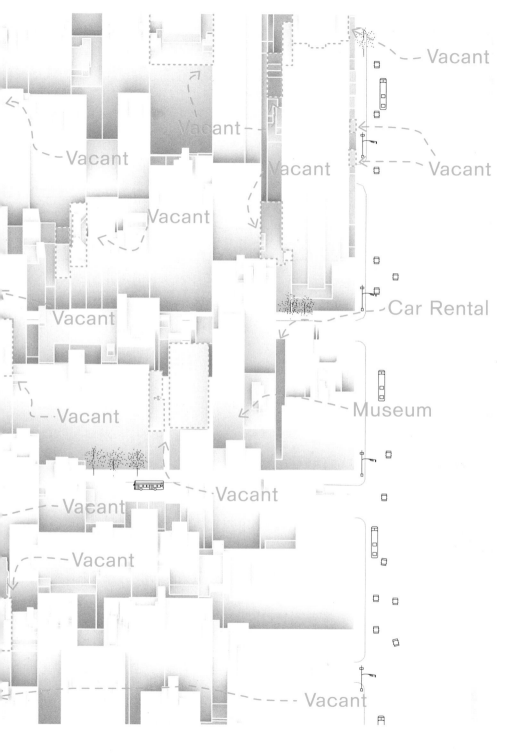

Vacant

Vacant

Vacant

Vacant

Vacant

Vacant

Car Rental

Vacant

Museum

Vacant

Vacant

Vacant

Vacant

445

Case Studies

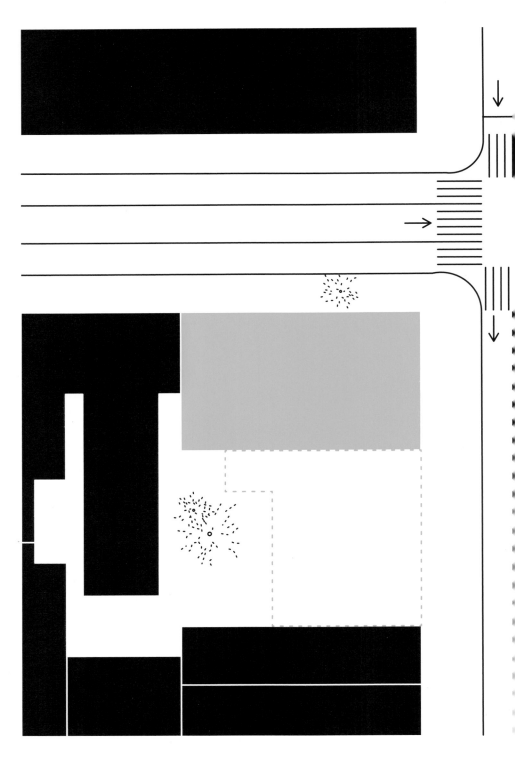

Case Studies

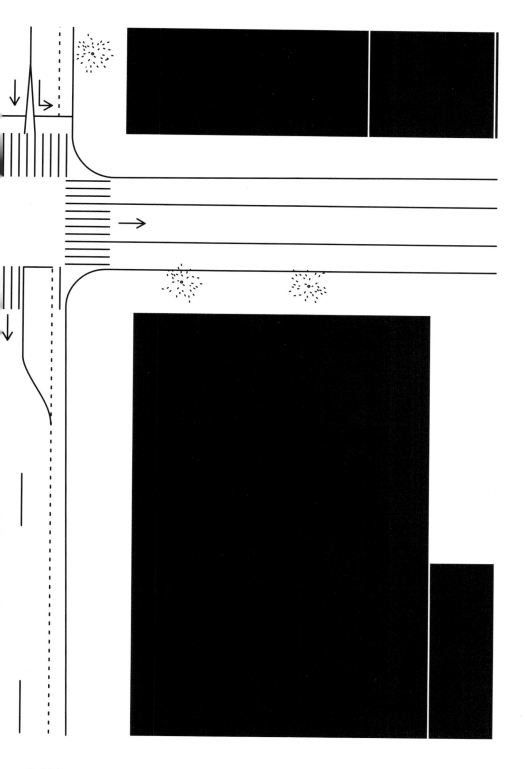

447   Case Studies

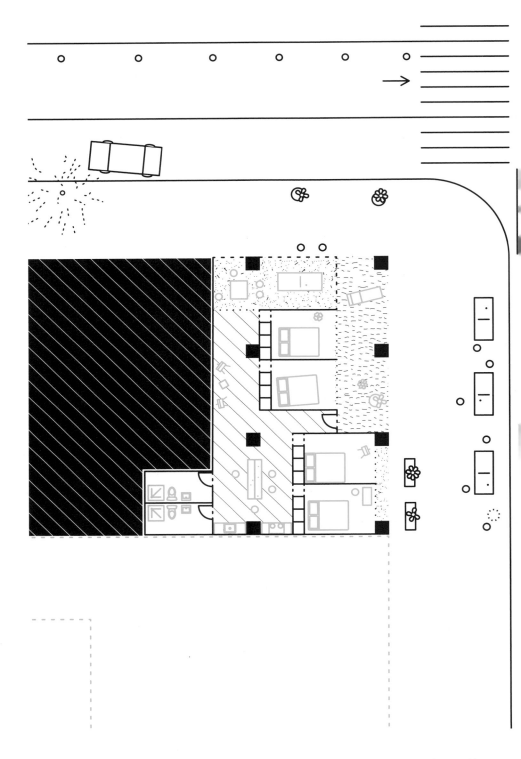

448   Case Studies

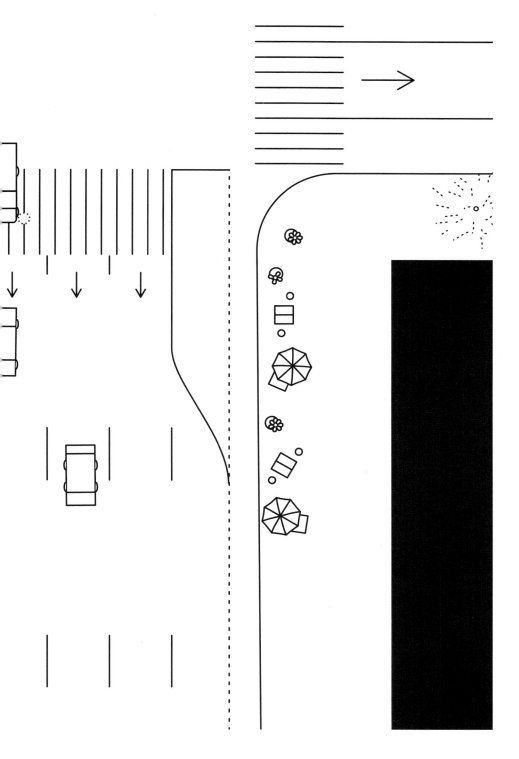

449   Case Studies

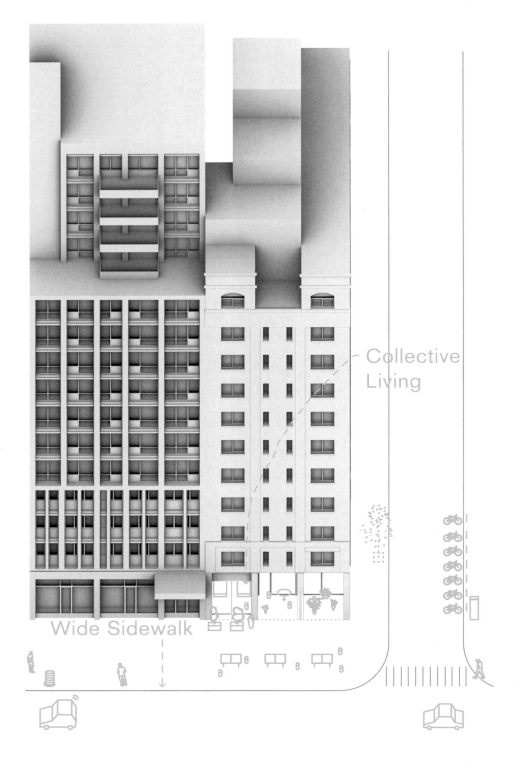

Collective
Living

Wide Sidewalk

Case Studies

Accessible
Community
Center

451   Case Studies

1345 St Nicholas Avenue

A long and narrow site located in the city's Little Dominican Republic, 2 blocks from Highbridge Park. This section of Saint Nicholas Avenue is also known as Juan Pablo Duarte Boulevard. The George Washington Bridge is to the left, and the Alexander Hamilton is to the right. There are 146 reported vacancies in Washington Heights South, although we observed many other vacancies that were unreported. The median gross income is 51,000 dollars. There are 1,513 units of affordable housing. 4 community gardens. Mainly restaurants and bodegas on the surrounding blocks.

A different type of retail space and home for 1, or 2 to share, are added. A flower shop and outdoor space in the front, a bedroom, bathroom, kitchen, and small yard in the back.

Nov 2019, 1341 Realty Group Llc, $212K Land Val, $1.2M Tot Val, 595 SF,
761 days since logged occupancy.

453   Case Studies

454

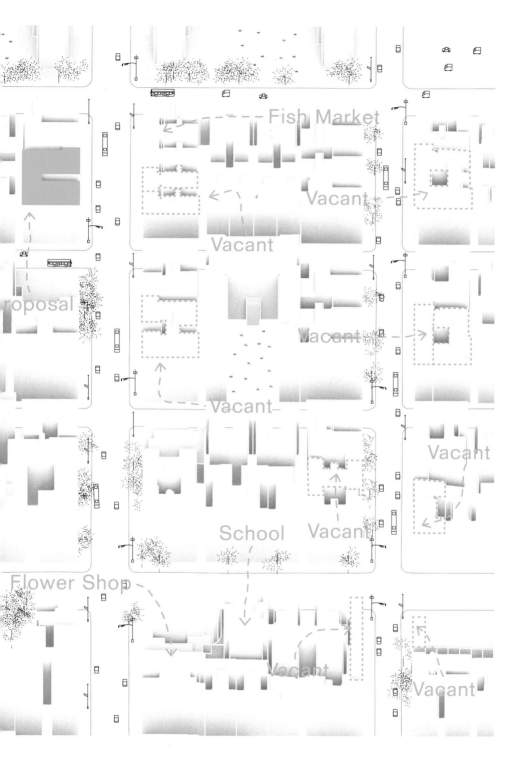

Fish Market

Vacant

Vacant

Proposal

Vacant

Vacant

Vacant

School

Vacant

Vacant

Flower Shop

Vacant

Vacant

455

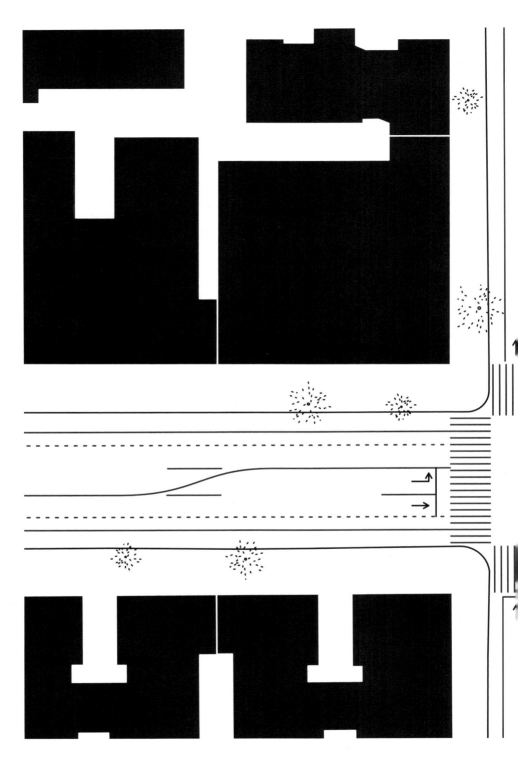

456

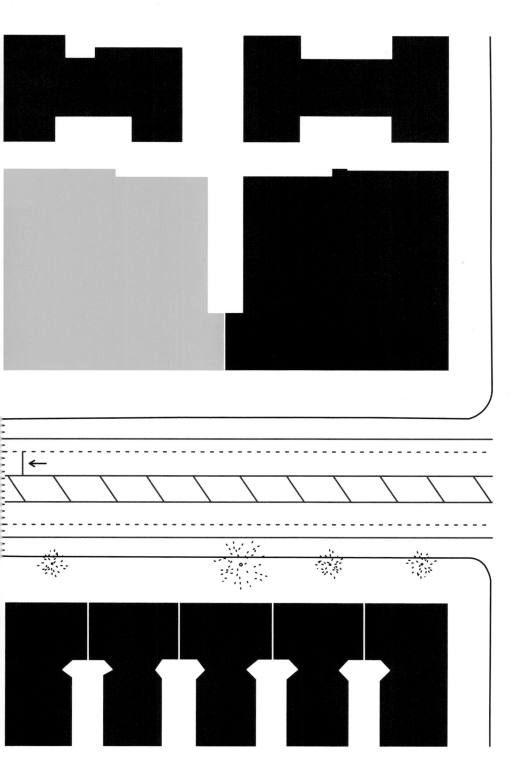

457   Case Studies

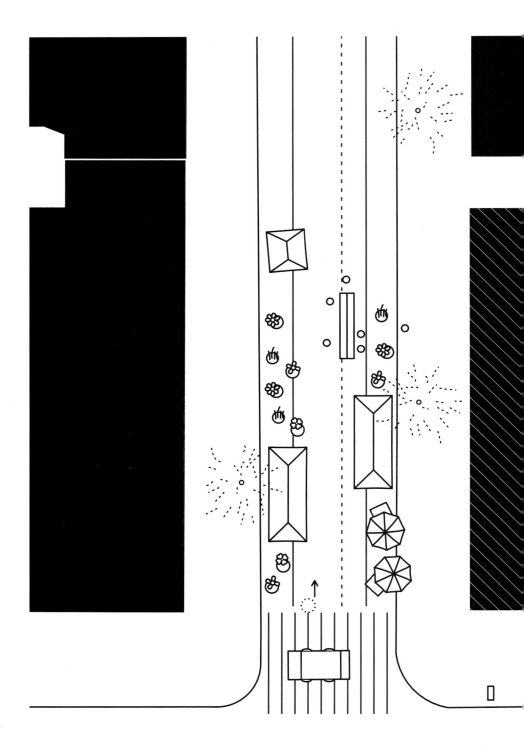

Case Studies

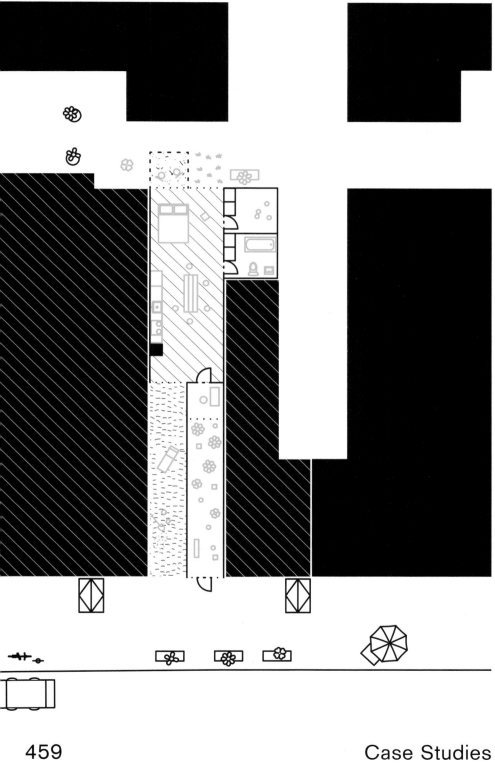

459

460   Case Studies

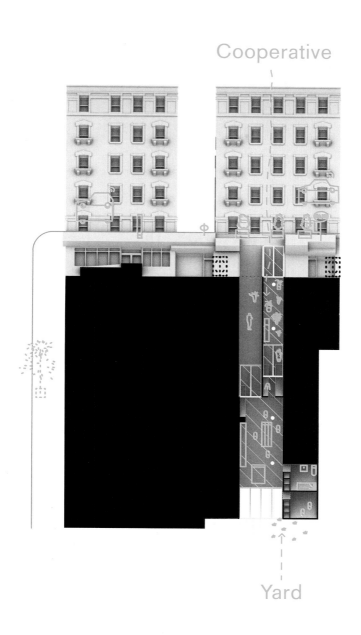

Cooperative

Yard

Case Studies

260 Park Avenue South

Another in Hudson Yards, Chelsea, Flatiron, Union Square. See also 238 7 Avenue. This one is a large space in the Flatiron District on the corner of Park Avenue South and East 21 Street. Park Avenue South has 2-way traffic divided by a narrow tree-lined barrier; there are no bike lanes. The building consists of 2 buildings – one built in 1910, the other 1930 – redeveloped into a single bourgeois condominium in 2014. 3 blocks to Bryant Park, and half of a block to Gramercy Park. There is another vacancy of equivalent size on the block, and a FedEx, furniture store, cafe, and restaurant across Park Avenue. There are 9 soup kitchens or food pantries, but none nearby. Small patches of affordable housing; everything else is the opposite.

Collective housing and a soup kitchen are added. Each bedroom shares a garden space with another, and they all share bathrooms and a communal kitchen. The soup kitchen has access to a yard in the back, where people can sit, eat, and relax.

Oct 2019, Unavailable Owner, $6.08M Land Val, $32.9M Tot Val, 8925 SF,
1064 days since logged occupancy.

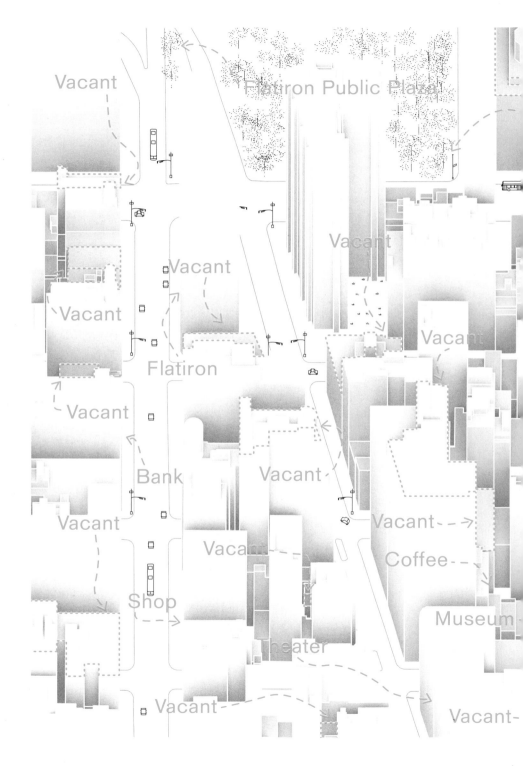

Vacant

Flatiron Public Plaza

Vacant

Vacant

Vacant

Vacant

Vacant

Flatiron

Vacant

Bank

Vacant

Vacant

Vacant

Vacant

Coffee

Shop

Museum

Theater

Vacant

Vacant

Case Studies

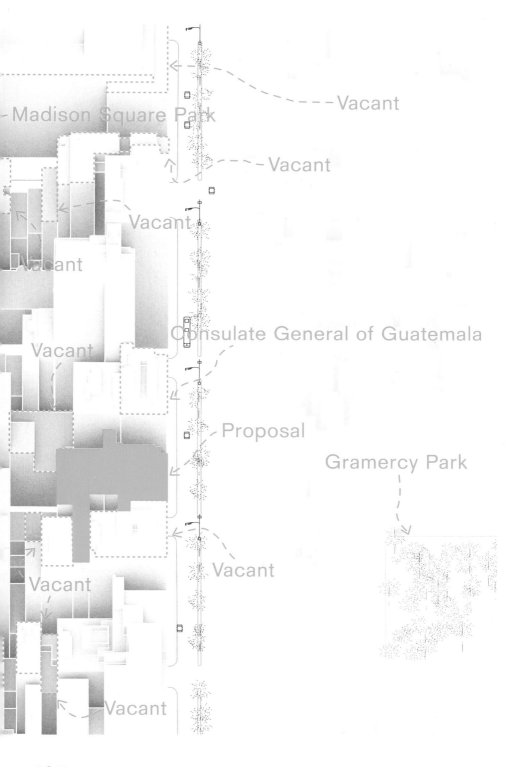

Madison Square Park

Vacant

Vacant

Vacant

Vacant

Vacant

Consulate General of Guatemala

Proposal

Gramercy Park

Vacant

Vacant

Vacant

465   Case Studies

Case Studies

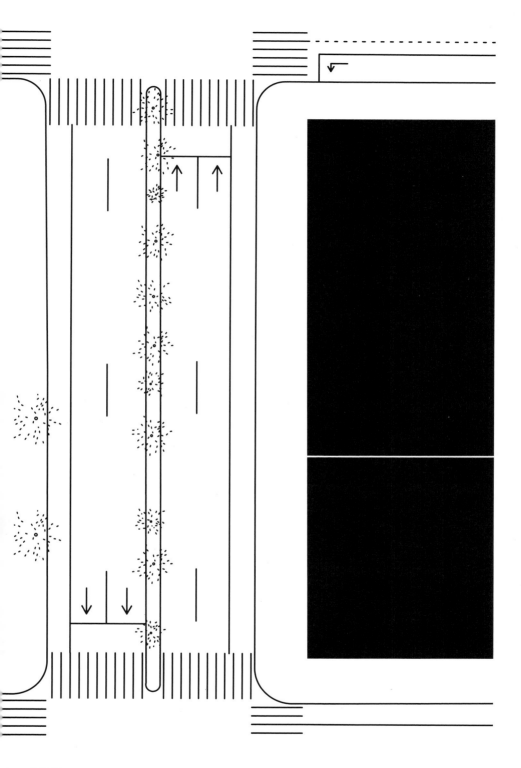

Case Studies

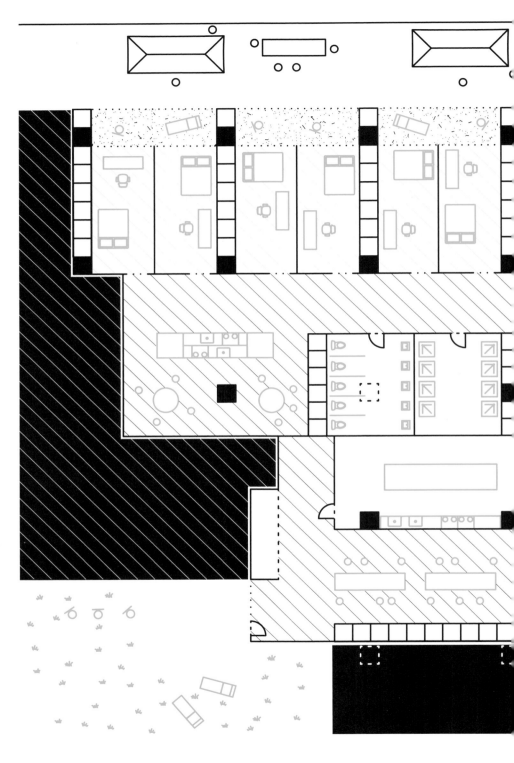

Case Studies

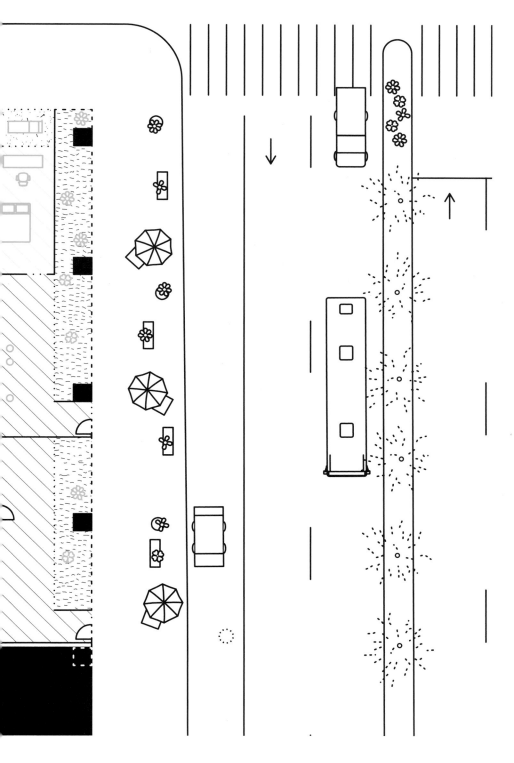

469   Case Studies

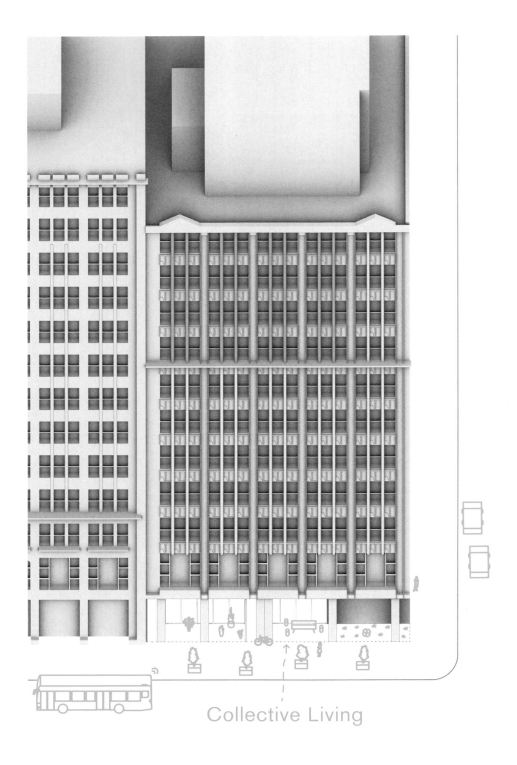

Collective Living

470   Case Studies

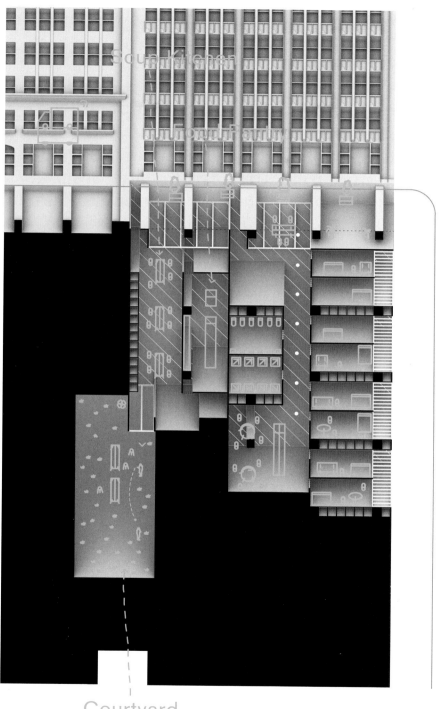

Soup Kitchen

Food Pantry

Courtyard

Case Studies

108 1 Avenue

A fast-food restaurant next door and a popular family-owned garden and hardware store 3 stores down. 2 vape shops and 6 restaurants are across the street. 1 block from Tompkins Park. 1st Avenue is busy, with a bike lane that is separated from traffic by a lane. There are 244 reported vacancies in the East Village. 761 units of affordable housing. The median household income is 78,000 dollars, although the median gross rent is 2,000 dollars and 22 percent of renters spend 50 percent more of their income on rent.

Collective housing for 4 is added. A row of bedrooms with a kitchen and bathroom share a common space on one side and an outdoor space on the other.

Jun 2019, 108 1 St Llc, $352K Land Val, $1.68M Tot Val, 1500 SF, 577 days since logged occupancy.

473   Case Studies

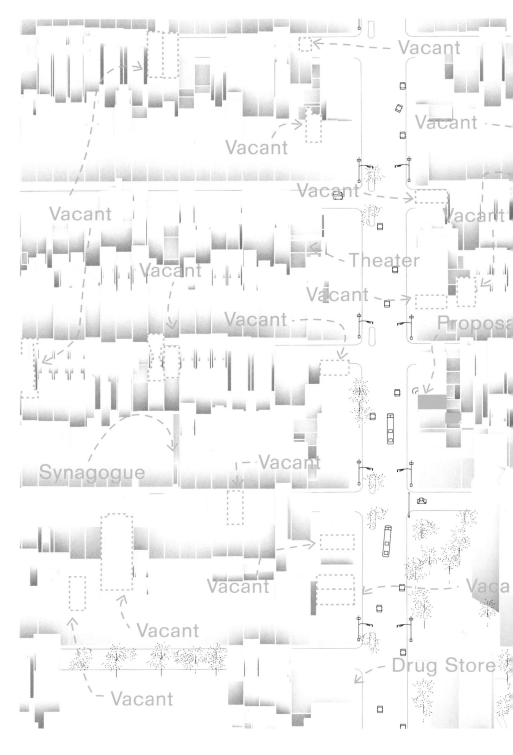

Vacant

Vacant

Vacant

Vacant

Vacant

Vacant

Theater

Vacant

Vacant

Proposa

Synagogue

Vacant

Vacant

Vaca

Vacant

Drug Store

Vacant

Case Studies

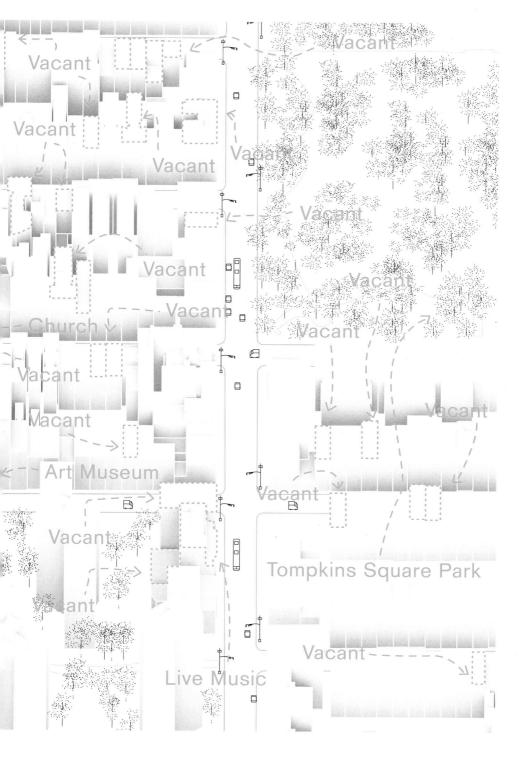

475   Case Studies

476   Case Studies

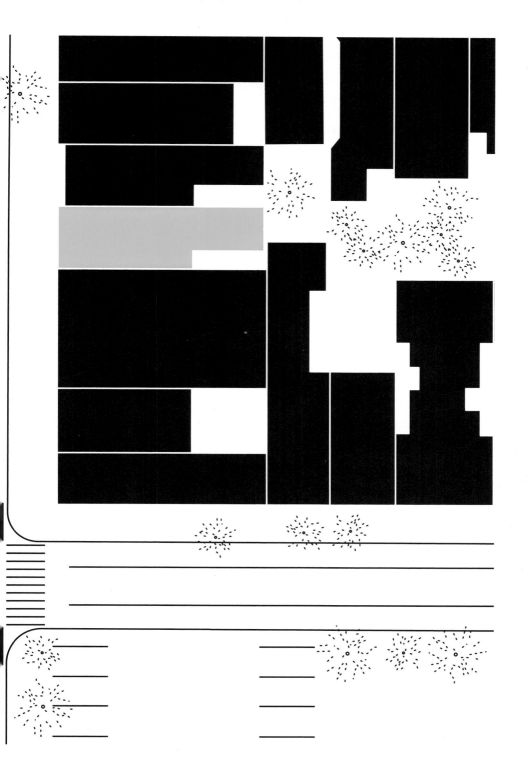

477   Case Studies

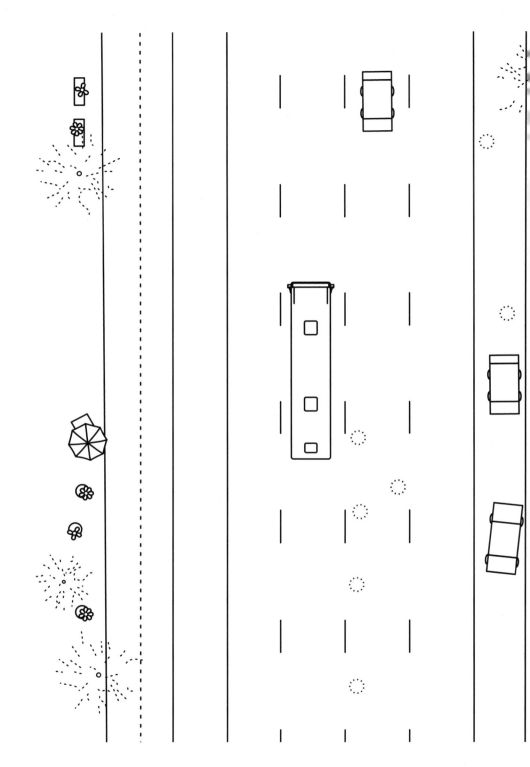

478

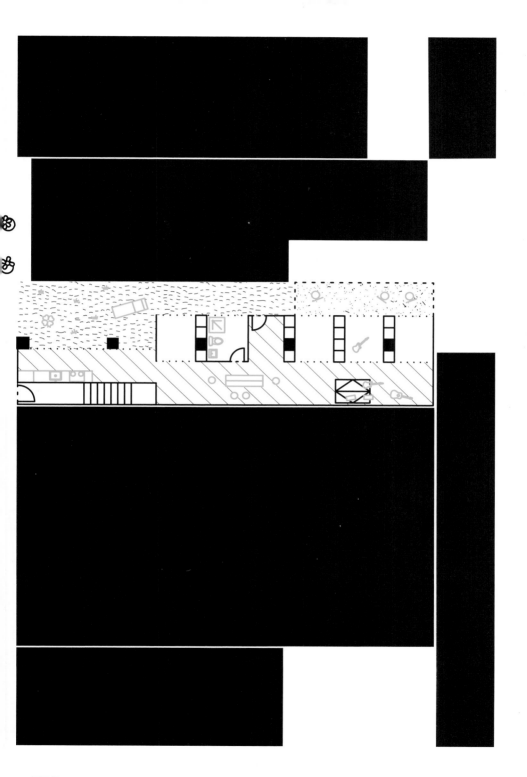

479

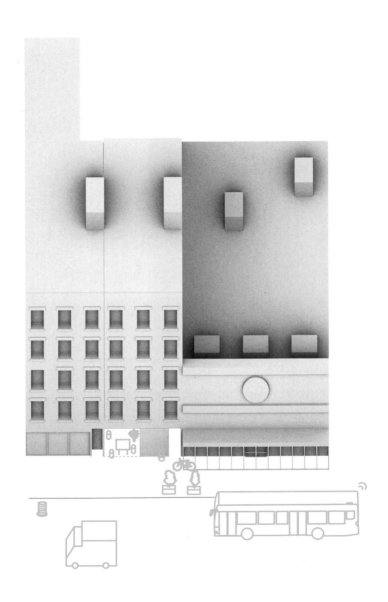

Case Studies

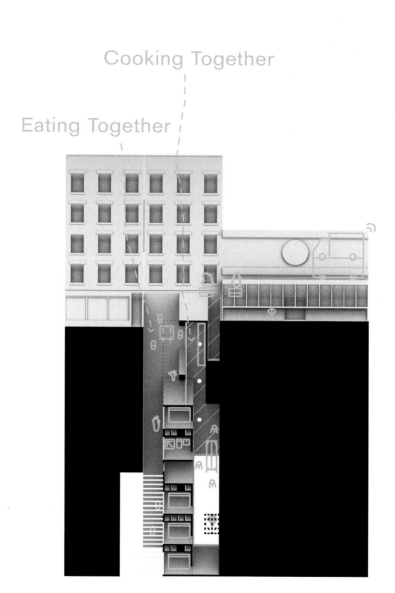

Cooking Together

Eating Together

481   Case Studies

195 Broadway

Also known as the Financial District. The building is sometimes called the Telephone Building, the place of the first transcontinental telephone call. Built in 1916, designed by William Bosworth, and 29-stories, the building supposedly uses the most marble of any building in New York City. Even the fire stairs are white Vermont granite. It is next to a cemetery, 1 block from the Oculus, and an Anthropologie and Starbucks are on the block. It has an entrance to the Fulton Street Subway stop, with 1 and 2 trains heading downtown and to Brooklyn. A mall is across the street. There is 1 public library. 12 percent of households make less than 35,000 dollars, and 53 percent make more than 150,000 dollars. Median gross rent is 3,200 dollars. The highest rent in Manhattan. 127 units of affordable housing. 0 affordable for extremely low income, 12 very low, 109 low, 0 moderate, 6 medium.

8 units of collective housing are introduced, buffered by large outdoor and common spaces. 4 bedrooms are on the ground floor, and because the ceilings are nearly 28 feet tall, a mezzanine is added for 4 additional rooms. A luxury commercial space repurposed for affordable housing.

Oct 2019, 195 Broadway Ground Owner Llc, $12.4M Land Val, $101M Tot Val, 9871 SF, 1826 days since logged occupancy.

483 Case Studies

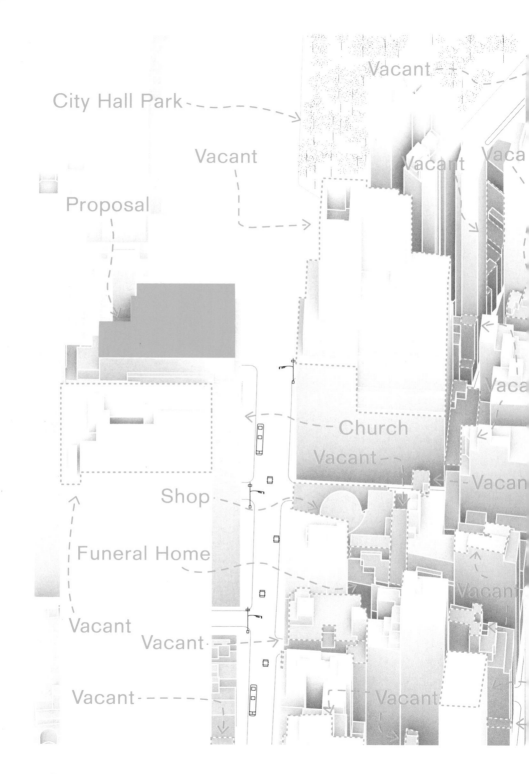

City Hall Park

Vacant

Vacant

Vacant

Vaca

Proposal

Vaca

Church

Vacant

Vacan

Shop

Funeral Home

Vacan

Vacant

Vacant

Vacant

Vacant

484

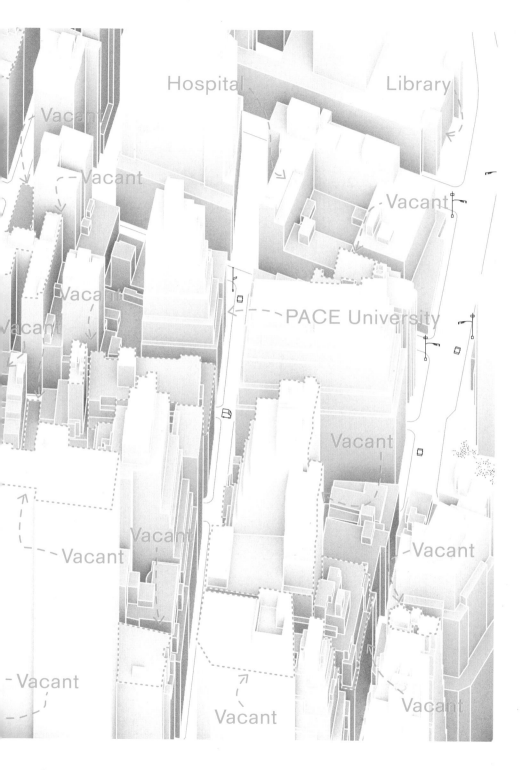

Hospital

Library

Vacant

Vacant

Vacant

Vacant

Vaca

acant

PACE University

Vacant

Vacant

Vacant

Vacant

Vaca

Vacant

Vacant

Vacant

485

Case Studies

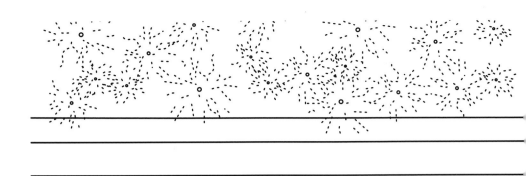

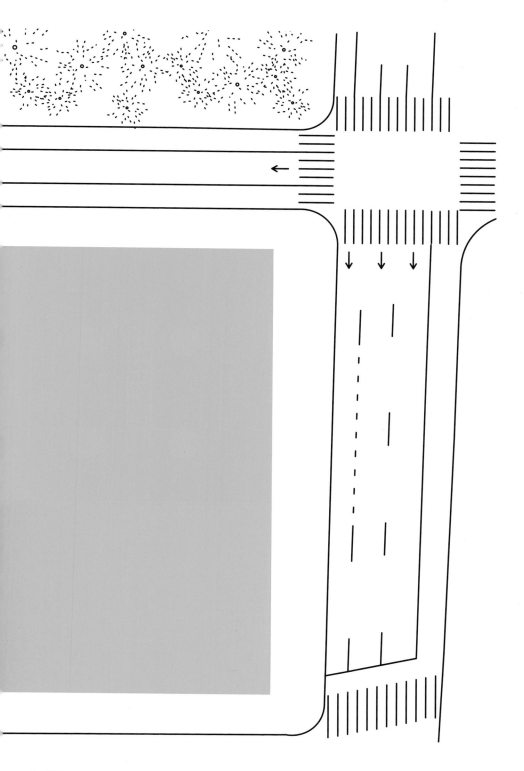

Case Studies

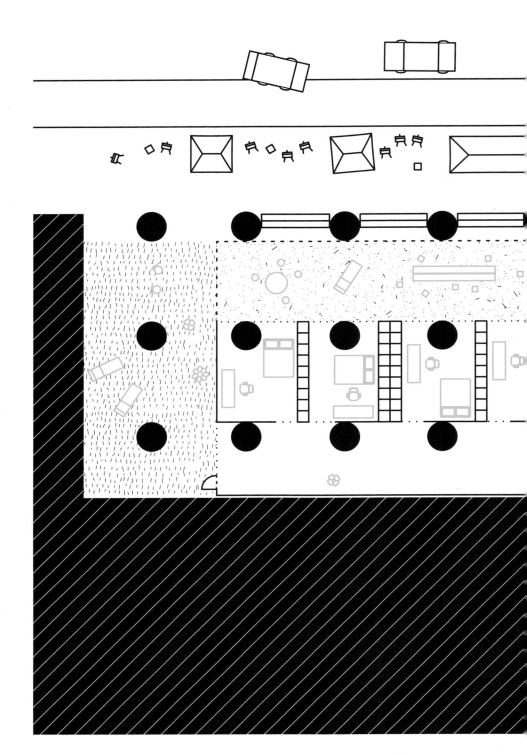

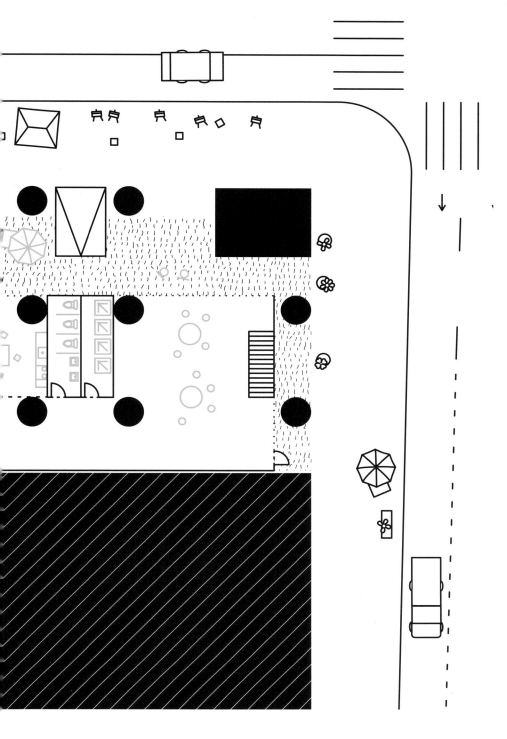

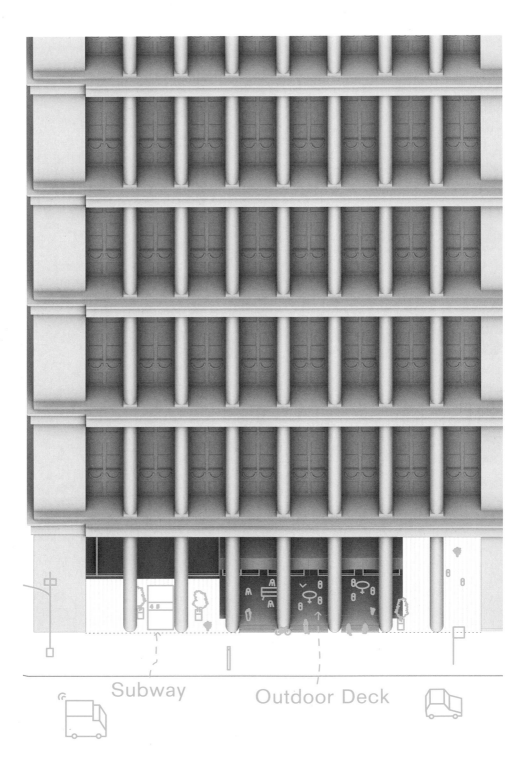

Subway   Outdoor Deck

490   Case Studies

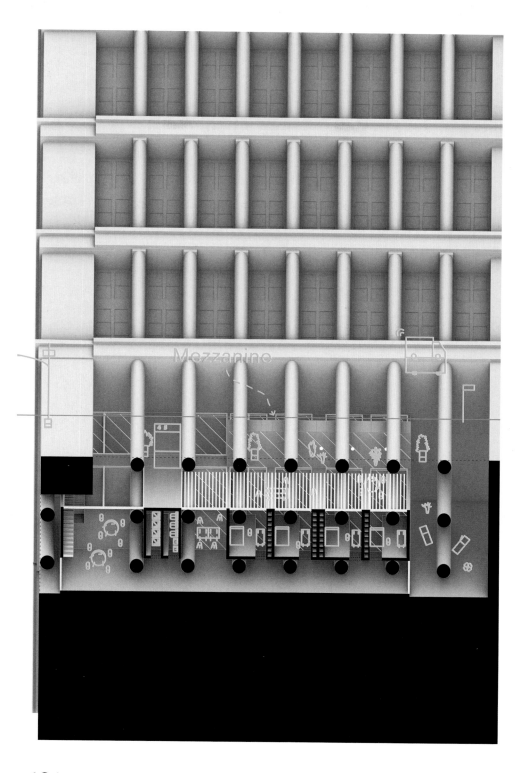

Mezzanine

491

2051–2057 Frederick Douglass Bl

A line of 4 row houses, all with vacant ground floors. Next to an anti-poverty nonprofit, with banks on each end of the block. There are 2 large parks both 1 block away, Morningside and Central. Close to Columbia University. Affordable housing is across the street. The median gross rent is 1,200 dollars in Central Harlem South.

23 percent of renters are severely rent burdened, spending more than 50 percent of their income on rent, so collective housing is added. Turned into a collective art residency for artists. A place for experimentation and other models of living.

May 2019, FDB 111 Street Llc, $338K Land Val, $2.92M Tot Val, 2450 SF,
942 days since logged occupancy

493   Case Studies

Vacant

Vacant

Pediatrician

Vacant

Morningside Park

Food

Vacant

Vacant

Bank

Vacant

Proposal

Veterinarian

Case Studies

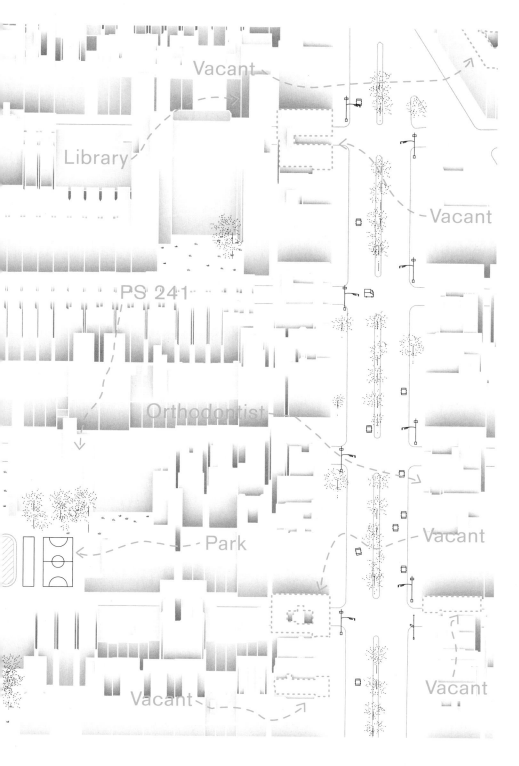

Vacant

Library

Vacant

PS 241

Orthodontist

Park

Vacant

Vacant

Vacant

495

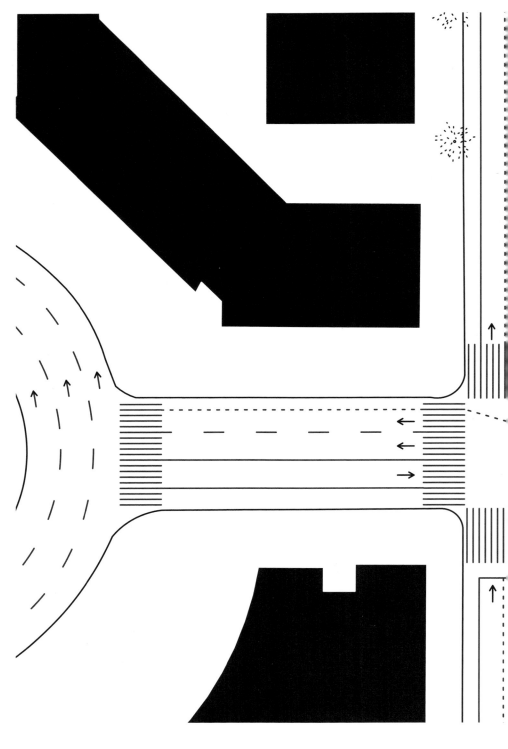

496   Case Studies

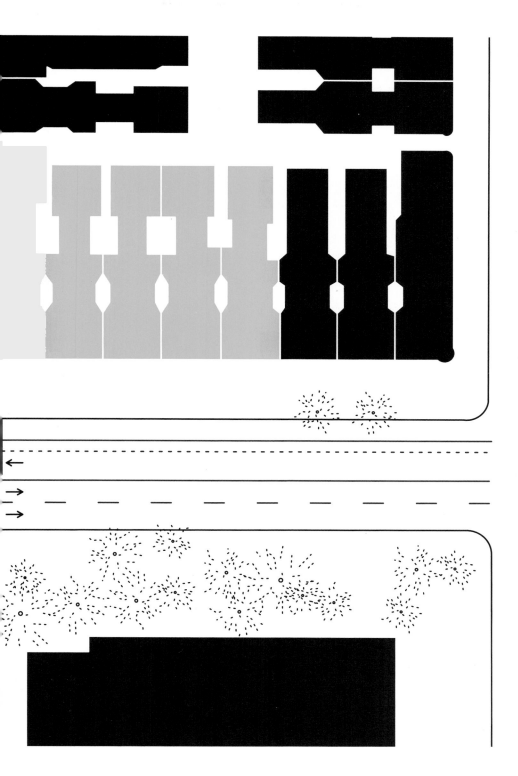

Case Studies

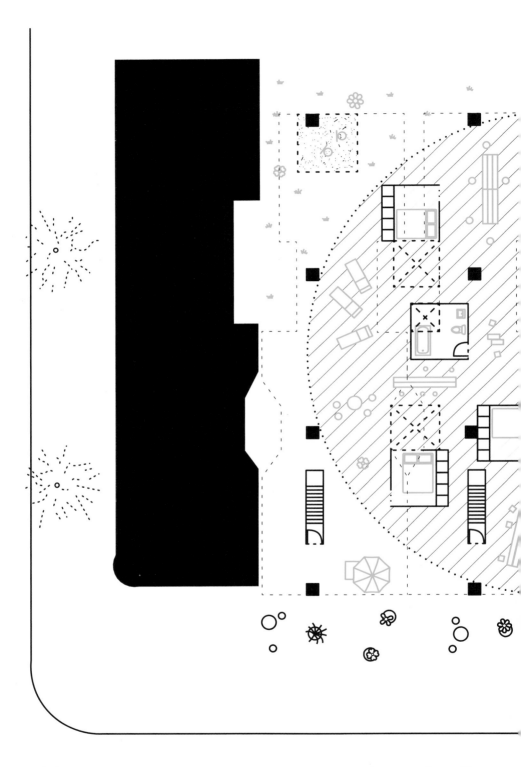

498   Case Studies

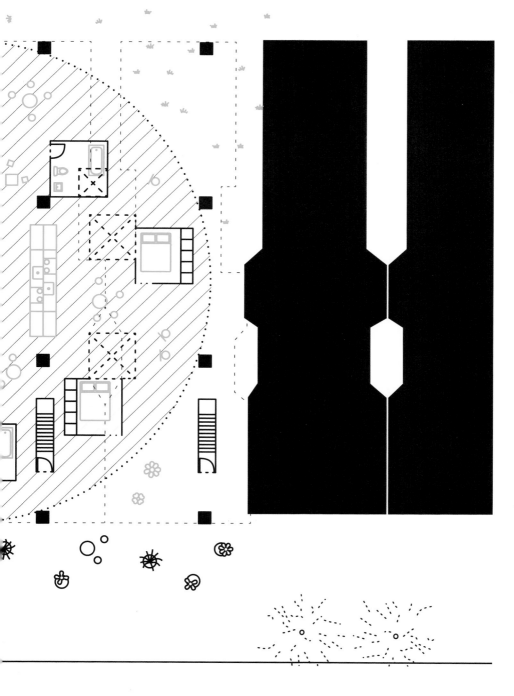

499

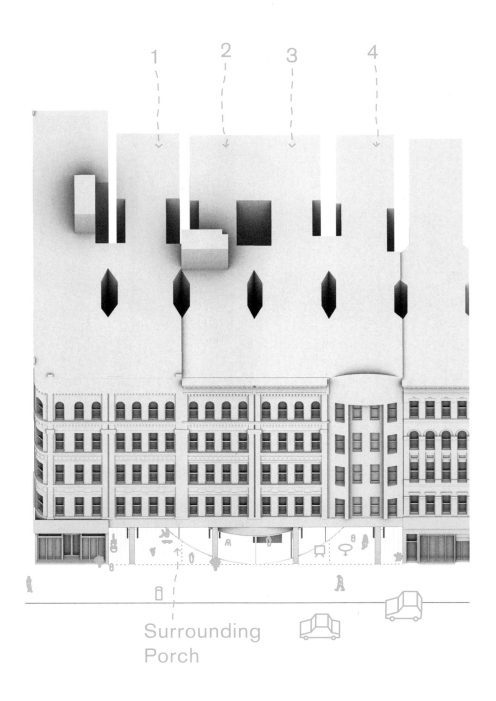

Surrounding
Porch

Case Studies

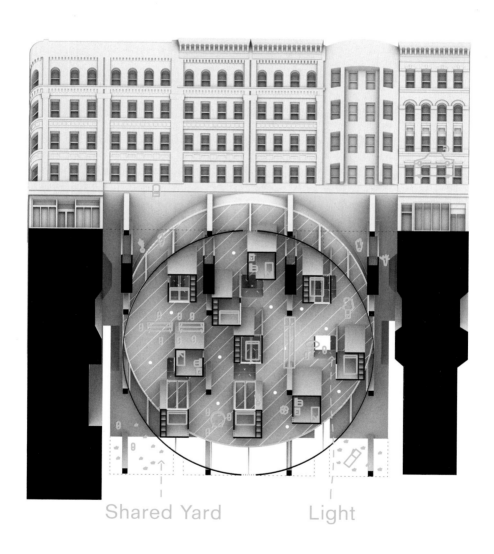

Shared Yard   Light

501   Case Studies

Chinatown

Chinatown is one of the Manhattan neighborhoods hardest hit by Covid 19. Many businesses have permanently closed, including Jing Fong, an iconic neighborhood restaurant that closed in March after being open for 28 years. Due to the coronavirus, which has fueled racism and violence against Asian Americans around the country, the recovery of Chinatown remains uncertain even after the end of the virus.

Prior to Covid 19, Chinatown was gentrifying, experiencing higher rent increases than average and changing demographics. 47 percent of households currently make less than 35,000 dollars, and there are 1,993 units of affordable housing – 38 extremely low income, 117 very low, 1,339 low, 460 moderate, and 39 medium. 30 percent of renters spend 50 percent or more of their income on rent, yet new developments often primarily add luxury units, marketing to individuals outside of the community. One Manhattan Square, completed in 2019, adds apartments beginning at 1 million dollars.

The following are 15 housing proposals, of Chinatown's 392 reported ground-floor vacancies. We propose an incremental horizontal housing development. Filling in instead of building up. A network currently 51-units, 25,000 square feet. More vacancies are available to expand into as the neighborhood changes.

503   Case Studies

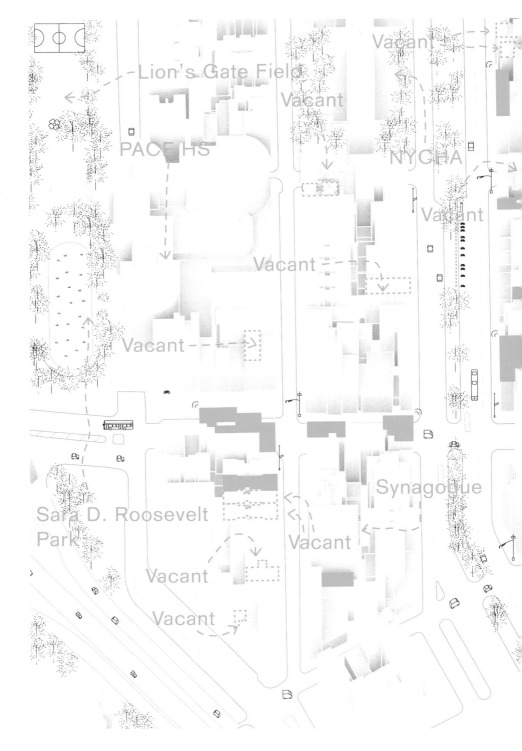

Lion's Gate Field

Vacant

Vacant

PACE HS

NYCHA

Vacant

Vacant

Vacant

Synagogue

Sara D. Roosevelt
Park

Vacant

Vacant

Vacant

504

PS 042

Vacant

Vacant

Vacant

Vacant

Vacant

Proposal

Tennis Court

Seward Park

Library

Straus Square

Post Office

505

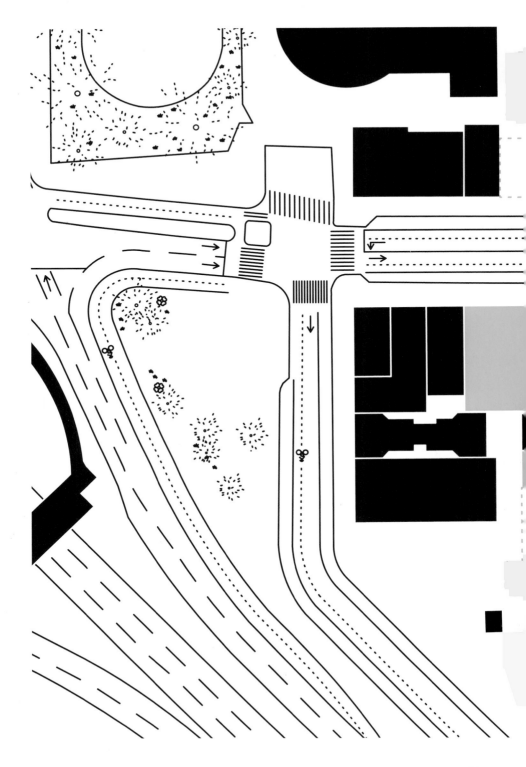

Case Studies

507   Case Studies

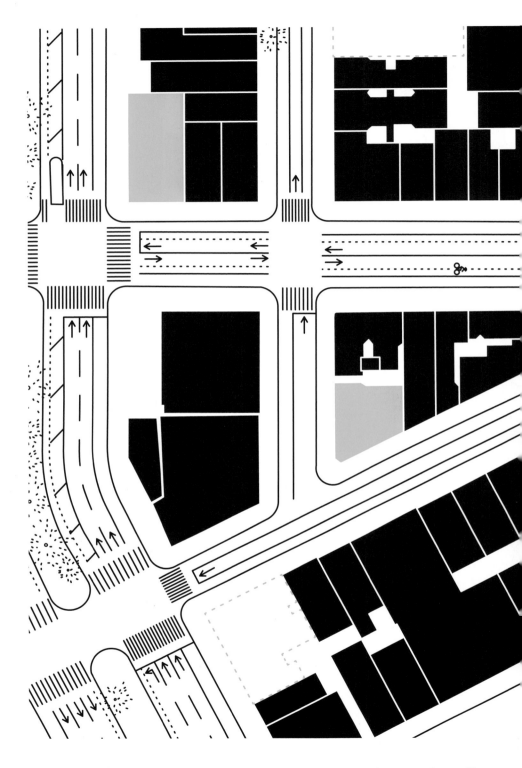

508   Case Studies

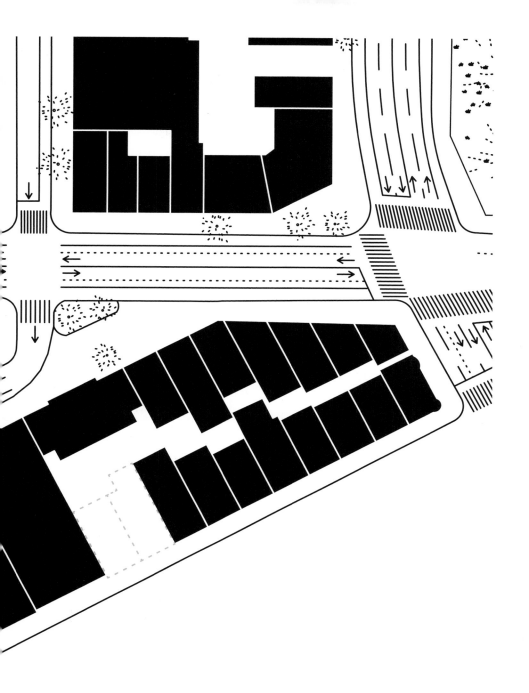

509   Case Studies

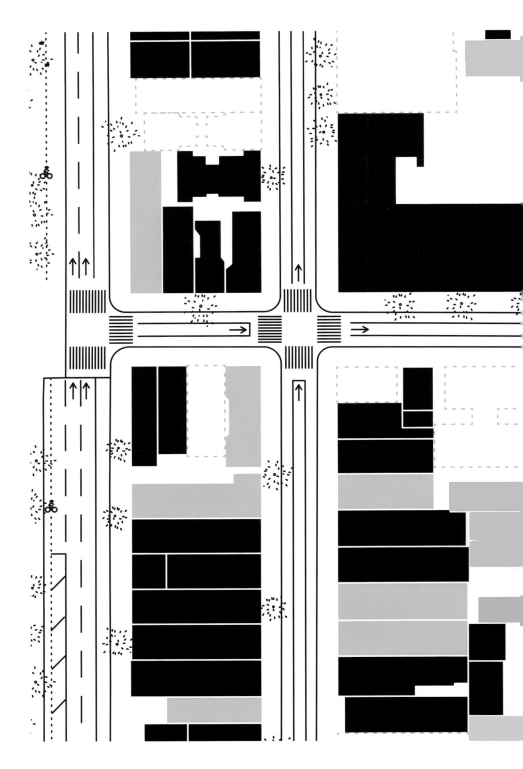

Case Studies

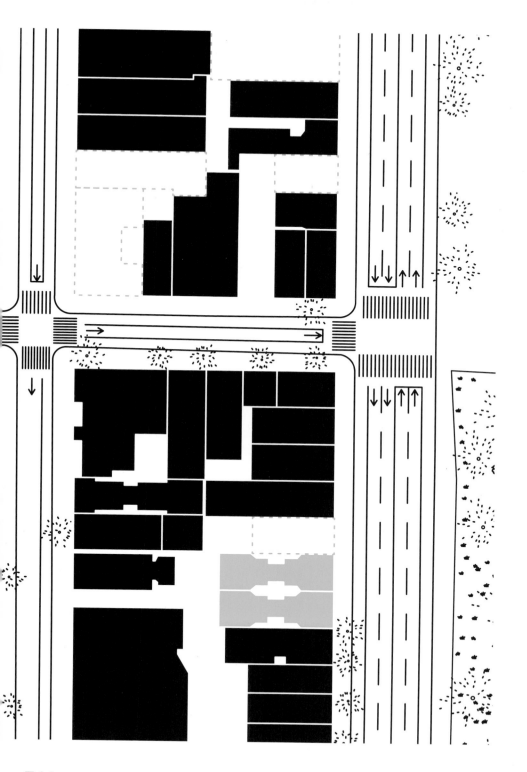

511

10 Eldridge Street

A single-story building constructed in 1945 with a large paved area behind it, near 19 Eldridge Street. A synagogue built in 1887 and designated a national historic landmark is on one side, a vacancy on the other. Otherwise the block is 6-story residential buildings. There are 9 restaurants, a hair salon, pharmacy, 99 cent store, and 8 other vacancies on the narrow, one-way street. Their store names on colorful red, yellow, and white signage. 1 block from Xu Bing Park.

An outdoor space and stair leading to a rooftop garden provide privacy for a home for 2 from the street. Light and air enters through skylights.

10 Eldridge Street, Jun 2019, 10 Eldridge Llc, $55K Land Val, $170K Tot Val, Unlisted SF, 1704 days since logged occupancy.

513   Case Studies

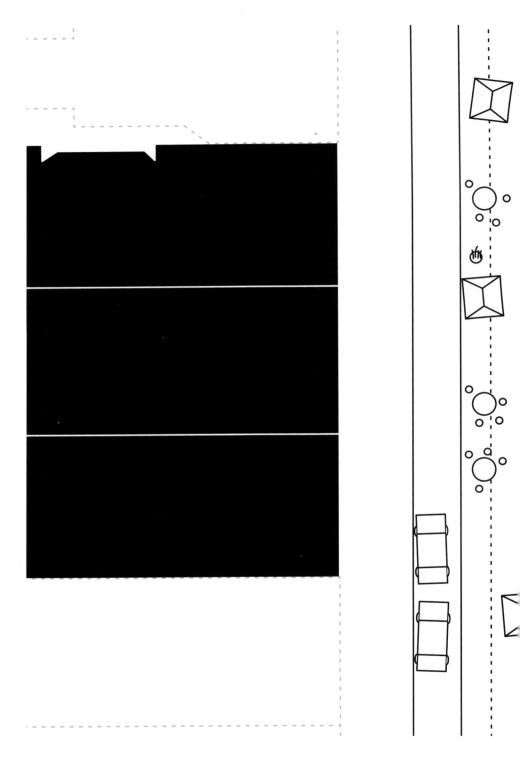

Case Studies

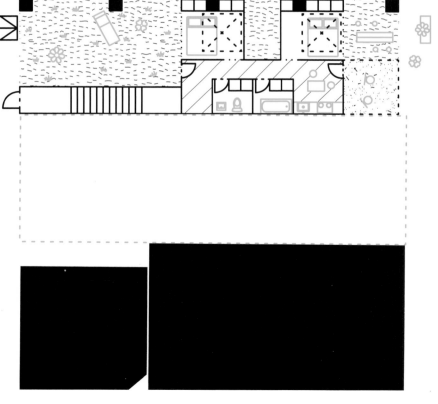

515   Case Studies

Case Studies

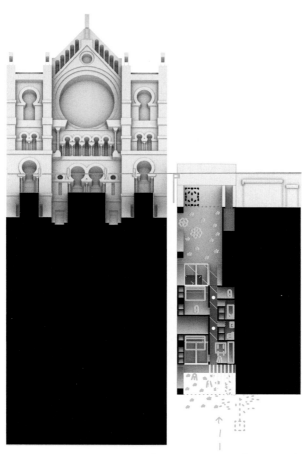

Communal Yard

Case Studies

19 Eldridge Street

A small vacancy in a residential building. Next to 2 other vacancies, and near 10 Eldridge Street. The Pu Chao Buddhist Temple is across the street, along with a synagogue 2 buildings down.

A bed and bath is added for a studio for 1. A small outdoor space brings as much light and air into the home as possible.

Jun 2019, TBF–19 Eldridge Llc, $128K Land Val, $1.16M Tot Val, Unlisted SF,
578 days since logged occupancy.

519   Case Studies

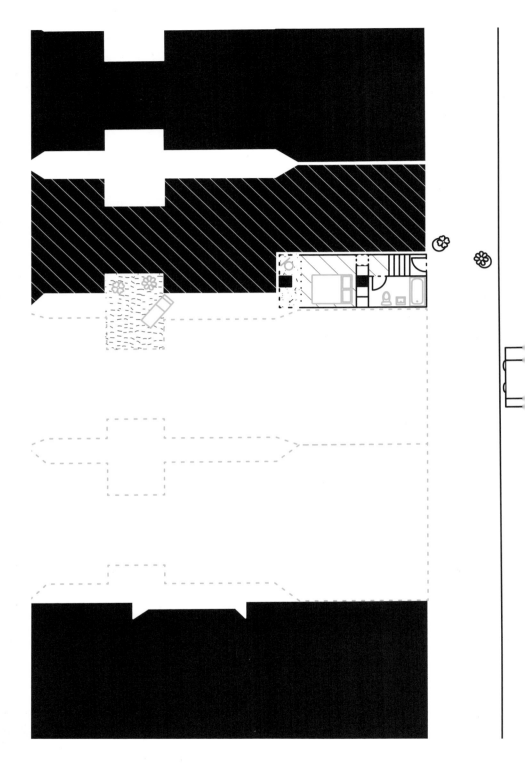

520

521   Case Studies

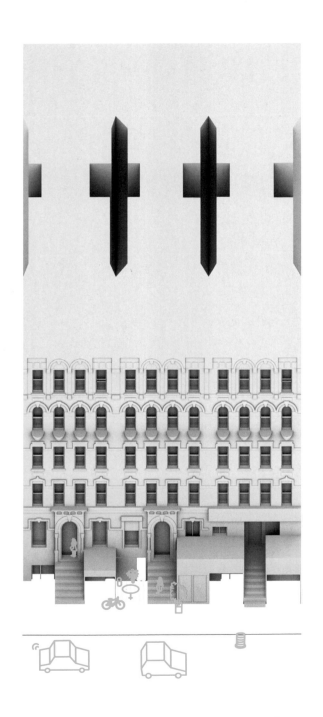

522   Case Studies

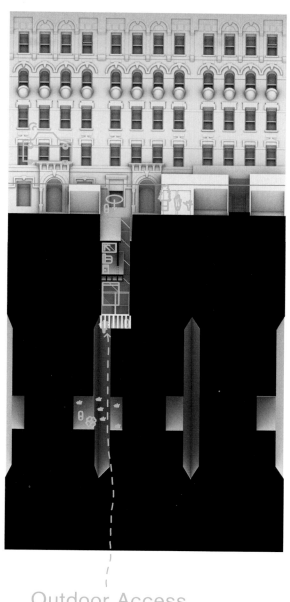

Outdoor Access

Case Studies

130 Division Street

On the corner of Division and Orchard Street, built in 1900, 5 stories tall. 2 blocks from Seward Park. There are restaurants, bakeries, a hair studio, and the Asian Americans For Equality neighborhood office across the street. The 7-story, glass building on the other side of Orchard was completed in 2012.

Collective housing for 6 and a community room that can hold different types of classes are added with a patio wrapping the living spaces.

Jun 2019, Sun Woohing Inc, $151K Land Val, $914K Tot Val, 1550 SF,
4383+ days since logged occupancy.

Case Studies

Case Studies

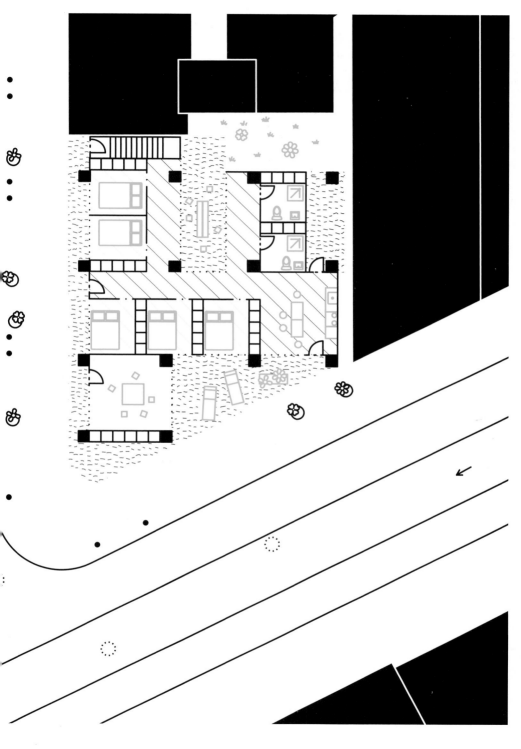

527

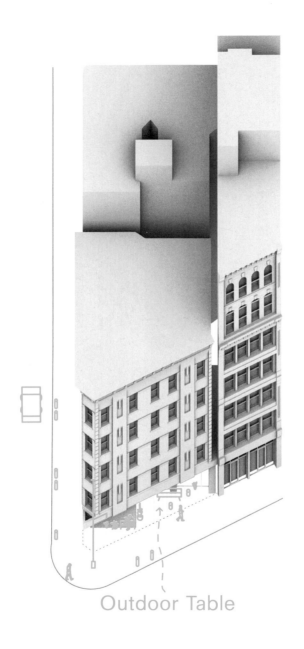

Outdoor Table

Case Studies

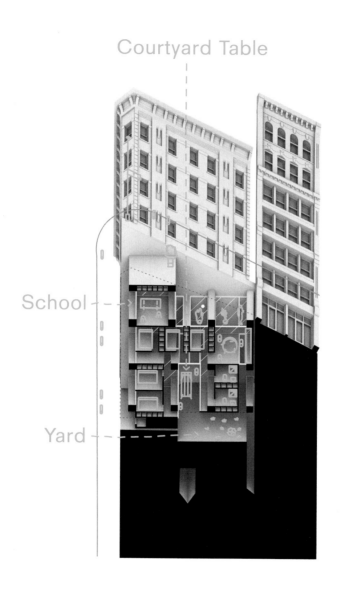

Courtyard Table

School

Yard

Case Studies

15 Essex Street

Seward Park is across Essex Street.
Constructed in 1897, it is the first permanent,
municipally built playground in the US. The
surrounding buildings were completed around
the same time. A public library is on the other
side of the park. There is a paint and signage
store, 3 bars, and a restaurant on the block.

2 current vacancies are combined to add
collective housing, with a third vacancy
available to expand into next door. Soon the
typical ground-level retail will become spaces
for living. 6 bedrooms share a kitchen and 3
bathrooms, allowing it to be for either 1 large
family, 2 different smaller families, 6 individuals,
and so on.

Case Studies

Jul 2020, 13–15 Essex Street Llc, $314K Land Val, $3.37M Tot Val, Unlisted SF, 1003 days since logged occupancy.

Case Studies

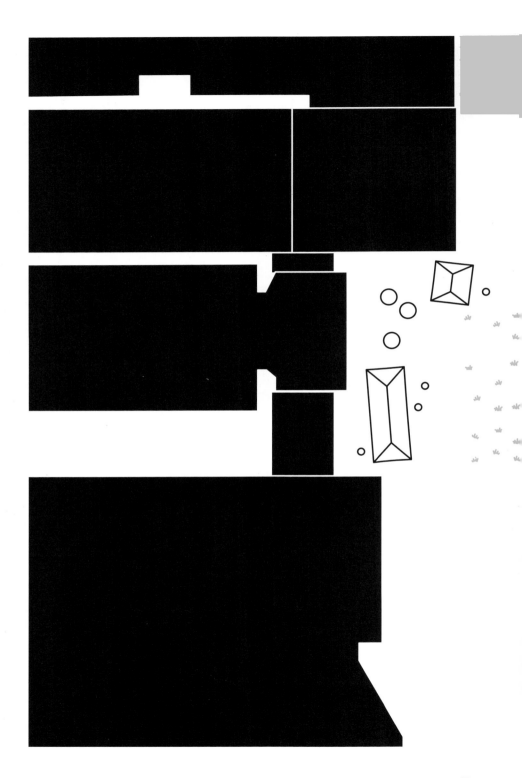

Case Studies

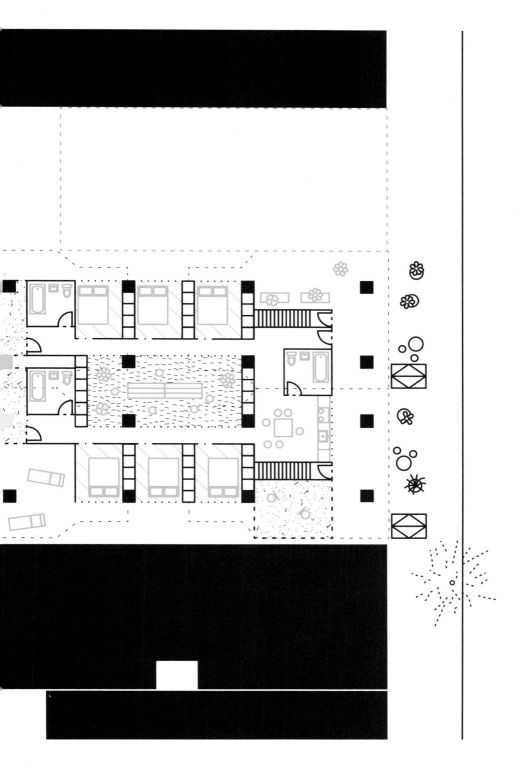

Case Studies

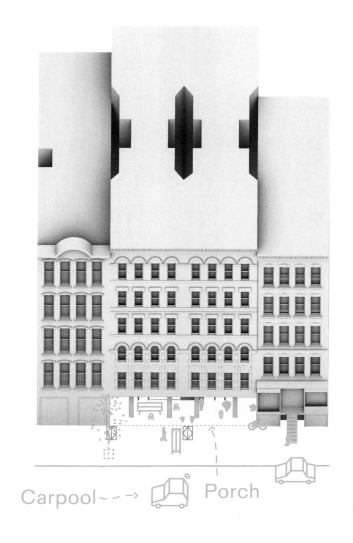

Carpool- - -> 🚐 Porch

Case Studies

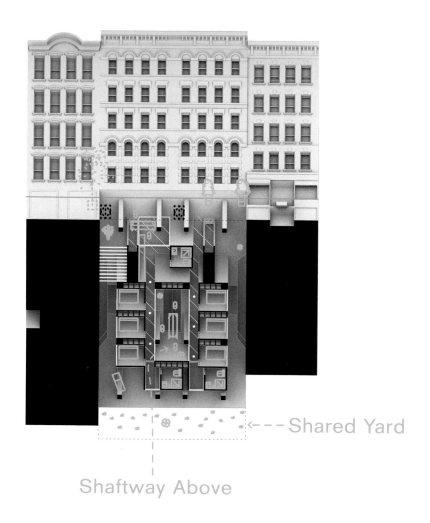

<--- Shared Yard

Shaftway Above

535   Case Studies

23 Orchard Street

There are art galleries, restaurants, and dry cleaners along both sides of Orchard Street, along with 24–26, 32 Orchard and 34 Allen. The building is 5 stories tall, built in 1900, with a glass addition facing Allen Street completed in 2018. The addition is rented periodically, a pop-up retail space available short and long term.

Housing for 2, sharing a kitchen and bath, is added. An outdoor space separates the beds from the street, allowing light and air to penetrate.

Case Studies

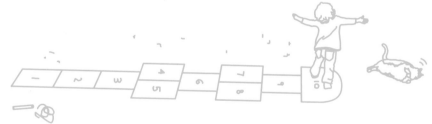

Jun 2019, Racson Group Inc, $402K Land Val, $993K Tot Val, Unlisted SF, 577 days since logged occupancy.

Case Studies

538   Case

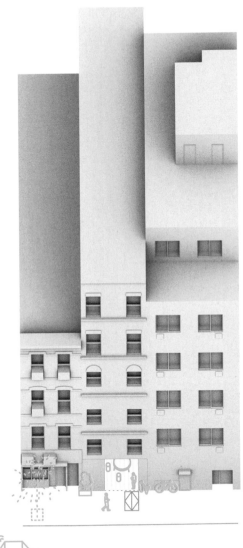

Case Studies

Porch with
Shared Table

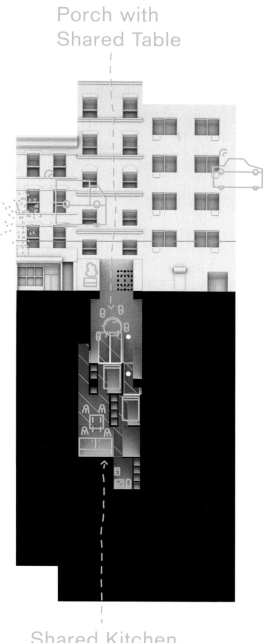

Shared Kitchen,
Dinner Together

541   Case Studies

24–26 Orchard Street

2 adjacent vacancies are combined to accommodate a larger housing collective. A 2- and 3-story building near 34 Allen, 23 and 32 Orchard Street.

7 beds share 3 bathrooms and 2 kitchens, as well as 2 patios and a garden in the back. The street-facing patio can hold large public and private events that spill out onto the narrow street. To provide flexibility in the future, the housing collective whole can be divided into 2 separate parts: 5 bedrooms that share 2 bathrooms and a kitchen, and 2 bedrooms that share a single bathroom and kitchen.

Jun 2019, Meitov Corp, $115K Land Val, $337K Tot Val, Unlisted SF, 1704 days since logged occupancy.

543   Case Studies

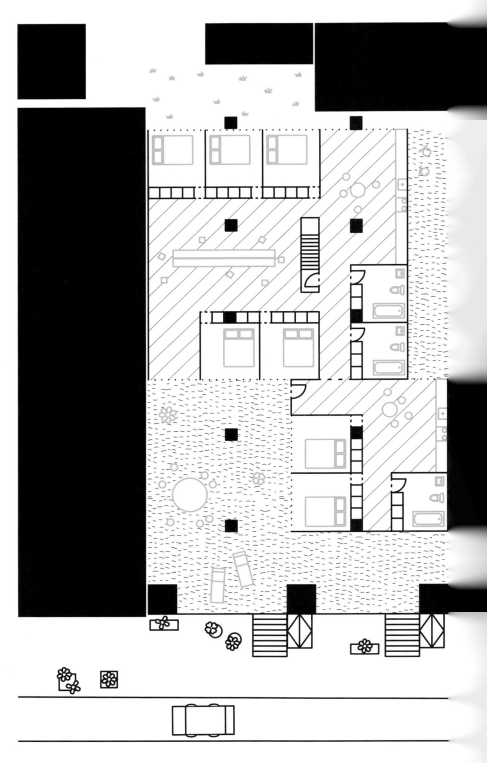

Case Stu

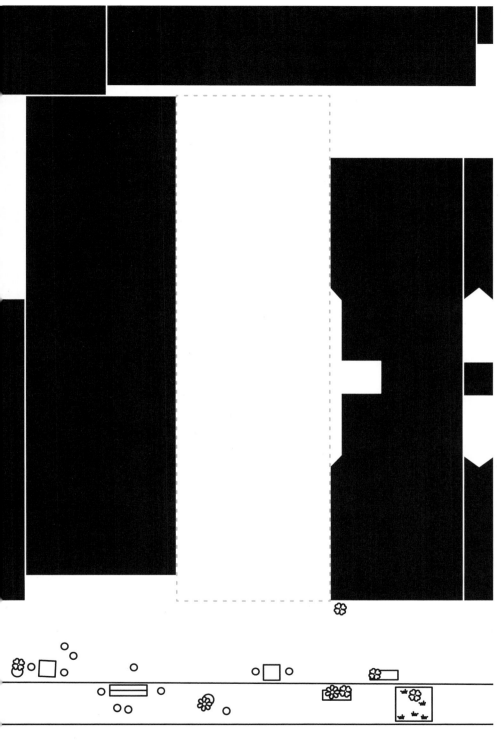

Case Studies

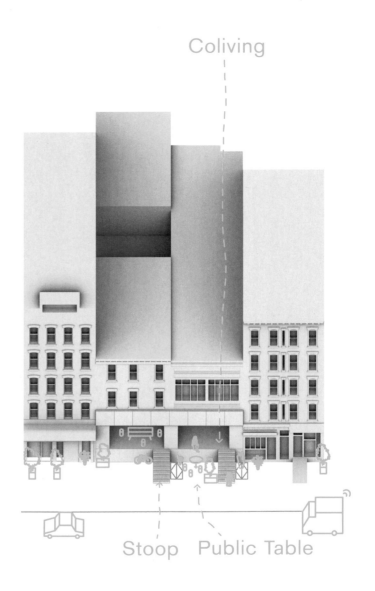

Coliving

Stoop   Public Table

546   Case Studies

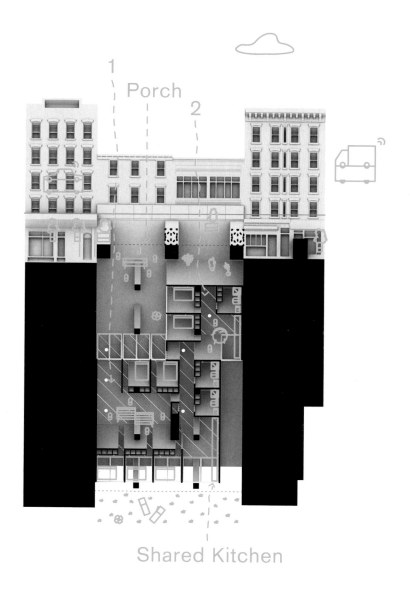

Porch

1

2

Shared Kitchen

547   Case Studies

29 Ludlow Street

Part of a 6-story mixed-use building on the corner of Ludlow and Hester Street, which also has a pharmacy and art gallery on the ground floor. There are laundromats, clothing stores, cafes, and art galleries on the nearby blocks. The Benjamin Altman School, a public elementary school built in 1900, is on the other side of Hester Street.

A studio for 1 is added, with a kitchen, bathroom, and small outdoor space. A porch creates an exterior space between the bedroom and sidewalk.

Jul 2020, A Wong Realty Corp, $115K Land Val, $1.04M Tot Val, Unlisted SF,
304 days since logged occupancy.

549   Case Studies

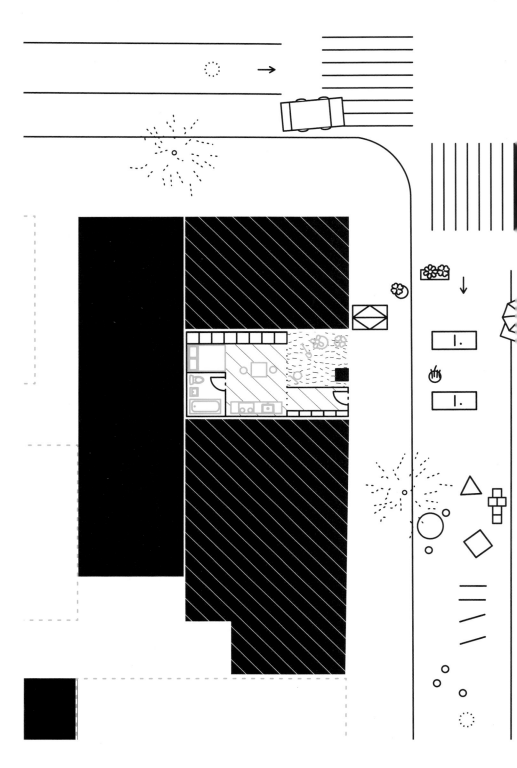

Case Studies

551   Case Studies

Street-Level Apartment

Case Studies

553

32 Orchard Street

A 3-story building across from 34 Allen and 68 Hester Street. The adjacent building, constructed from 2006 to '10, is 11 stories tall. Parts of the street parking are reserved for outdoor seating areas and places for children to play in the summer.

Housing for 3 is added, sharing a kitchen and bathroom, buffered by a patio in the front and back. A small yard can be used to grow a garden or sit in the sun. The street is not only a place for commerce but also a place for people to play and live.

Jun 2019, Globalserv Property One Llc, $139K Land Val, $767K Tot Val, 1300 SF, 638 days since logged occupancy.

555   Case Studies

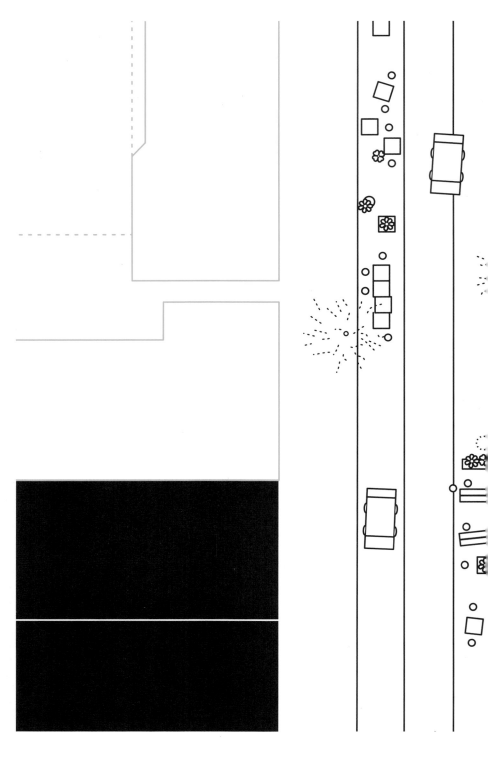

Case Studies

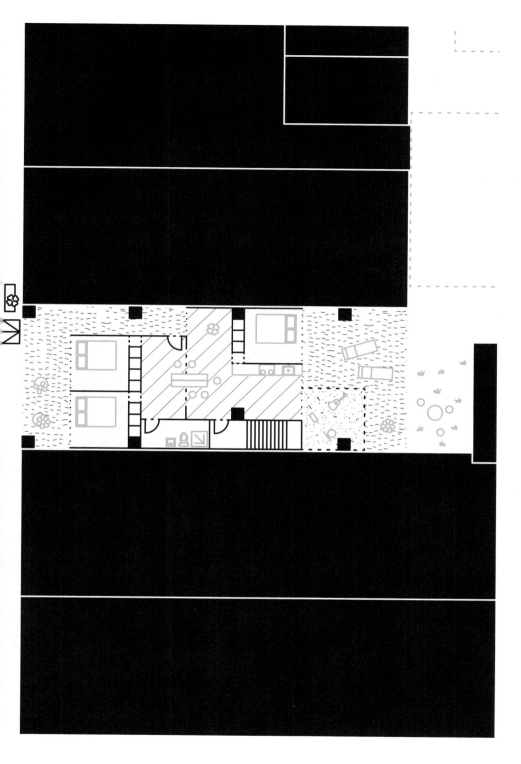

557

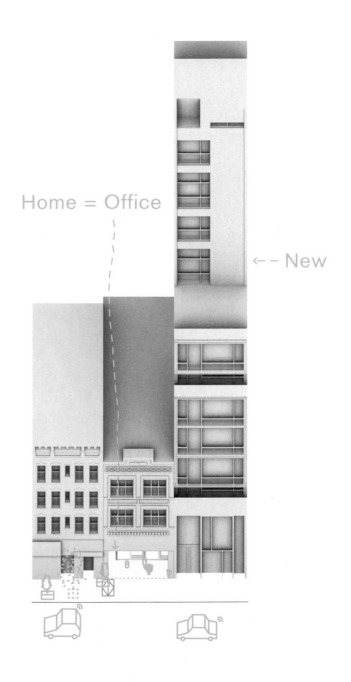

Home = Office

← – New

Case Studies

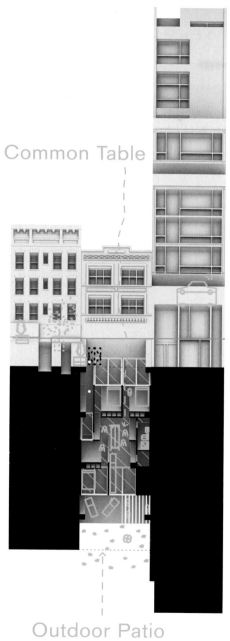

Common Table

Outdoor Patio

Case Studies

34 Allen Street

A 6-story building spanning between Allen and Orchard Street. The case studies along Orchard Street and 68 Hester Street are nearby. A signage company, travel agency, printing shop, and wall and flooring company are on Allen Street, along with a Citi Bike station in the Allen Street road median.

Bedrooms are added on either side to maximize light, buffered by outdoor patios. Each bedroom has its own office and shares a central kitchen and bathroom.

Oct 2019, Happy Spring Realty Inc, $182K Land Val, $698K Tot Val, Unlisted SF, 122 days since logged occupancy.

561   Case Studies

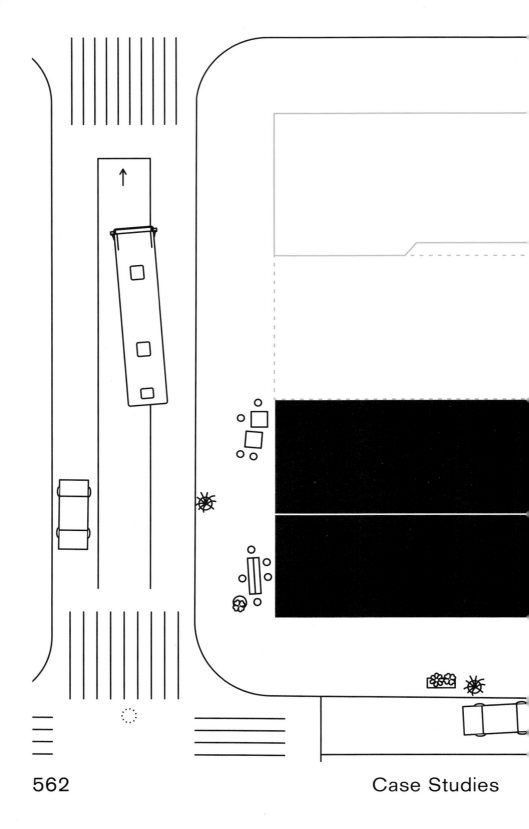

Case Studies

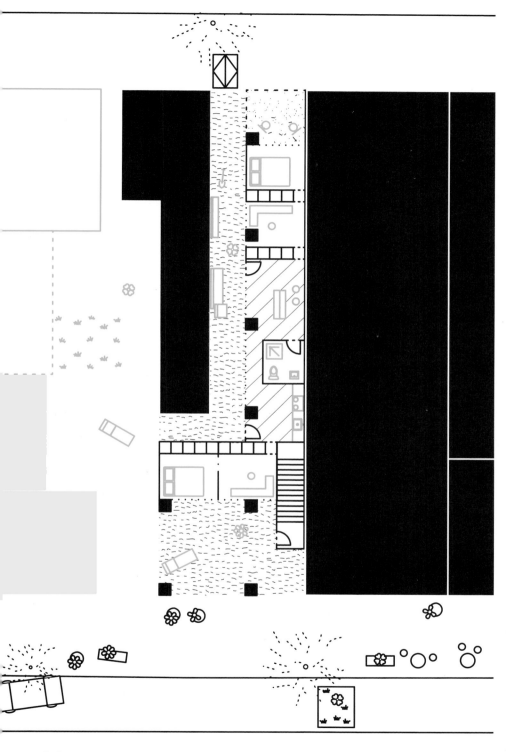

Case Studies

Alley

Case Studies

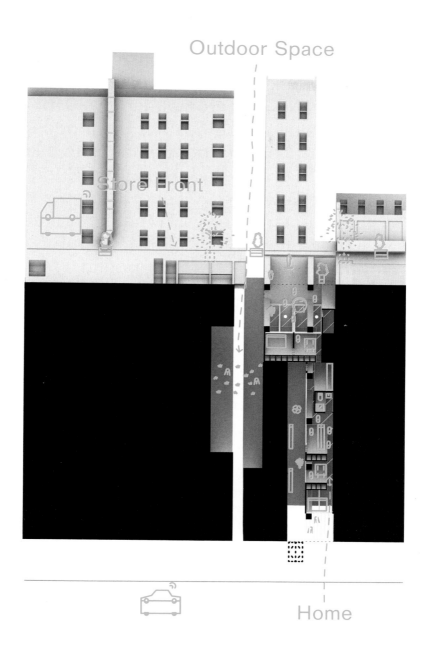

Outdoor Space

Store Front

Home

565   Case Studies

42–44 Allen Street

2 vacancies on the corner of Allen and Hester Street combined for a larger housing collective, with a vacancy next door to expand into. The 8-story building is new, completed in 2016. The ground floor retail space has not been occupied yet. Allen Street has a large median with bike lanes, benches, grass, and trees. The Buddhist Association of New York, Guang Ji Temple is next to it on Hester Street. On the other side of Allen is NYCHA housing. 2 blocks from Seward Park and the Hester Street Playground.

2 pairs of beds have their own kitchen and bathroom. They share a yard in the back and patios in the front. As more ground-floor retail spaces are repurposed for living, new ways of sharing and forming communities will be possible.

Case Studies

Oct 2019, Unlisted Owner, $0 Land Val, $0 Tot Val, Unlisted SF, 1125 days since logged occupancy.

567   Case Studies

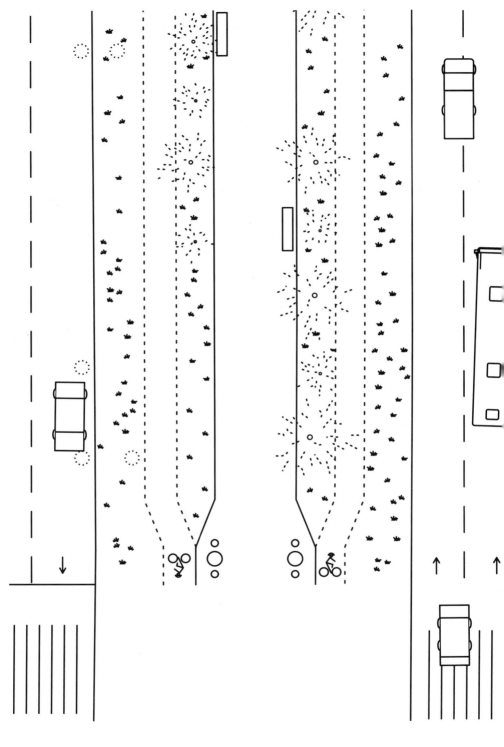

Case Studies

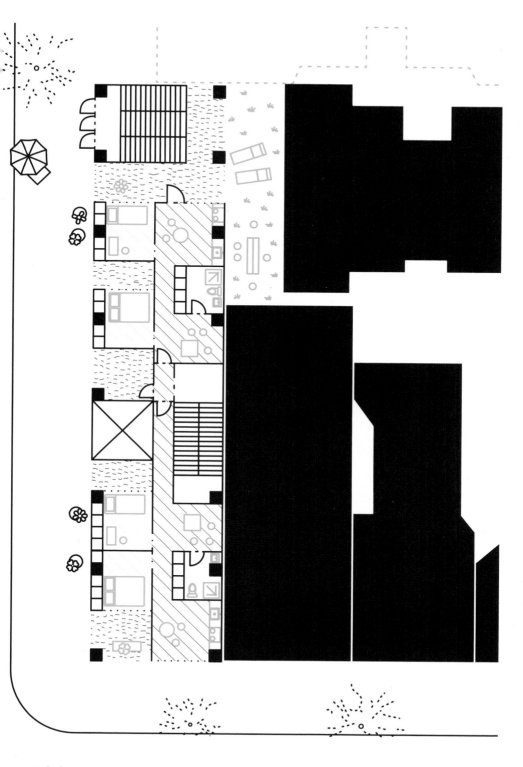

569

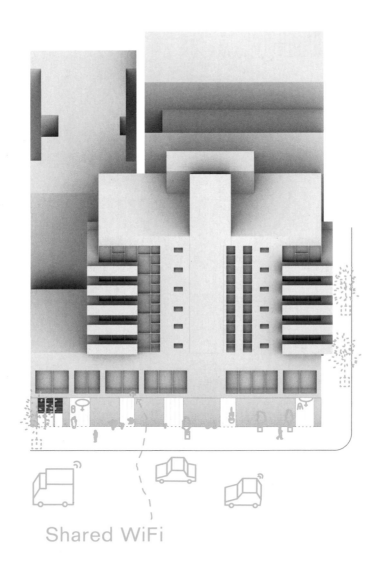

Shared WiFi

Case Studies

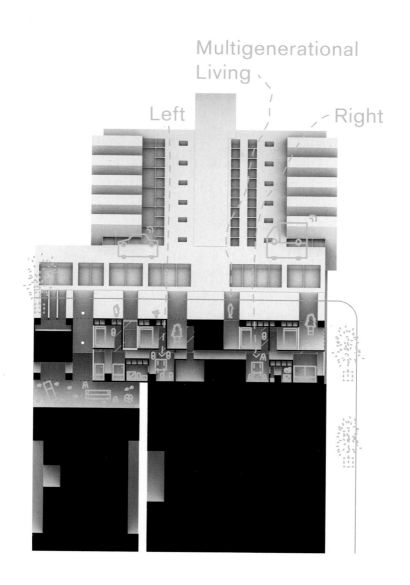

Multigenerational
Living

Left   Right

Case Studies

63 Canal Street

On the corner of Allen and Canal Street across from 70 Canal Street. There is another vacancy next to it on Allen Street, and the Canal Street Bus Stop on Canal Street, which goes to Virginia, Maryland, Delaware, Kentucky, Ohio, and West Virginia. The Allen Street median continues to run from 42–44 Allen Street.

5 bedrooms share 2 bathrooms and a kitchen. It is on a busy street corner, so outdoor space the same size as the indoor was added to cushion bedrooms from noise and crowds. It helps light and air enter. Plants help shield the interior from view.

Oct 2019, Yuan Tong Buddhist Tmpl, $294K Land Val, $895K Tot Val, Unlisted SF, 3075 days since logged occupancy.

573   Case Studies

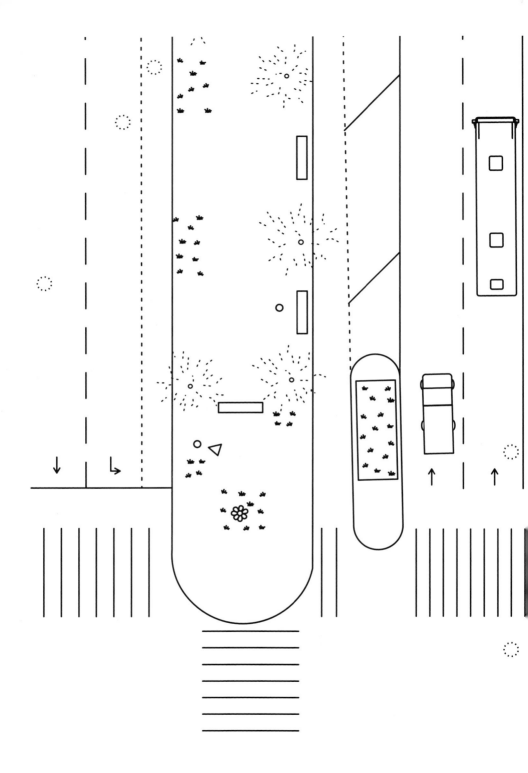

Case Studies

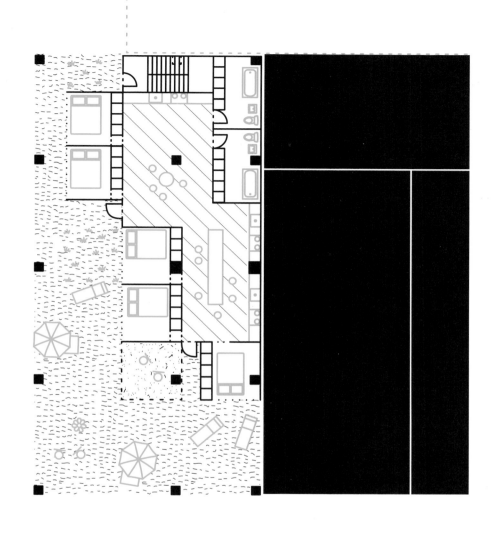

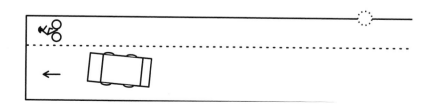

Case Studies

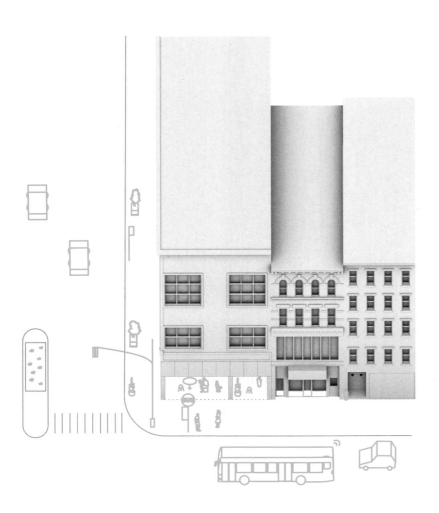

Case Studies

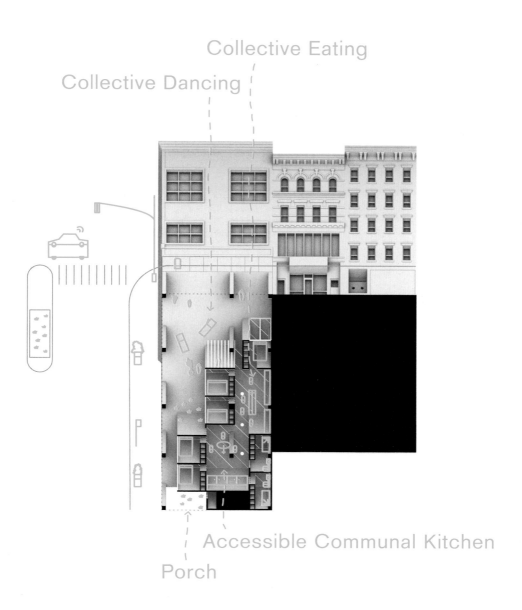

Collective Eating

Collective Dancing

Accessible Communal Kitchen

Porch

Case Studies

68 Hester Street

A smaller space in a larger 4-story, mixed-use building on the corner of Hester and Orchard Street. It also houses a furniture store and ice cream shop on the ground floor. There is an adjacent vacancy available to expand into, a fabric store, and a restaurant on the block. Near 34 Allen, 32 Orchard.

A single bedroom, kitchen, and bathroom are added. Living at the street level is intimate, a human-oriented view of the city. Interacting with neighbors, friends, and strangers. Being a part of your environment. Screens, curtains, and plants are there when needed.

Oct 2019, 37 Re Llc, $128K Land Val, $387K Tot Val, Unlisted SF, 2648 days since logged occupancy.

579 Case Studies

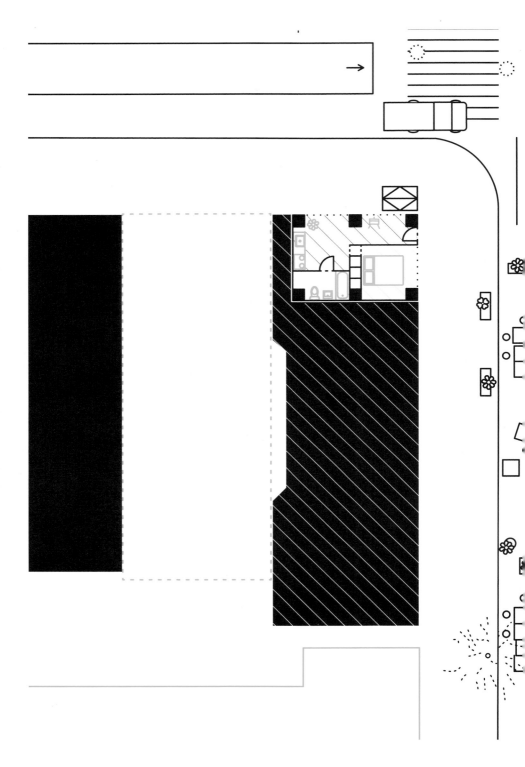

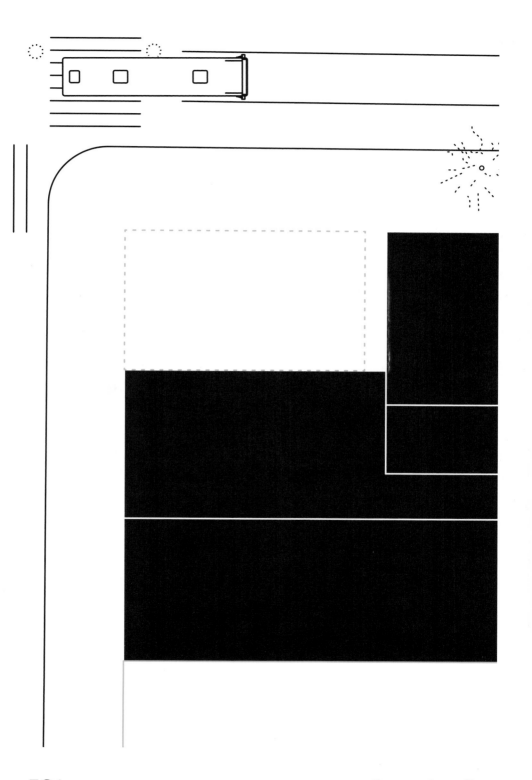

581

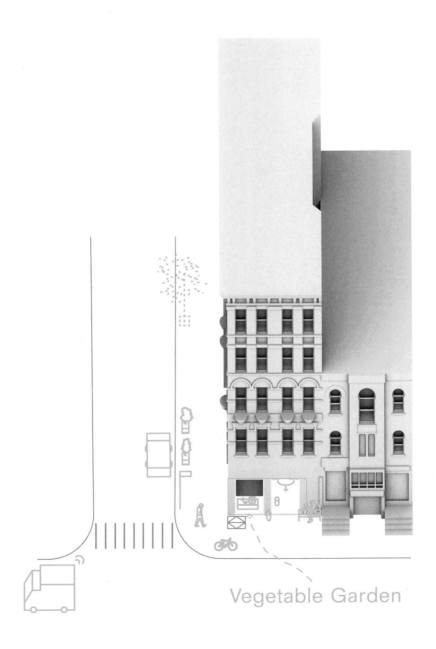

Vegetable Garden

Case Studies

Shared Table

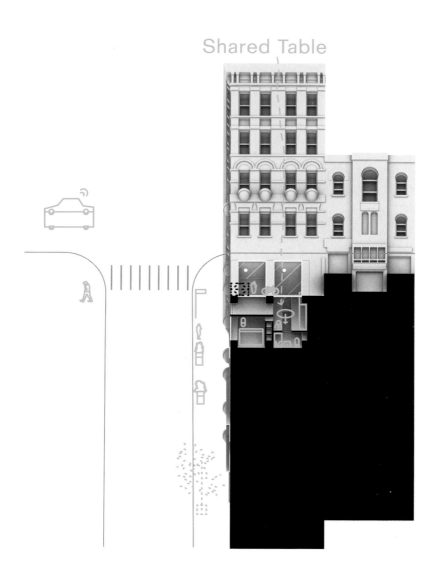

Case Studies

70 Canal Street

On the corner of Canal and Allen Street across from 63 Canal Street. Half of the footprint of a mixed-use building built in 1910. The other half is a bicycle shop. Surrounding buildings are between 6 and 8 stories tall, the Allen Street median park separates 2-way traffic, one heading uptown, the other toward the Manhattan Bridge. A megabus stop is on the same corner, where people form lines at regular intervals throughout the day. The street is hectic, with bicycle riders, tourists, cars, and buses late into the night.

An outdoor yard and patio are added to set back 2 bedrooms from the street. They share a kitchen and bathroom.

Oct 2019, Friberg Realty Company Llc, $236K Land Val, $1.09M Tot Val, Unlisted SF, 1826 days since logged occupancy.

585   Case Studies

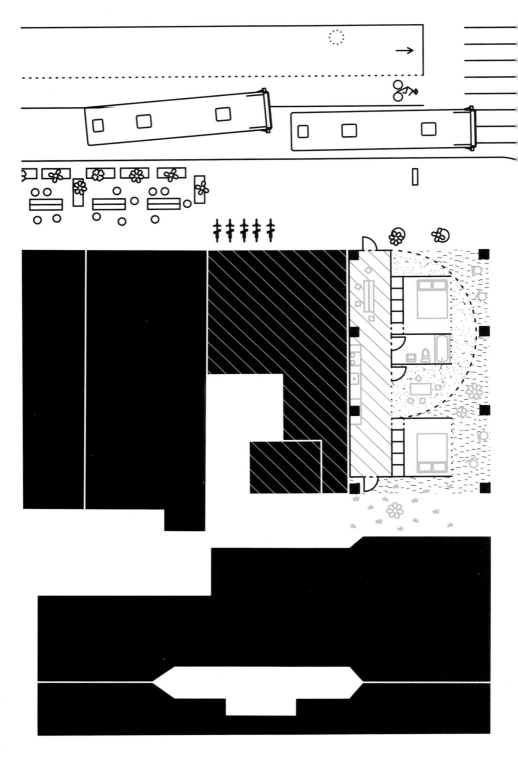

Case Studies

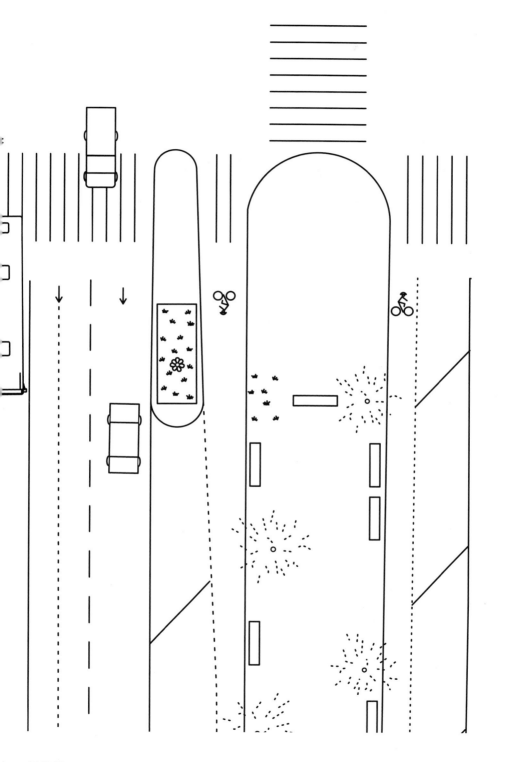

Case Studies

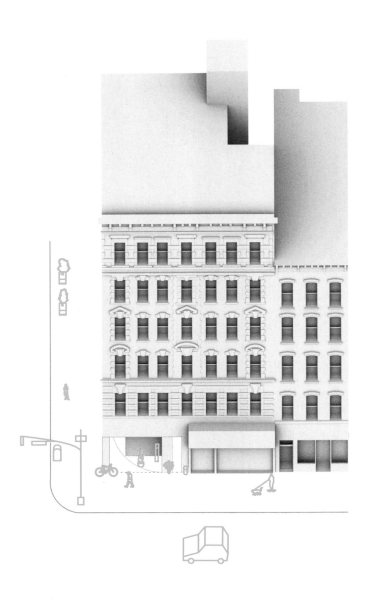

588   Case Studies

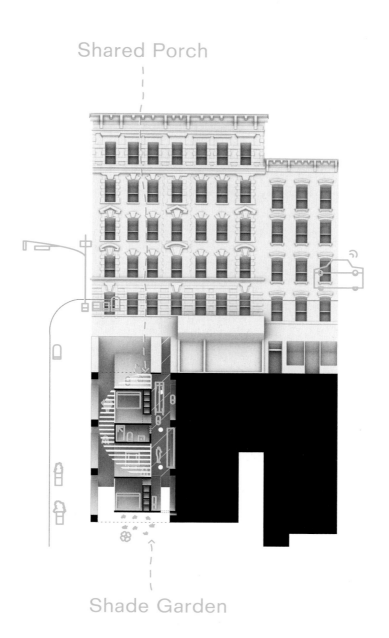

Shared Porch

Shade Garden

589   Case Studies

80–82 Canal Street

A 5-story building with 2 vacant units on the corner of Canal and Eldridge Street. The previous tenants were a depot for tables and chairs and gold, silver, and diamond shop. PACE High School, the Xu Bing Park, and the Sara D. Roosevelt Park Track are all a block away. Near 86 Canal Street. There are restaurants, a hotel, and a print shop on the block.

4 bedrooms share a bathroom and kitchen, which are cushioned by an outdoor space. A corner activated by people living and working at the street level.

Oct 2019, HCKD Canal Realty Corp, $122K Land Val, $957K Tot Val, Unlisted SF, 1826 days since logged occupancy.

591   Case Studies

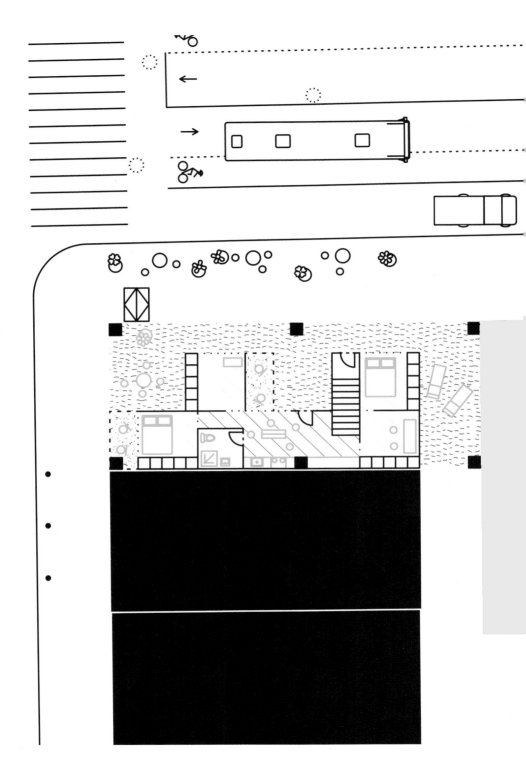

Case Studies

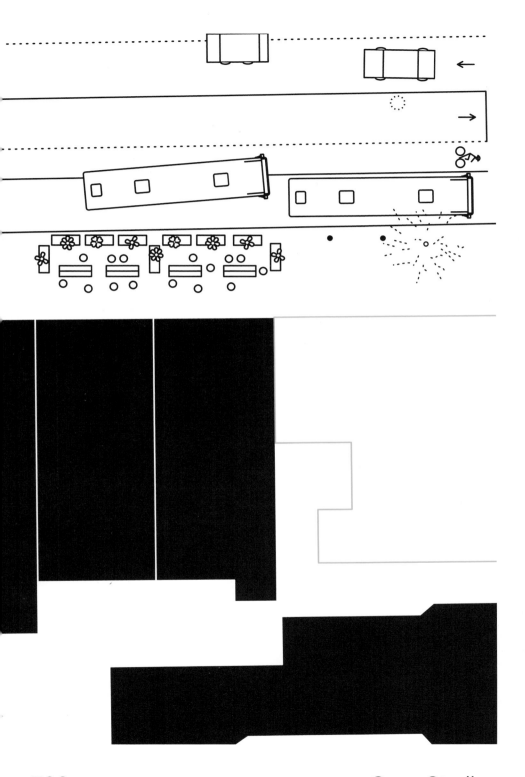

Case Studies

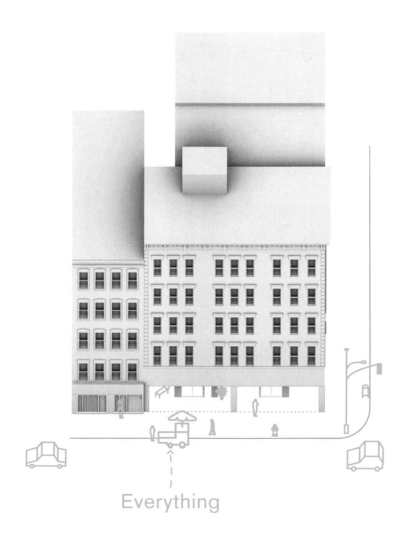

Everything

Case Studies

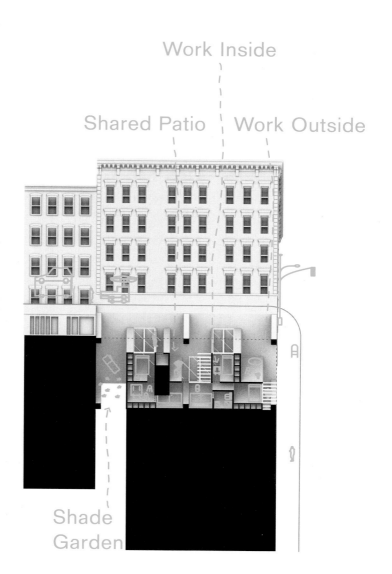

Work Inside

Shared Patio | Work Outside

Shade
Garden

Case Studies

86 Canal Street

On the corner of Canal and Eldridge Street.
Part of a larger mixed-use building whose other
tenants include a salon, tea shop, and hotel.
Eldridge Street is closed for a weekend street
fair. On the same block as 80–82 Canal Street.

An outdoor space is added between the
sidewalk and collective housing. 6 bedrooms
share a kitchen and 2 bathrooms. Plants and
greenery help separate domestic spaces from
the busy street.

Jun 2019, Unavailable Owner, $2.05M Land Val, $9.22M Tot Val, Unlisted SF, 1767 days since logged occupancy.

597   Case Studies

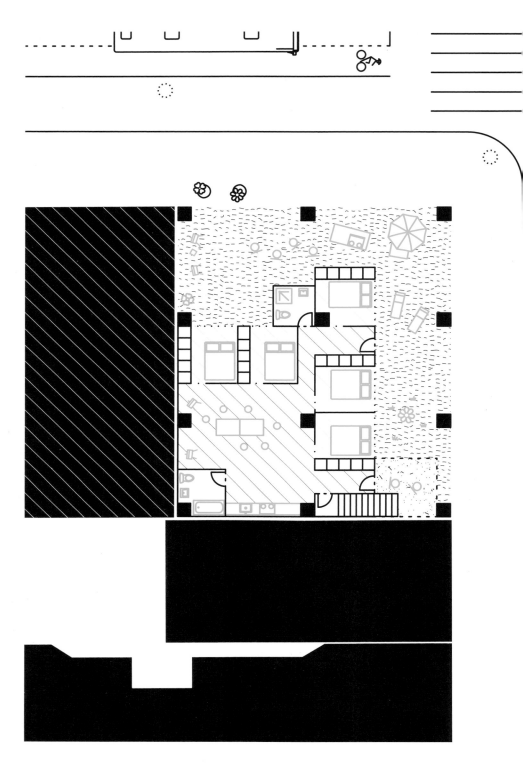

Case Studies

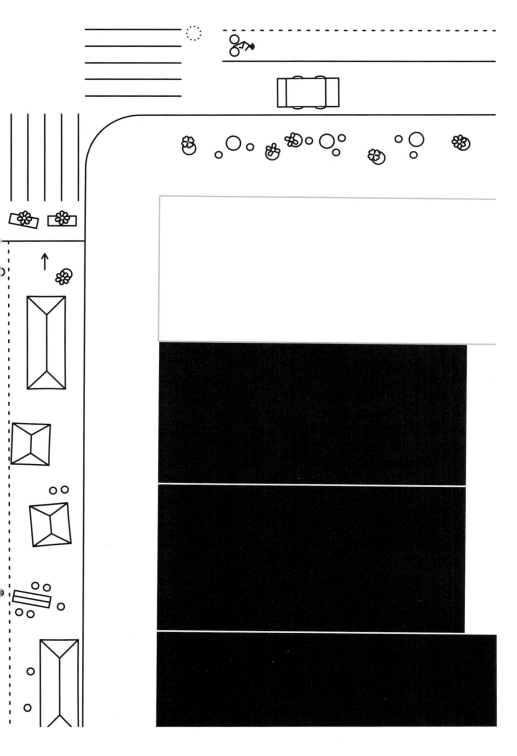

Case Studies

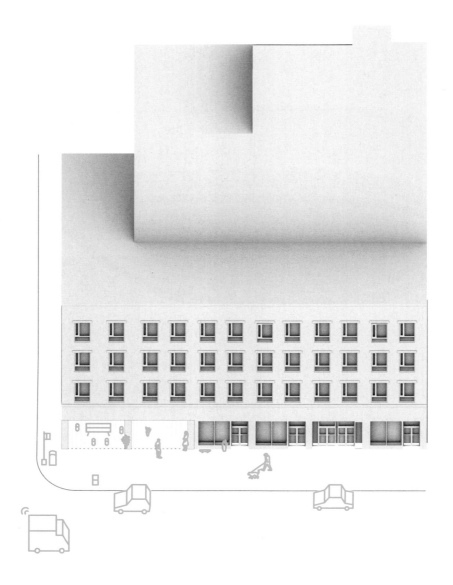

Case Studies

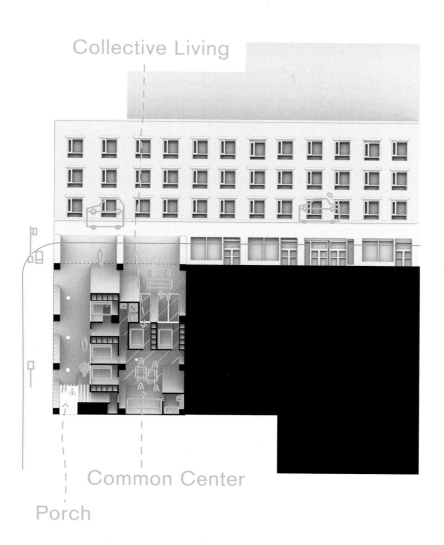

Collective Living

Common Center

Porch

601   Case Studies

Conclusion

The city is a never-ending project. Always editing. Always revising. At the time of writing, we remain in the midst of a pandemic with an unprecedented amount of vacant space growing throughout New York City – offices, business storefronts, luxury housing, etc. We've also seen the resilience of the small scale. Speculative real estate investment, large-scale development, corporations, retail chains, financial institutions, and wealthy individuals quickly deserted the city only to be replaced by new, even larger corporations hoping to take advantage of the real estate market to consolidate more and more space. All the while small businesses faced tremendous hardships. Bodegas and corner delis remain open, individually managed and owned restaurants have socially distanced lines in front of them, closed streets have become public spaces, and local stores are visited daily by neighbors wearing masks. The investments these businesses and individuals make are not simply strategic and financial. They live here. They aren't ready to pick up and leave for a better deal elsewhere. They make a difference to their block, to their neighborhood, to the larger community, to New York.

We illustrated this growing inequity through publicly available data, and, when collected together, this research connects the dots to form a picture of the various crises facing New

York: a housing shortage, especially severe for affordable housing; racial and economic inequalities; the growing number of those experiencing homelessness; vacant spaces. All of these problems are connected: The primary cause of houselessness, particularly among families, is lack of affordable housing. The popularity of e-commerce has made many retail stores reduce their physical presence or go out of business, while 500,000 households in the city do not have internet access. The inequitable distribution of services and economic diversity, furthers inequity. Reductions in federal funding give real estate developers more leverage to negotiate the amount and types of affordable rental units they build, typically in areas with lower property values. Of the new residential building permits issued in 2019, 72 percent of nearly 25,000 total units in New York City were in buildings with 50 or more units.[1] More unneeded luxury housing stock is built, correlating with higher vacancy rates, while rent-stabilized and rent-controlled units are deregulated. All of this is further evidence of the small being displaced by the large.

Covid 19 has compounded these issues and increased public awareness of them, but they were growing for years before it. The majority of our research predates the coronavirus for this reason. As the city begins to reopen, it turns its

Conclusion

attention back to the same rezoning strategies and new kinds of developments, as if this past year did not happen. The same strategies that caused these problems in the first place. Even once the effects of Covid 19 are gone, these issues will persist.

The problem of vacancies clearly demonstrates the need to support a diverse, smaller scale. Diversity requires the small scale. By investing in solving one problem, we can solve others. Vacant space is an opportunity to design our city to be more healthy, more vibrant, and more equitable. An opportunity to imagine something other than ground-floor retail. To resist homo-geneity through individual local interventions, creating more flexible, diverse, and embedded spaces in specific communities. Our 26 case studies repurpose 58,000 square feet of space split between 10 different neighborhoods. If proposals were done for all 560 documented vacancies, we could repurpose over 1.25 million square feet of space. Understanding the city through this kind of development calls attention to a different economic and development model, one that requires engaging every building, every block, every neighborhood. Together. This instead of abstracting properties into global assets and investment vehicles. The inability of financial institutions, real estate companies, and governments to think at the human scale is central to many of the problems presented here. They are more attuned to large scales, large numbers, large distances, large profits. They are interested in consolidating more and more with little financial incentive or reward to pay attention to the small scale. Holding them accountable demands starting here, in the city, at the small urban and economic level. It demands finding and organizing around common ground. Cities bring us together. Economics, media and public discourse is fragmented, pulling us apart, but the physical proximity and diversity within cities is essential to our society, and becoming more so. We cannot allow them to become vacant, or enclaves of wealth. As architects, we must collectively imagine and represent possibilities to begin a conversation. To bring everyone to the table, not just other architects. It may seem impossible to combat large problems through the small-scale redevelopment of existing vacant spaces, but we hope these case studies offer a place to start.

1. "2019 Data on New York City's Housing Stock," *The Stoop: NYU Furman Center Blog*, April 22, 2020.

Conclusion

Vacant Spaces NY

Published by
Actar Publishers, New York,
Barcelona
www.actar.com

Distribution
Actar D, Inc. New York, Barcelona.

New York
440 Park Avenue South, 17th Floor
New York, NY 10016, USA
T +1 2129662207
salesnewyork@actar-d.com

Barcelona
Roca i Batlle 2
08023 Barcelona, Spain
T +34 933 282 183
eurosales@actar-d.com

Credits
MOS Architects
Michael Meredith
Hilary Sample
Ben Dooley
Andy Kim
Vicky Cao
Reese Lewis
Jacqueline Mix
Hannah Lucia Terry
Cristina Terricabras
Carly Richman

Graphic Design
Studio Lin and MOS Architects

Printing and Binding
die Keure

Indexing
ISBN: 978-1-948765-99-2
Library of Congress Control
Number: 2021937080

Special thanks to Princeton
University School of Architecture.
This publication is made possible
in part from the Barr Ferree
Foundation Fund for Publications,
Department of Art and
Archaeology, Princeton University.